# che guevara

## reminiscences of the cuban revolutionary war

# che guevara

## reminiscences of the cuban revolutionary war

*Translated by Victoria Ortiz*

Monthly Review Press
New York

Library of Congress Catalog Card Number 68-13655

Monthly Review Press
122 West 27th Street
New York, NY 10001

Manufactured in Canada


10   9   8   7   6   5   4   3   2

## GUERRILLA ROUTE IN THE SIERRA MAESTRA
### December 1956 – December 1957

1. Las Coloradas Beach: landing place
2. Alegría de Pío: defeat and dispersion
3. Ojo de Buey Bay
4. Puercas Gordas, where Almeida's men abandoned their arms
5. Mongo Pérez's farm: where the dispersed troops regrouped, under Fidel Castro's command
6. Caracas Hill
7. La Plata: First victory
8. The Arroyo del Infierno
9. Caracas Hill
10. Surprise attack on the heights of Espinosa
11. El Lomón: arrival of reinforcements sent by Frank País
12. Mt. Turquino
13. Pino del Agua
14. El Uvero

# Contents

*"In our country the individual knows that the glorious period in which it has befallen him to live is one of sacrifice; he has learned its meaning.*

*"The men in the Sierra Maestra—and wherever else there was fighting—learned it first; later, all Cuba came to know it. Cuba, the vanguard of America, must make sacrifices, because it points the way to full freedom for the Latin American peoples.*

*". . . the true revolutionary is moved by strong feelings of love. It is impossible to conceive of an authentic revolutionary who lacks this quality. Herein lie what are perhaps the great dramatic challenges to a leader: he must combine an impassioned spirit with coolness of mind; and he must make painful decisions unfalteringly.*

*"The love our vanguard revolutionaries bear for the people and for the most hallowed causes must be the same indivisible, spiritualized love. Not for them the routine expressions of finite love as expressed by ordinary men.*

*"Revolutionary leaders are not often present to hear their children's first hesitant words; their wives must also share in their sacrifice if the revolution is to reach its goal; their friends are to be found only among their comrades in revolution. For them there is no life outside the revolution. If they are to sidestep dogmatic extremes, sterile scholasticism, and isolation from the people, they must possess a full measure of humanity and a sense of justice and truth. Theirs is a daily struggle to transform their love of living humanity into concrete deeds, into acts that will serve as a mobilizing force and an example."*

—CHE GUEVARA
*Socialism and Man in Cuba*

# From Rosario to Cuba

Ernesto Che Guevara was born on the night of June 14, 1928, in Rosario, one of Argentina's most important cities. At the age of two he suffered his first attack of asthma, that couldn't be cured and brought with it a fatigue, a choking sensation that would always accompany him, a wheezing that persisted and echoed throughout the classrooms of the School of Medicine, in the heart of the Sierra Maestra and the jungles of Latin America.

His parents, Ernesto Guevara Lynch, civil engineer, and Celia de la Serna, descendants of Irish and Spanish families respectively, decided to move to Buenos Aires.

Celia said that "at the age of 4, Ernesto could no longer stand the climate of the capital. His father slept sitting on Ernesto's bed because Che weathered the asthma attacks better sleeping with his head resting on his father's chest." Ernesto got worse; the doctors said that his was a difficult case, and later they said he needed a change of climate.

The Guevara family moved again. They went to Córdoba, where the child improved. The attacks lessened. They settled in Alta Gracia after having traveled throughout the province.

Before her eldest son was eight, Mrs. Guevara received a letter

---

This biographical sketch appeared in the Cuban weekly review, *Granma,* Oct. 24, 1967.

from the Ministry of Education stating that Ernesto Guevara de la Serna, seven years of age, was not registered in any primary school.

"I answered immediately. I was proud that they were concerned with children learning to read and write. I taught him his ABC's, but he could not attend school because of his asthma. He only attended classes regularly during the second and third grades; the fifth and sixth he attended sporadically. His brothers and sisters would copy the lessons, and he did them at home."

Then came high school, and he traveled to Córdoba every day in a tiny auto filled with fellow students. The chauffeur: Celia de la Serna.

He lived at Villa Nidia, in the "better" section of town. Those were the days of pleasure and economic prosperity. Later the situation changed, and it was necessary to sell the large farm that his mother owned on the outskirts of town and move to the city. Ernesto had room and board, but the family budget did not allow any spending money, and he found his first job.

He was already an adolescent, independent, careful, attracted by books, determined. With incredible effort he had overcome his illness and practiced sports with his brother Roberto and some others. He had three other brothers and sisters: Celia, Ana María and Juan Martín.

Some athletes today remember young Guevara, who was well known around the Atalaya Athletic Club. Sometimes he left the field to use his vaporizer. Interest in Baudelaire as well as sports tempered him both spiritually and physically.

In 1941, while in high school, he became friends with Alberto Granados, now a biochemist, who was graduated three years later.

On December 29, 1951, Che and Granados began a long trip by motorcycle. They had decided to proceed up the Pacific Coast. Guevara wanted to tour the continent, to get to know it, to seek out ancient civilizations that existed prior to the arrival of the conquistadores, to see people, travel, even if he had to go on foot.

The Guevara family had moved to Buenos Aires at the end of 1944. Ernesto continued his studies. His fellow students felt that because of his aptitude for mathematics he should become an engineer, and it surprised them when he told them that he had enrolled in the School of Medicine.

Before his trip with Granados, he had traveled to the north and west of the country, spurred on by his interest in leprosy and other tropical diseases. Once he went from one end of the country to the other by bicycle. He walked through the valleys of Calchaquíes and the Andes, passed through Tucumán and Mendoza, Salta, Jujuy and La Rioja.

Granados and Ernesto arrived in Santiago de Chile; later they crossed the highlands on foot. "This gave us an opportunity to know the people. We worked at odd jobs to earn a few pesos, and then we'd continue on our way. We worked as stevedores, porters, sailors, doctors, and dishwashers. We were capable of peeling potatoes and doing other odd chores, one of us with a university degree and the other nearly a graduate doctor."

They arrived in Peru and realized an old aspiration to visit a leper colony. Guevara also visited Machu Picchu and, later, the heart of the Peruvian jungles, where the patients of a leper colony had built a dam that changed the course of the river, deflecting it to Colombia.

Problems, difficulties with papers, money, absurd trivialities, kept popping up.

"In Iquitos," recalls Granados, "we were football coaches and earned enough money for our plane fares. In Bogotá they deported us."

A collection made by students permitted them to make a trip to Venezuela. Alberto stayed there. Ernesto went to Miami aboard a cargo plane filled with thoroughbred horses. He originally intended to stay there two days, but remained a month. He was so careful of his money that he survived completely on reading at the community library and limiting himself to a diet of coffee laced with milk once a day.

He returned to Buenos Aires and was called by the draft, but was declared unfit for military service on the first call. He was told they would recall him on graduation.

With his strange method of studying and his rare ability and intelligence, he passed 11 or 12 subjects in less than a year. He was graduated as a doctor in March 1953. He was 25, and had already been an active militant against all forms of tyranny. He already suffered the pain of knowing the terrible truth about the conditions in which the Latin American Indians lived, and he decided to work for them. He decided to return to Caracas, where he was expected by Granados. There he intended to work at the Cabo Blanco leper colony.

Not wanting to ask anybody for money, he decided to leave Buenos Airés by train. In Ecuador, lawyer Ricardo Rojo convinced him that Guatemala was the place to see. He arrived there in December 1953. Later he went to Mexico and after that aboard the "Granma" to Cuba.

# In Tribute to Che

## By Fidel Castro

REVOLUTIONARY COMRADES:

I first met Che one day in July or August, 1955. And in one night—as he recalls in his writings—he became one of the future expeditionaries of the "Granma," although at that time that expedition possessed neither ship, nor arms nor troops.

And that was how, together with Raúl, Che became one of the first two on the "Granma" list. And twelve years have passed since then—they have been twelve years filled with struggle and historical significance. During this time death has cut down many brave and invaluable men, but, at the same time, throughout those years of our revolution, extraordinary persons have arisen, forged from among men of the revolution, and between those men and the people, bonds of affection and of friendship have emerged which surpass all description.

Tonight we are meeting to try to express, in some degree, our feelings toward him who was one of the closest, the most beloved and, without doubt, the most extraordinary of our revolutionary

This is the text of the speech made by Major Fidel Castro Ruz, first secretary of the Central Committee of the Communist party of Cuba and prime minister of the revolutionary government, in memory of Major Ernesto Che Guevara, at the Plaza de la Revolución, on October 18, 1967. The translation is that furnished by the Cuban government.

comrades—to express our feelings for him and for the heroes who
have fought with him and fallen with him, his internationalist
army that has been writing a glorious and never to be effaced
historical epic.

Che was one of those people who is liked immediately, for his
simplicity, his character, his naturalness, his comradely attitude,
his personality, his originality, even when one had not yet learned
of his other characteristic and unique virtues.

In those first days he was our troop doctor. And so the bonds of
friendship and warm feelings for him were ever increasing.

He was filled with a profound spirit of hatred and loathing for
imperialism, not only because his political awareness was already
considerably developed, but also because shortly before, he had
had the opportunity of witnessing the criminal imperialist intervention in Guatemala through the mercenaries who aborted the
revolution in that country.

A man like Che did not require elaborate arguments. It was
sufficient for him to know that there were men determined to
struggle against that situation, arms in hand; it was sufficient for
him to know that those men were inspired by genuinely revolutionary and patriotic ideals. That was more than enough.

One day, at the end of November, 1956, he set out on the expedition toward Cuba with us. I recall that that trip was very hard
for him, since, because of the circumstances under which it was
necessary to organize the departure, he could not even provide
himself with the medicine he needed and throughout the trip
he suffered from a severe attack of asthma, with nothing to alleviate
it, but also without ever complaining.

We arrived, set out on our first march, suffered our first setback
and, at the end of some weeks, as you all know, a group of those
who had survived from the expedition of the "Granma" was able
to reunite. Che continued to be the doctor of our group.

We came through the first battle victorious, and Che was already a soldier of our troop and, at the same time, still our doctor. We came through the second victorious battle and Che was not only a soldier, but the most outstanding soldier in that battle, carrying out for the first time one of those singular feats that characterized him in all military action. Our forces continued to develop and we faced another battle of extraordinary importance at that moment.

The situation was difficult. The information we had was erroneous in many respects. We were going to attack, in full daylight—at dawn—a strongly defended, well-armed position at the edge of the sea. Enemy troops were at our rear, not very distant, and in that confused situation it was necessary to ask the men to make a supreme effort.

Comrade Juan Almeida had taken on one of the most difficult missions, but one of our flanks remained completely without forces —one of the flanks was left without an attacking force, placing the operation in danger. And at that moment, Che, who was still functioning as our doctor, asked for two or three men, among them one with a machine gun, and in a matter of seconds rapidly set off to assume the mission of attack from that direction.

On that occasion, he was not only an outstanding combatant but, also, an outstanding doctor, attending the wounded comrades and, at the same time, attending the wounded enemy soldiers.

After all the weapons had been captured and it became necessary to abandon that position, undertaking a long return march under the harassment of diverse enemy forces, it was necessary for someone to stay behind with the wounded, and Che stayed with the wounded. Aided by a small group of our soldiers, he took care of them, saved their lives and later rejoined the column with them.

From that time forward, he stood out as a capable and valiant leader, of that type of men who, when a difficult mission is pending, do not wait to be asked to carry it out.

Thus it was at the battle of El Uvero, but he had acted in a similar way on a not previously mentioned occasion in the first

days when, following a betrayal, our little troop was surprised by
a number of airplanes and we were forced to retreat under the
bombardment. We had already walked some distance when we
remembered some rifles of some peasant soldiers who had been
with us in the first actions and had then asked permission to visit
their families at a time when there was still not much discipline
in our embryonic army. And right then it was thought that pos-
sibly the rifles were lost.

I recall that the problem was not brought up again and, during
the bombardment, Che volunteered, and having done so, quickly
went out to recuperate those rifles.

This was one of his principal characteristics: his willingness to
instantly volunteer for the most dangerous mission. And naturally
this aroused admiration, and twice the usual admiration, for a
fellow combatant, fighting alongside us, who had not been born
here, a man of profound ideas, a man in whose mind stirred the
dream of struggle in other parts of the continent and who was,
nonetheless, so altruistic, so disinterested, so willing to always do
the most difficult things, to constantly risk his life.

And that was how he won the rank of major and leader of the
Second Column, organized in the Sierra Maestra. Thus his prestige
began to increase; he began to gain fame as a magnificent combatant
who was to reach the highest posts in the course of the war.

Che was an incomparable soldier. Che was an incomparable
leader. Che was, from a military point of view, an extraordinarily
capable man, extraordinarily courageous, extraordinarily aggressive.
If, as a guerrilla, he had his Achilles' heel it was this excessively
aggressive quality, his absolute contempt for danger.

The enemy believes it can draw certain conclusions from his
death. Che was a master of warfare. He was a virtuoso in the art
of guerrilla struggle. And he showed that an infinite number of
times. But he showed it especially in two extraordinary deeds. One
of these was in the invasion, in which he led a column, a column

pursued by thousands of enemy soldiers, over flat and absolutely unknown terrain, carrying out—together with Camilo [Cienfuegos] —an extraordinary military accomplishment. He also showed it in his lightning campaign in Las Villas Province, especially in the audacious attack on the city of Santa Clara, entering, with a column of barely 300 men, a city defended by tanks, artillery, and several thousand infantry soldiers.

Those two heroic deeds stamped him as an extraordinarily capable leader, as a master, as a virtuoso in the art of revolutionary war.

However, now after his heroic and glorious death, some attempt to deny the truth or value of his concepts, his guerrilla theories.

The master may die—especially when he is a virtuoso in an art as dangerous as revolutionary struggle—but what will surely never die is the art to which he dedicated his life, the art to which he dedicated his intelligence.

What is so strange about the fact that this master died in combat? What is stranger is that he did not die in combat on one of the innumerable occasions when he risked his life during our revolutionary struggle. And many times it was necessary to take steps to keep him from losing his life in actions of minor significance.

And so it was in a combat—in one of the many battles he fought —that he lost his life. We do not have sufficient evidence to enable us to make deductions about what circumstances preceded that combat, to imagine how far he may have acted in an excessively aggressive way, but—we repeat—if as a guerrilla he had an Achilles' heel that Achilles' heel was his excessive daring, his complete contempt for danger.

And this is where we can hardly agree with him, since we consider that his life, his experience, his capacity as a seasoned leader, his prestige and everything his life signified, were more valuable, incomparably more valuable than he himself, perhaps, believed.

His conduct may have been profoundly influenced by the idea that men have a relative value in history, the idea that causes are not defeated when men fall, that the powerful march of history cannot and will not be halted when leaders fall.

And that is true, there is no doubt about it. It shows his faith in men, his faith in ideas, his faith in examples. However, with all our heart we would have liked to see him as a forger of victories, to see victories forged under his leadership, since men of his experience, men of his caliber, of his really unique capacity, are not common.

We have a full understanding of the value of his example. We are absolutely convinced that many men will strive to live up to his example, that men like him will emerge from the heart of the peoples.

It is not easy to find a person with all the virtues that were combined in him. It is not easy for a person, spontaneously, to develop a personality like his. I would say that he is one of those men who are difficult to match and virtually impossible to surpass. But I would say that the example of men like him contributes to the appearance of men of the same caliber.

In Che, we not only admire the fighter, the man capable of performing great feats. And what he did, what he was doing, the very fact of his rising, with a handful of men, against the army of the ruling class, trained by Yankee advisers sent in by Yankee imperialism, backed by the oligarchies of all neighboring countries—in itself constitutes an extraordinary feat.

And if we search the pages of history, it is likely that we will find no other case in which a leader, with such a limited number of men, has set about a task of such import; a case in which a leader, with such a limited number of men, has set out to fight against such large forces. Such proof of confidence in himself, such proof of confidence in the people, such proof of faith in men's capacity to fight, can be looked for in the pages of history—but the like of it will never be found.

And he fell.

The enemy believes it has defeated his ideas, his guerrilla concepts, his point of view on revolutionary armed struggle. And what they accomplished, by a stroke of luck, was to eliminate him physically—what they accomplished was to gain an accidental advantage that an enemy may gain in war.

And we do not know to what degree that stroke of luck, that stroke of fortune, was helped along, in a battle like many others, by that characteristic of which we spoke before—his excessive aggressiveness, his absolute disdain for danger.

This also happened in our war of independence. In a battle at Dos Ríos they killed the apostle of our independence. In a battle at Punta Brava, they killed Antonio Maceo, a veteran of hundreds of battles.* Countless leaders, countless patriots of our war of independence were killed in similar battles. And, nevertheless, that did not spell defeat for the Cuban cause.

The death of Che is a hard blow for the revolutionary movement, in that it deprives it, without a doubt, of its most experienced and able leader.

But those who are boasting of victory are mistaken. They are mistaken when they think that his death is the end of his ideas, the end of his tactics, the end of his guerrilla concepts, the end of his thesis. For the man who fell, as a mortal man, as a man who faced bullets time and again, as a soldier, as a leader, was a thousand times more able than those who killed him by a stroke of luck.

However, how must revolutionaries face this serious setback? How must they face this loss? If Che had to express an opinion on this point, what would it be? He gave his opinion, he expressed that opinion quite clearly when he wrote in his message to the Latin American Conference of Solidarity that if death surprised him anywhere, it would be welcome as long as his battle cry had reached

---

* "The apostle of our independence" referred to in this paragraph is José Martí; for Maceo, see footnote to chapter called "Lydia and Clodomira."

a receptive ear and another hand was stretched out to take up his rifle.

And his battle cry will reach not just one receptive ear, but millions of receptive ears. And not one hand but millions of hands will be stretched out to take up arms.

New leaders will emerge. And the men—of the receptive ears and the outstretched hands—will need leaders who emerge from the ranks of the people, just as leaders have emerged in all revolutions.

Those hands will not have available a leader of Che's extraordinary experience and enormous ability. Those leaders will be formed in the process of struggle—those leaders will emerge from among the millions of receptive ears, from the millions of hands that will sooner or later be stretched out to take up arms.

It isn't that we feel that his death will necessarily have immediate repercussions in the practical sphere of revolutionary struggle, that his death will necessarily have immediate repercussions in the practical sphere of development of this struggle. The fact is that when Che took up arms again he was not thinking of an immediate victory—he was not thinking of a speedy victory against the forces of the oligarchies and of imperialism. As an experienced fighter, he was prepared for a prolonged struggle of five, ten, fifteen, or twenty years, if necessary. He was ready to fight five, ten, fifteen, twenty years, or all his life if need be!

And within this time perspective, his death—or rather his example —will have tremendous repercussions. The force of that example will be invincible.

Those who cling to the idea of luck try in vain to deny his experience and his capacity as a leader. Che was an extraordinarily able military leader. But when we remember Che, when we think of Che, we do not think fundamentally of his military virtues. No! Warfare is a means and not an end—warfare is a tool of revolutionaries. The important thing is the revolution—the important thing is the revolutionary cause, revolutionary ideas, revolutionary objectives, revolutionary sentiments, revolutionary virtues!

And it is in that field, in the field of ideas, in the field of sentiments, in the field of revolutionary virtues, in the field of intelligence, that—apart from his military virtues—we feel the tremendous loss that his death means to the revolutionary movement.

Because Che's extraordinary personality was made up of virtues which are rarely found together. He stood out as an unsurpassed man of action, but Che was not only an unsurpassed man of action —he was a man of visionary intelligence and broad culture, a profound thinker. That is, in his person the man of ideas and the man of action were combined.

But it is not only that Che possessed the double characteristic of the man of ideas—of profound ideas—and the man of action, but that Che as a revolutionary united in himself the virtues which can be defined as the fullest expression of the virtues of a revolutionary: A man of total integrity, a man of supreme sense of honor, of absolute sincerity—a man of stoic and Spartan living habits, a man in whose conduct not one stain can be found. He constituted, through his virtues, what can be called a truly model revolutionary.

When men die it is usual to make speeches, to emphasize their virtues, but rarely as on this occasion can one say of a man, with greater justice, with greater accuracy, what we say of Che: that he was a pure example of revolutionary virtues.

But he possessed another quality, not a quality of the intellect nor of the will, not a quality derived from experience, from struggle, but a quality of the heart: he was an extraordinarily human man, extraordinarily sensitive.

That is why we say, when we think of his life, that he constituted the singular case of a most extraordinary man, able to unite in his personality not only the characteristics of the man of action, but also of the man of thought, of the man of immaculate revolutionary virtues and of extraordinary human sensibility, joined with an iron character, a will of steel, indomitable tenacity.

And because of this, he has left to the future generations not only his experience, his knowledge as an outstanding soldier, but also, at the same time, the fruits of his intelligence. He wrote with the virtuosity of a master of our language. His narratives of the war are incomparable. The depth of his thinking is impressive. He never wrote about anything with less than extraordinary seriousness, with less than extraordinary profundity—and we have no doubt that some of his writings will pass on to posterity as classic documents of revolutionary thought.

And thus, as fruits of that vigorous and profound intelligence, he left us an infinity of memories, an infinity of narratives that, without his work, without his efforts, might have been lost forever.

An indefatigable worker, during the years that he served our country he did not know a single day of rest. Many were the responsibilities assigned to him: as president of the National Bank, as director of the National Planning Board, as Minister of Industries, as commander of military regions, as the head of political or economic or fraternal delegations.

His versatile intelligence was able to undertake with maximum assurance any task of any kind. And thus he brilliantly represented our country in numerous international conferences, just as he brilliantly led soldiers in combat, just as he was a model worker in charge of any of the institutions that he was assigned to, and for him there were no days of rest, for him there were no hours of rest!

And if we looked through the windows of his offices, he had the lights on until all hours of the night, studying, or rather, working or studying. For he was a student of all problems, he was a tireless reader. His thirst for learning was practically insatiable, and the hours he stole from sleep he devoted to study.

He devoted his scheduled days off to voluntary work. He was the inspiration and provided the greatest incentive for that work which is today carried out by hundreds of thousands of persons throughout the country; he stimulated that activity in which our people are making greater and greater efforts.

And as a revolutionary, as a communist revolutionary, a true communist, he had a boundless faith in moral values. He had a boundless faith in moral values, he had a boundless faith in the conscience of man. And we should say that he saw, with absolute clarity, moral resources as the fundamental lever in the construction of communism in human society.

He thought, worked out and wrote many things. And it is fitting to bring out, on a day like today, that Che's writings, Che's political and revolutionary thinking, will be of permanent value in the Cuban revolutionary process and in the Latin American revolutionary process. And we do not doubt that his ideas, as a man of action, as a man of thought, as a man of untarnished moral virtues, as a man of unexcelled human sensitivity, as a man of spotless conduct, have and will continue to have universal value.

The imperialists boast of their triumph at having killed this guerrilla fighter in action—the imperialists boast of a triumphant stroke of luck that led to the elimination of such a splendid man of action. But perhaps the imperialists do not know or pretend not to know that the man of action was only one of the many facets of the personality of that combatant. And if we speak of sorrow, we are saddened not only at having lost a man of action, we are saddened at having lost a morally superior man, we are saddened at having lost a man of exquisite human sensitivity, we are saddened at having lost such a mind. We are saddened to think that he was only thirty-nine years old at the time of his death.

We are saddened at missing the additional fruits that we would have received from that intelligence and that ever richer experience.

We have an idea of the dimensions of the loss for the revolutionary movement. But, nevertheless, here is the weak side of the imperialist enemy: they think that by eliminating a man physically they have eliminated his thinking—that by eliminating him physically they have eliminated his ideas, eliminated his virtues, eliminated his example.

And so shameless are they in this belief that they have no hesitation in publishing, as the most natural thing in the world, the by now almost universally accepted circumstances in which they murdered him after he had been seriously wounded in action. They do not even seem aware of the repulsiveness of the procedure, they do not even seem aware of the shamelessness of the admission. They have published it as if thugs, oligarchs, and mercenaries had the right to shoot a seriously wounded revolutionary combatant.

And even worse, they explain why they did it. They assert that Che's trial would have been quite an earthshaker, that it would have been impossible to place this revolutionary in the dock.

And not only that, but neither have they hesitated to spirit away his remains. And be it true or false, they certainly announced they had cremated his body, thus beginning to show their fear, beginning to show that they are not so sure that by physically eliminating the combatant they can liquidate his ideas, liquidate his example.

Che fell defending the interests, defending the cause of the exploited and the oppressed peoples of this continent—Che fell defending the cause of the poor and disfranchised of this earth. And the exemplary manner and the selflessness with which he defended that cause cannot be disputed by even his most bitter enemies.

And before history, men who act as he did, men who do and give all for the cause of the oppressed, grow in stature with each passing day, and find a deeper place in the heart of the peoples with each passing day. The imperialist enemies are beginning to see this, and it will not be long before it will be proved that his death will, in the long run, be like a seed which will give rise to many men determined to imitate him, many men determined to follow his example.

And we are absolutely convinced that the revolutionary cause on this continent will recover from the blow, that the revolutionary movement on this continent will not be crushed by this blow.

From the revolutionary point of view of our people, how must we view Che's example? Do we feel we have lost him? It is true that we will not see new writings of his, true that we will never again hear his voice. But Che has left a heritage to the world, a great heritage, and we who knew him so well can become in great degree his beneficiaries.

He left us his revolutionary thinking, his revolutionary virtues—he left us his character, his will, his tenacity, his spirit of work. In a word, he left us his example! And Che's example will be a model for our people—Che's example will be the ideal model for our people!

If we wish to express what we expect our revolutionary combatants, our militants, our men to be, we must say, without hesitation: "Let them be like Che!" If we wish to express what we want the men of future generations to be, we must say: "Let them be like Che!" If we wish to say how we want our children to be educated we must say without hesitation: "We want them to be educated in Che's spirit!" If we want the model of a man, the model of a man who does not belong to our time, the model of a man who belongs to the future, I say from the depths of my heart that such a model, without a single stain on his conduct, without a single stain on his actions, is Che! If we wish to express what we want our children to be, we must say from our very hearts as ardent revolutionaries: "We want them to be like Che!"

Che has become a model of what men should be, not only for our people but also for people everywhere in Latin America. Che carried to its highest expression revolutionary stoicism, the revolutionary spirit of sacrifice, revolutionary combativeness, the revolutionary's spirit of work.

Che brought the ideas of Marxism-Leninism to their freshest, purest, most revolutionary expression. No other man of our time has carried the spirit of internationalism to its highest possible level as Che did.

And in the future, when an example of a proletarian internationalist is sought, that example, high above any other, will be

Che's example! National flags, prejudices, chauvinism, and egoism had disappeared from his mind and heart. And he was ready to shed his generous blood spontaneously and immediately, in behalf of any people, for the cause of any people!

And thus, his blood fell on our soil when he was wounded in several battles—and his blood was shed in Bolivia, for the redemption of the exploited and the oppressed. That blood was shed for the sake of all the exploited and all the oppressed—that blood was shed for all the peoples of America and for the people of Vietnam, because while fighting there in Bolivia, fighting against the oligarchies and imperialism, he knew that he was offering Vietnam the highest possible expression of his solidarity!

It is for this reason, comrades of the revolution, that we must face the future with optimism. And in Che's example, we will always look for inspiration, inspiration in struggle, inspiration in tenacity, inspiration in intransigence toward the enemy, inspiration in internationalist sentiment!

Therefore, after tonight's impressive ceremony, after this incredible demonstration of multitudinous recognition—incredible for its magnitude, discipline, and spirit of devotion—which demonstrates that our people are a sensitive, grateful people who know how to honor the memory of the brave who die in combat, that our people recognize those who serve them, which demonstrates the people's solidarity with the revolutionary struggle and how this people will raise aloft and maintain ever higher aloft the revolutionary banners and revolutionary principles—in these moments of remembrance, let us lift our spirits, with optimism for the future, with absolute optimism in the final victory of the peoples, and say to Che and to the heroes who fought and died with him: Ever onward to victory!

PATRIA O MUERTE! VENCEREMOS!

# che guevara

## reminiscences of the cuban revolutionary war

# Prologue

For a long time we have wanted to write a history of our Revolution which would encompass all its many facets and aspects. Many of the leaders of the Revolution have often privately or publicly expressed their desire to write such a history, but the tasks are many, the years pass, and the memory of the insurrection is dissolving in the past. We have not yet definitively set down these events, which already belong to the history of America.

For this reason I am starting a series of personal reminiscences of attacks, battles, and skirmishes in which we all participated. It is not my intention that this fragmentary history, based on remembrances and a few hasty notes, should be taken as a full account. On the contrary, I hope that each theme will be developed by those who lived it.

The fact that I personally was limited to the fighting at a given point on the map of Cuba during the entire struggle prevented me from participating in battles and events in other places. I believe that to bring to life our revolutionary actions and to do this in an orderly manner, I can best begin with the first battle, the only one in which Fidel participated which went against our forces: the surprise attack at Alegría de Pío.*

---

* In this volume, the account of the battle at Alegría de Pío is preceded by two chapters dealing with the beginning of the expedition and the voyage of the "Granma." (*All footnotes have been added by the editor.*)

There are many survivors of this battle and each of them is encouraged to contribute his recollections so that the story may thus be filled out. I ask only that the narrator be strictly truthful. He should not pretend, for his own aggrandizement, to have been where he was not, and he should beware of inaccuracies. I ask that after having written a few pages to the best of his ability, depending on his education and his disposition, he then criticize them as seriously as possible in order to remove every word which does not refer to a strict fact, or those where the fact is uncertain. With this intention I begin my reminiscences.

ERNESTO CHE GUEVARA

# "El Patojo"

A few days ago a cable brought the news of the death of some Guatemalan patriots, among them Julio Roberto Cáceres Valle.

In this difficult job of a revolutionary, in the midst of class wars which are convulsing the entire continent, death is a frequent accident. But the death of a friend, a comrade during difficult hours and a sharer in dreams of better times, is always painful for the person who receives the news, and Julio Roberto was a great friend. He was short and frail; for that reason we called him "El Patojo," Guatemalan slang meaning "Shorty" or Kid.

El Patojo had witnessed the birth of our Revolution while in Mexico and had volunteered to join us. Fidel, however, did not want to bring any more foreigners into that struggle for national liberation in which I had the honor to participate.

A few days after the Revolution triumphed, El Patojo sold his few belongings and, with only a small suitcase, appeared in Cuba. He worked in various branches of public administration, and he was the first Chief of Personnel of the Department of Industrialization of INRA [the National Institute of Agrarian Reform]. But he was never happy with his work. El Patojo was looking for something different; he was seeking the liberation of his own country. The Revolution had changed him profoundly, as it had all of us. The bewildered boy who had left Guatemala without fully under-

31

standing the defeat had changed now to the fully conscious revolutionary.

The first time we met we were on a train, fleeing Guatemala, a couple of months after the fall of Arbenz. We were going to Tapachula, from where we could reach Mexico City. El Patojo was several years younger than I, but we immediately formed a lasting friendship. Together we made the trip from Chiapas to Mexico City; together we faced the same problems—we were both penniless, defeated, and forced to earn a living in an indifferent if not hostile environment.

El Patojo had no money and I only a few pesos; I bought a camera and, together, we undertook the illegal job* of taking pictures of people in the city parks. Our partner was a Mexican who had a small darkroom where we developed the films. We got to know all of Mexico City, walking from one end to another, delivering the atrocious photographs we had taken. We battled with all kinds of clients, trying to convince them that the little boy in the photo was really very cute and it was really a great bargain to pay a Mexican peso for such a marvel. Thus we ate for several months. Little by little the contingencies of revolutionary life separated us. I have already said that Fidel did not want to bring him to Cuba, not because of any shortcomings of his, but so as not to turn our army into an international force.

El Patojo had been a journalist, had studied physics at the University of Mexico, had left his studies and then returned to them, without ever getting very far ahead. He earned his living in various places, at various jobs, and never asked for anything. I still do not know whether that sensitive and serious boy was immensely timid, or too proud to recognize his weaknesses and his personal problems to approach a friend for help. El Patojo was an introvert, highly intelligent, broadly cultured, sensitive. He matured steadily and in his last days put his great sensibilities at the service

---

* As foreigners, they did not have permission to work.

of his people. He belonged to the Partido Guatemalteco de Trabajo [Guatemalan Labor Party] and had disciplined himself in that life —he was developing into a fine revolutionary. By then, little remained of his earlier hypersensitivity. Revolution purifies men, improves and develops them, just as the experienced farmer corrects the deficiencies of his crops and strengthens the good qualities.

After he came to Cuba we almost always lived in the same house, as was proper for two old friends. But we no longer maintained the early intimacy in this new life, and I only suspected what was going on in his mind when I sometimes saw him earnestly studying one of the native Indian languages of his country. One day he told me he was leaving, that the time had come for him to do his duty.

El Patojo had had no military training; he simply felt that duty called him. He was going to his country to fight, gun in hand, somehow to reproduce our guerrilla struggle. It was then that we had one of our few long talks. I limited myself to recommending strongly these three things: constant movement, absolute mistrust, and eternal vigilance. Movement: that is, never stay put; never spend two nights in the same place; never stop moving from one place to another. Mistrust: at the beginning, mistrust even your own shadow, friendly peasants, informants, guides, contacts; mistrust everything until you hold a liberated zone. Vigilance: constant guard duty, constant reconnaissance; establishment of a camp in a safe place and, above all, never sleep beneath a roof, never sleep in a house where you can be surrounded. This was the synthesis of our guerrilla experience, the only thing—along with a warm handshake—which I could give to my friend. Could I advise him not to do it? With what right? We had undertaken something at a time when it was believed impossible, and now he saw that it had succeeded.

El Patojo left and, in time, the news of his death came. At the beginning we hoped that there had been a confusion of names, that there had been some mistake, but unfortunately his body had been identified by his own mother; there is no doubt that he is dead. And not only he, but a group of comrades with him, all of them as brave, as selfless, as intelligent perhaps as he, but not personally known to us.

Once again we taste the bitterness of defeat and we ask the unanswered question: why did he not learn from the experience of others? Why did those men not heed more carefully the simple advice which was given? We still do not know exactly what happened, but we do know that the region was poorly chosen, that the men were not physically prepared, that they were not mistrustful enough and, of course, that they were not vigilant enough. The repressive army surprised them, killed a few, dispersed the rest, then returned to pursue them, and virtually annihilated them. They took some prisoners; others, like El Patojo, died in battle. After losing their unity, the guerrillas were probably hunted down, as we had been after Alegría de Pío.

Once again young blood has fertilized the fields of America, to make freedom possible. Another battle has been lost; we must make time to weep for our fallen comrades while we sharpen our machetes. From the valuable and tragic experience of the cherished dead, we must firmly resolve not to repeat their errors, to avenge the death of each one of them with many victories, and to bring about total liberation.

When El Patojo left Cuba, he left nothing behind, nor did he leave any messages; he had few clothes or personal belongings to worry about. However, old mutual friends in Mexico brought me some poems he had written and left there in a notebook. They are the last verses of a revolutionary; they are, in addition, a love song to the Revolution, the homeland, and to a woman. To that woman whom El Patojo knew and loved in Cuba, are addressed these final verses, this injunction:

Take it, it is only my heart
Hold it in your hand
And when the day dawns,
Open your hand
And let the sun warm it. . . .

El Patojo's heart has remained among us, in the hands of his beloved and in the loving hands of an entire people, waiting to be warmed beneath the sun of a new day which will surely shine for Guatemala and for all America. Today, in the Ministry of Industry where he left many friends, there is a small school of statistics, called in his memory "Julio Roberto Cáceres Valle." Later, when Guatemala is free, his beloved name will surely be given to a school, a factory, or a hospital, to any place where people fight and work in the building of a new society.

# A Revolution Begins

The history of the military takeover of March 10, 1952—the blood-less coup directed by Fulgencio Batista—does not, of course, begin on the very day of the coup. Its antecedents must be sought further back in the history of Cuba: much further back than the interven-tion of U.S. Ambassador Sumner Wells in 1933; even further back than the Platt Amendment of 1901; further back than the landing of the "hero" Narciso López, sent directly by the North American annexationists. We reach the roots of the matter in the period of John Quincy Adams who, at the beginning of the nine-teenth century, announced the posture which his country was to take with regard to Cuba. The island was seen as an apple which, cut from Spain's branches, was fated to fall into Uncle Sam's hands. These are all links in a long chain of continental aggression which has been directed against others as well as Cuba.

This tide, this imperial ebb and flow, is marked by the rise or fall of new governments under the uncontrollable pressure of the masses. The history of all Latin America exhibits these characteris-tics: dictatorial governments representing a small minority come to power through coups d'état; democratic governments with a wide popular base arise laboriously and often, even before assuming power, are compromised by a series of pre-arranged concessions which had been necessary to their survival.

The Cuban revolution in this respect was an exception, and it becomes necessary here to present a little background, for the author of these words, tossed by the waves of these social movements convulsing America, thus had the opportunity to meet another American exile: Fidel Castro.

I met him on one of those cold nights in Mexico, and I remember that our first discussion was on international politics. A few hours later that same night—at dawn—I was one of the future expeditionaries. But I should like to clarify how and why I met the present head of the Cuban government in Mexico. It was in 1954, during the ebb of the democratic governments, when the last revolutionary American democracy maintaining itself upright in the area—that of Jacobo Arbenz Guzmán—succumbed before the cold, premeditated aggression of the USA, hidden behind a smokescreen of continental propaganda. Its apparent leader was the Secretary of State, John Foster Dulles, who by a strange coincidence was also the lawyer for and a stockholder in the United Fruit Company, the major imperialist concern in Guatemala.

I was on my way back from there, defeated, united in my pain to all the Guatemalans, hoping, seeking a way to recreate a future for that bleeding land. And Fidel came to Mexico seeking neutral territory on which to prepare his men for the big push. The assault on the Moncada barracks in Santiago de Cuba had already pared away all those of weak will, who for one reason or another joined political parties or revolutionary groups demanding less sacrifice. The recruits were joining the brand-new ranks of the 26th of July Movement (named for a date marking the 1953 attack on the Moncada barracks). A very hard task was beginning for those in charge of training these people under necessary conditions of secrecy in Mexico. They were fighting against the Mexican government, against American FBI agents, and also against Batista's spies; they were fighting against these three forces which in one way and another joined together, money and personal sellouts playing a large role. In addition, they had to fight against Trujillo's spies, against the poor selection of human material (especially in Miami). And, after overcoming all of these difficulties, we had also to manage the all-important departure, and then arrival, and all that these entailed. At that time, this seemed easy to us. Today we can measure the cost in effort, in sacrifices, and in lives.

Fidel Castro, helped by a small group of intimates, gave himself over entirely, with all his capacity and his extraordinary spirit of work, to the task of organizing the armed expedition to Cuba. He almost never gave lessons in military tactics, for there was little time. The rest of us were able to learn a good bit from General Alberto Bayo.* My almost immediate impression, on hearing the first lessons, was of the possibility for victory, which I had seen as very doubtful when I joined the rebel commander. I had been linked to him, from the outset, by a tie of romantic adventurous sympathy, and by the conviction that it would be worth dying on a foreign beach for such a pure ideal.

Thus several months passed. Our marksmanship became more exact, and sharpshooters emerged. We found a ranch in Mexico where, under the direction of General Bayo—I was Chief of Personnel—the final preparations for a March 1956 departure were made. However at that time two Mexican police forces, both paid by Batista, were hunting Fidel Castro, and one of them had the good fortune—financially speaking—to capture him. But they committed the error—also financially speaking—of not killing him after making him prisoner.† Many of Fidel's followers were captured some days later. Our ranch on the outskirts of Mexico City also fell to the police, and we all went to jail.

This postponed the beginning of the last part of the first stage. There were some who spent fifty-seven days in prison, with the

---

* A veteran of the Spanish Civil War.
† In order to collect the reward.

threat of extradition hanging constantly over us (Major Calixto García and I can testify to this). But at no time did we lose our personal trust in Fidel Castro. For Fidel did some things which we might almost say compromised his revolutionary attitude for the sake of friendship. I remember making my own case clear: I was a foreigner in Mexico illegally, and with a series of charges against me. I told Fidel that under no circumstances should the Revolution be held back for me; that he could leave me behind; that I understood the situation and would try to join their fight from wherever I was sent; that the only effort they should make on my behalf was to have me sent to a nearby country and not to Argentina. I also remember Fidel's brusque reply: "I will not abandon you." And so it was, for they had to use precious time and money to get us out of the Mexican jail. The personal attitude of Fidel toward the people he esteems is the key to the absolute devotion which is created around him; loyalty to the man, together with an attachment to principles make this Rebel Army an indivisible unit.

The days passed, we worked secretly, hid where we could, avoided public appearances as much as possible, and in fact almost never went out into the street.

When a few months had passed, we found there was a traitor in our ranks. We did not know who it was, but he had sold an arms shipment of ours. We also knew that he had sold the yacht and a transmitter, although the "legal contract" of the sale had not yet been completed. This first betrayal proved to the Cuban authorities that their agent was doing his job and knew our secrets. This is also what saved us, for we were shown the same thing. From that moment on, frenzied activity was necessary: the "Granma" was prepared with extraordinary speed, and we stocked as much food as we could get (not very much, of course), as well as uniforms, rifles, equipment, and two anti-tank rifles with almost no ammunition.

Finally, on November 25, 1956, at two in the morning, Fidel's words, which had been derided by the official press, began to take on reality: "In 1956 we shall be free or we shall be martyrs."

With our lights extinguished we left the port of Tuxpan amid an infernal mess of men and all sorts of materiel. The weather was very bad and navigation was forbidden, but the river's estuary was calm. We traversed the entrance into the Gulf and a little later turned on our lights. We began a frenzied search for the anti-seasickness pills, which we did not find. We sang the Cuban national anthem and the "Hymn of the 26th of July" for perhaps five minutes and then the entire boat took on an aspect both ridiculous and tragic: men with anguished faces holding their stomachs, some with their heads in buckets, others lying in the strangest positions, immobile, their clothing soiled with vomit.

Apart from two or three sailors and four or five other people, the rest of the eighty-three crew members were seasick. But by the fourth or fifth day the general panorama had improved a little. We discovered that what we had thought was a leak in the boat was actually an open plumbing faucet. We had thrown overboard everything superfluous in order to lighten the load.

The route we had chosen made a wide circuit south of Cuba, windward of Jamaica and the Grand Cayman islands, in order to reach the point of disembarkation somewhere near the town of Niquero, in the province of Oriente. The plan was carried out quite slowly. On the 30th we heard over the radio the news of riots in Santiago de Cuba, which our great Frank País had organized, hoping to coincide with the arrival of our expedition. The following night, December 1, without water, fuel, and food, we were pointing our bow on a straight course toward Cuba, desperately seeking the lighthouse at Cabo Cruz. At two in the morning, on a dark and tempestuous night, the situation was worrisome. The watches moved about, looking for the beam of light which did not appear on the horizon. Roque, an ex-lieutenant in the Navy, once again mounted the small upper bridge looking for the light at Cabo. He lost his footing and fell into the water. A while later, as we set out once again, we did see the light, but the wheezing progress of our yacht made the last hours of the trip interminable. It was already daylight when we landed in Cuba, at a place known as Belic, on the Las Coloradas beach.

A coast guard cutter spotted us and telegraphed Batista's Army. No sooner had we disembarked and entered the swamp, in great haste and carrying only the indispensable, when we were attacked by enemy planes. Since we were walking through mangrove-covered marshes, we were not visible, nor were we hit by the planes, but the Army of the dictatorship was now on our trail.

We took several hours to get through the swamp. We were delayed in this by the lack of experience and irresponsibility of a comrade who had claimed he knew the way. We were on solid ground, disoriented and walking in circles, an army of shadows, of phantoms, walking as if moved by some obscure psychic mechanism. We had had seven days of continual hunger and sickness at sea, followed by three days on land which were even more terrible. Exactly ten days after leaving Mexico, at dawn on December 5, after a night's march interrupted by fainting, exhaustion, and rest stops, we reached a place known—what a paradox!—as Alegría [Happiness] de Pío.

# Alegria de Pio

Alegría de Pío is in the province of Oriente, in the Niquero zone, near Cabo Cruz. It was there, on December 5, 1956, that we were set upon by Batista's troops.

We were much weakened after a march more arduous than long. On December 2 we had landed in a place called Playa de las Coloradas, losing almost all our equipment and walking for endless hours through salt-water marshes. We all wore new boots which had blistered our feet. But our footwear and the resulting fungal infections were not our only enemies. We had left the Mexican port of Tuxpan on November 25, a day on which the north wind (a norther) made navigation hazardous. We landed in Cuba after seven days of crossing the Gulf of Mexico and the Caribbean. We sailed without food, our boat was in poor repair, and most of us, unused to sea travel, were seasick. All this had left its mark on the troop of rookies who had never known combat.

Nothing remained of our equipment but a few rifles, cartridge belts, and some wet bullets. Our medical supplies had disappeared, our packs had for the most part been left in the swamps. The previous day we had walked by night along the border of the cane fields of Niquero sugar mill, which in those days belonged to Julio Lobo. We satisfied our hunger and thirst by eating cane as we walked, and, inexperienced as we were, we left the peelings behind. We found out years later that the enemy did not in fact need these careless clues to our presence since our guide, one of the principal traitors in the Revolution, brought them to us. The guide had been given the night off, an error we were to repeat several times during the war, until we learned that civilians of unknown background were always to be closely watched when we were in danger zones. We should never have allowed our treacherous guide to leave.

At dawn on the 5th only a few of us could go a step further; our exhausted men could walk only short distances, and then needed long rests. A halt at the edge of a cane field was ordered. Most of us slept through the morning in a thicket near the dense woods.

At noon we became aware of unusual activity. Piper Cub planes as well as other military and private aircraft began to circle in the vicinity. Some of our men were calmly cutting and eating cane as the planes passed overhead, without thinking how visible they were to the low-flying aircraft.

As the troop's doctor, it was my job to treat the men's blisters. I think I remember my last patient on that day. He was Humberto Lamotte, and as it turned out, it was his last day on earth. I can still see his tired and anxious face as he moved from our primitive clinic toward his post, carrying the shoes he could not wear.

Comrade Montané and I were leaning against a tree, talking about our respective children; we were eating our meager rations —half a sausage and two crackers—when we heard a shot. In a matter of seconds a hurricane of bullets—or at least this is what it seemed to my anxious mind during that trial by fire—rained on the troop of eighty-two men. My rifle was not of the best—I had deliberately asked for it because a long asthma attack during the crossing had left me in a deplorable state and I did not want to waste a good weapon. I do not know exactly when or how things happened; the memories are already hazy. I do remember that during the cross fire, Almeida—Captain in those days—came to ask for orders, but there was no longer anyone there to give them. As I found out later, Fidel tried in vain to regroup his men in the nearby cane field, which could be reached simply by crossing a small clearing. The surprise attack had been too massive, the bullets too abundant. Almeida went back to take charge of his group. At that moment a comrade dropped a cartridge box at my feet. I pointed questioningly to it and the man answered me with a face I remember perfectly, for the anguish it reflected seemed to say, "It's too late for bullets," and he immediately left along the path through the cane field (he was later murdered by Batista's thugs). This was perhaps the first time I was faced with the dilemma of choosing between my dedication to medicine and my duty as a revolutionary soldier. At my feet were a pack full of medicines and a cartridge box; together, they were too heavy to carry. I chose the cartridge box, leaving behind the medicine pack, and crossed the clearing which separated me from the cane field. I distinctly remember Faustino Pérez kneeling on the edge of the field, firing his machine pistol. Near me a comrade named Arbentosa was walking toward the plantation. A burst of gunfire, nothing special about it, hit us both. I felt a terrible blow on the chest and another in the neck, and was sure I was dead. Arbentosa, spewing blood from his nose, mouth, and an enormous wound from a .45 bullet, shouted something like, "They've killed me," and began to fire wildly, although no one was visible at that moment. From the ground I said to Faustino, "They've got me" (but I used a stronger expression). Still firing, Faustino glanced at me and told me it was nothing, but in his eyes I read a sentence of death from my wound.

I stayed on the ground; following the same obscure impulse as Faustino, I fired once toward the forest. I immediately began to wonder what would be the best way to die, now that all seemed lost. I remembered an old story of Jack London's in which the hero, knowing that he is condemned to freeze to death in the icy reaches of Alaska, leans against a tree and decides to end his life with dignity. This is the only image I remember. Someone, crawling near me, shouted that we'd better surrender, and behind me I heard a voice, which I later learned belonged to Camilo Cienfuegos, shouting back: "Here no one surrenders. . ." followed by an oath. Agitated and short of breath, Ponce approached me. He had a wound, apparently through the lung. He told me he was wounded and, indifferently, I showed him that I was also. Ponce continued dragging himself toward the cane field, together with the unwounded men. For a moment I was alone, stretched out waiting for my death.

Almeida came over to me and urged me to move. In spite of my pain, I did so and we entered the field. There I saw our comrade Raúl Suárez near a tree, his thumb shattered by a bullet and Faustino Pérez bandaging it for him. After this everything became confused. The light planes flew low over us, firing a few shots from their machine guns. This only added to the Dantesque and grotesque scenes around us: a stout *guerrillero* trying to hide behind a single stalk of sugar cane; and another, without really knowing why, crying out for silence in the midst of the tremendous uproar.

A group was formed, led by Almeida, and including Lieutenant Ramiro Valdés (now a major), comrades Chao and Benítez, and myself. With Almeida at the head, we crossed the last row in the cane field in order to reach a small sheltering forest. At that moment we heard the first shouts of "Fire!" from the cane field and columns of smoke and flames rose from it; I am not sure of this, for I was thinking more of the bitterness of our defeat and the imminence of my death than of the specific incidents of the battle. We walked until night prevented us from going any further, and we decided to sleep huddled together. We were attacked by mosquitoes, tortured by thirst and by hunger. Such was our baptism of fire on December 5, 1956, in the district of Niquero. Such was the beginning of what would become the Rebel Army.

# Adrift

The day after the Alegría de Pío surprise attack, we were marching through the brush in a zone where red earth alternated with "dog-tooth" rocks. We heard the crack of a few isolated shots, and we never managed to find a real road. Chao, a veteran of the Spanish war, pointed out that by groping our way, as we were doing, we would surely end up falling into an enemy ambush. He proposed to find a place where we could wait for night to come, so that we could continue our journey under cover of darkness.

We were virtually without water and we had had a mishap with the only container of milk we had. Benítez, to whom it had been entrusted, had slipped it into his pocket, bottom side up. The little holes we had made in it for drinking purposes were thus upside down; and when we went to serve our ration—a vitamin tube of condensed milk with a sip of water—we realized with dismay that it had spilled all over Benítez' pocket and uniform.

We succeeded in installing ourselves in a kind of cavern; we had a broad view to one side, but on the other, unfortunately, it was impossible to intercept an enemy advance. However, since we were more concerned with not being seen than with defending ourselves, we decided to stay there all day. All five of us made a formal pledge to fight to the death. The names of those who made this pledge: Ramiro Valdés, Juan Almeida, Chao, Benítez, and the author of this account. All five of us survived the terrible experience of the defeat and the subsequent battles.

Night fell and we set out again. Drawing on my recollections of astronomy, I spotted the North Star, and for two days we guided ourselves by it, moving eastward toward the Sierra Maestra. Months later I was to learn that the star we used to find our way was not the North Star! It was simply good luck that we took the right direction and arrived in front of some cliffs near the coast at dawn.

Between us and the sea there was a cliff, about fifty meters high. On the other side rose into view the tempting sight of a pool of water, sweet water it appeared to us. That night a swarm of land crabs crawled around us and, driven by hunger, we massacred them. Since building a fire was out of the question, we swallowed the gelatinous part of their carcasses raw, which made us terribly thirsty.

It took us a good while to discover a passage by which we could descend to the water. But in the confusion of our comings and goings, we lost sight of the pond we had spotted from above. We had to make do with some little puddles of rain water, found in the hollows of the "dog-tooth" rocks.

We used the tiny pump of an anti-asthma vaporizer for extracting the water, of which there was scarcely a few drops for each of us.

We marched on, in no particular direction, demoralized. From time to time a plane flew over the sea. Walking among the rocks was extremely tiring; one of us suggested that we move along the coastal cliffs, but there was a serious drawback to that: the enemy could see us. So we remained in the shade of a cluster of shrubs, waiting for sundown. At nightfall, we found a small beach, where we swam.

I tried to put into practice a trick which I had once read about in a popular science magazine or in a novel. It was explained that sweet water mixed with a third of sea water increased the quantity and gave a very good potable water. I experimented, using a gourd, but the result was lamentable: a brackish beverage of which my comrades took a dim view. Somewhat refreshed by the swim, we resumed our march. It was night and, if I remember correctly, there was quite a good moon. Almeida and I, marching at the van, suddenly noticed that in one of the little shanties that fishermen put up at the sea's edge to protect themselves from bad weather, there were shadows of sleeping men. We were sure they were soldiers, but we were already too close to retrace our steps. We strode ahead. Almeida was going to demand that they surrender, but we had a happy surprise: they were three comrades from the "Granma": Camilo Cienfuegos, Pancho González, and Pablo Hurtado. At once we began to exchange impressions, news, opinions about the little each of us knew concerning the other comrades and the battle. Camilo's group offered us sticks of sugar cane, which they had pulled up before fleeing. This sweet and juicy substance was a good hunger-appeaser. Meanwhile, they were chewing crabs avidly. They had found a way to appease their thirst by drawing water directly from the little hollows in the rocks with a tube or a scooped-out stick.

We trekked on, all together. The surviving combatants of the "Granma" army numbered eight at that point, and we had no information about the existence of other survivors! We thought that, according to all logic, there must be other groups such as ours. But we hadn't the least idea of where to find them. All we knew was that by marching with the sea to our right we were going east, that is, toward the Sierra, where we were to take refuge. We did not try to hide from ourselves the fact that in the case of an encounter with the enemy, trapped as we were between the craggy cliffs and the sea, our chances of flight were nil. I no longer remember whether we marched along the coast for one day or two. I simply have a recollection of our eating little prickly pears which grew along the shore. There were only one or two apiece with which to stave off hunger. And we were tortured by thirst, since we had to ration our few drops of water with the greatest strictness.

One morning at dawn we arrived, dog-tired, at the sea coast; we stopped there to doze, while waiting to see clearly enough to find a passage before facing the too-steep cliffs.

When it was light, we began to explore. We stopped in surprise before a big house of palmwood, which appeared to belong to some fairly prosperous peasant. My immediate reaction was that we should not approach this sort of house, since its inhabitants would probably be hostile to us; indeed, the house might even be occupied by the Army. Benítez did not share my opinion and we ended up going toward the house together.

I stayed outside while he climbed over a barbed-wire fence. Someone else was with us, I don't remember who. Suddenly I noticed, in the dim light, a clearly outlined silhouette of a uniformed man holding an M-1 rifle. I thought that this was curtains for us, at least for Benítez, but since he was closer to the man, I was unable to warn him. Benítez, within two steps of the soldier, wheeled and returned toward me, saying with complete naïveté that he had returned because he saw "a man with a gun" and that it was his opinion that it was wiser not to ask the man any questions.

In actual fact, we felt as if we had been raised from the dead, especially Benítez! But our odyssey did not end there. After a discreet inspection of the locality, we saw that it would be necessary to scale the cliffs, which were not so steep at this point. In fact, we were coming close to the Ojo de Buey [Ox-Eye] zone, thus named because of a small stream of water which flowed down to the sea, cutting right through the cliff.

Night came upon us before the end of our climb. We had time only to find a cave, a magnificent observation post for the entire panorama. Absolute calm reigned on the landscape. We saw some men come ashore from a Navy skiff—we counted about thirty of them—and others embark, in what appeared to be a relief operation.

We learned later that these men were Laurent's—that fearful Navy murderer—who, once he had accomplished his mission of executing a group of our comrades, was engaged in relieving his men.

Before the astounded eyes of Benítez the "men with the guns" appeared, in all their tragic reality. The situation was not good. If we were discovered, not the slightest chance of escape; we would have no alternative but to fight it out on the spot to the end.

We hadn't eaten a mouthful all day; we rationed our water— and with what precision! We distributed it in the eyepiece of a pair of field-glasses; nothing could be fairer.

At night we resumed our march, aiming to get out of this locality where we had spent some of the most anguished days of the war, victims of hunger and thirst, of our sense of defeat, and the imminence of real and overwhelming danger, which gave us the sensation of rats in a trap.

After much groping, we came upon a famous torrent that empties into the sea, or of one of its tributaries. Throwing ourselves to the ground, we drank for a long time with the avidity of horses; we would have continued but our stomachs, empty of food, refused to absorb another drop. We filled our flasks and kept going. At dawn we reached the top of a hillock crowned with a clump of trees. So that we could resist and hide most effectively, the group spread out; we spent the entire day watching small planes equipped with loudspeakers emitting incomprehensible noises as they buzzed us. Almeida and Benítez, veterans of Moncada, realized that they were calling on us to surrender. From time to time, unidentifiable noises came from the forest.

That night our peregrinations led us near a house from which emerged the sound of music. Once more, we had differences of opinion. Ramiro, Almeida, and I were of the firm opinion that we must absolutely avoid showing ourselves at a dance or any such festive occasion because the peasants would announce our presence far and wide, not necessarily out of ill-will but for the pleasure of spreading news. Benítez and Camilo felt that we had to enter, at any price, so that we could eat. Finally Ramiro and I were chosen to go to the house, glean the news, and procure food. We were on our way there when suddenly the music stopped and we distinctly heard the voice of a man saying something like "And now, let us drink to our comrades-in-arms whose exploits were so brilliant," etc. That was enough for us; we did an about-face, stealthily but on the double, and reported to our comrades in which waters these men were at home.

We took up our march but the men balked at every turn. That night, or perhaps it was the next one, all the comrades with few exceptions decided that they did not want to continue. We were obliged, at that moment, to knock at the door of a peasant near the road, at Puercas Gordas, nine days after the surprise attack at Alegría de Pío.

We were warmly received. That peasant hut became the scene of endless feasting. Hours passed and yet we ate, so much and so well that dawn found us still revelling. It was impossible to leave. During the morning there was a constant procession of peasants who, filled with curiosity and solicitude, came to make our acquaintance, offer us food, or bring us some gift.

Then, the little house that sheltered us turned into an inferno. Almeida was the first to be overcome by diarrhea; and, in a flash, eight inappreciative intestines gave evidence of the blackest ingratitude. Some of the comrades began to vomit. Pablo Hurtado, exhausted by seasickness, by days of marching, by thirst and hunger, could no longer stand.

We decided to leave that night. The peasants told us that according to the news they had picked up, Fidel was alive. They proposed to take us to a place where, in all probability, we could find him and Crescencio Pérez. But they made one condition: we must leave our weapons and uniforms behind. Almeida and I kept our two Star Tommy guns. The eight guns and all the cartridges stayed in the peasant's hut as security. We planned to make it to the Maestra in stages, stopping over with peasants; we therefore divided into two groups, one of three men, one of four.

Our group, if I remember correctly, was composed of Pancho González, Ramiro Valdés, Almeida, and myself. In the other were Camilo, Benítez, and Chao. Pablo Hurtado was too sick to leave the house.

We were scarcely on our way when the owner gave in to the temptation of passing on the news to a friend, under pretext of asking his advice concerning the best way to hide our arms. The latter convinced him to sell them. They haggled with a third thief and it was he who denounced us to the police. As a result, a few hours after our departure from the first hospitable Cuban hearth, there was an enemy raid; they took Pablo Hurtado prisoner and seized our weapons.

We were staying with an Adventist named Argelio Rosabal, known as "Pastor." This comrade, hearing the bad news, promptly got in touch with another peasant who knew the zone thoroughly and was a rebel sympathizer. That same night we left for another, safer shelter. The peasant whom we met on that occasion was Guillermo García: today he is the commander of the Oriente army and a member of the national leadership of our Party.

Subsequently we were welcomed at several peasant homes: Carlos Mas, who later joined our ranks; Perucho, and other comrades whose names I have forgotten. One morning at daybreak, after crossing the road to Pilón and after marching without any guide at all, we reached the farm of Mongo Pérez, Crescencio's brother. There we found all the comrades of our landing troop who had survived and who were, for the time being, free: Fidel Castro, Universo Sánchez, Faustino Pérez, Raúl Castro, Ciro Redondo, Efigenio Ameijeiras, René Rodríguez, and Armando Rodríguez. A few days later we were joined by Morán, Crespo, Julito Díaz, Calixto García, Calixto Morales, and Bermúdez.

Our little band was without uniforms and without weapons. In fact, aside from the two Tommy guns, we had salvaged nothing from the disaster. Fidel reproached us bitterly.

For the duration of the campaign and even today his words remain engraved on my mind: "You have not paid for the error you committed, because the price you pay for the abandonment of your weapons under such circumstances is your life. The one and only hope of survival that you would have had, in the event of a head-on encounter with the Army, was your guns. To abandon them was criminal and stupid."

# The Battle of La Plata

The attack on the small barracks at the mouth of the La Plata river in the Sierra Maestra brought us our first victory, and had repercussions which reached far beyond the craggy region where it took place. It came to everyone's attention, proving that the Rebel Army existed and was ready to fight. For us, it was the reaffirmation of the possibility of our final triumph.

On January 14, 1957, a little over a month after the surprise attack at Alegría de Pío, we stopped at the Magdalena river which is separated from the La Plata by a range of the Sierra which ends in the ocean, separating the two small river valleys. Here, on Fidel's order, we trained the men in the elements of marksmanship; some of them held guns for the first time in their lives. Here we also washed, after many days of ignoring hygiene, and those who could changed their clothes. At that time we had twenty-three usable weapons: nine rifles with telescopic sights, five semi-automatics, four bolt-action rifles, two Thompson submachine guns, two machine pistols, and a 16-gauge shotgun. That afternoon we climbed the last hillock to reach the environs of the La Plata. We walked along a narrow, deserted footpath in the woods, following machete slashes left especially for us by a local peasant named Melquiades Elías. His name had been given to us by our guide, Eutimio, who at that time was indispensable to us and was a model peasant rebel. Some time later Eutimio was captured by Casillas who, instead of killing him, bribed him with the offer of 10,000 pesos and a rank in the Army if he would murder Fidel. He came very close to carrying out this plan, but he lacked the courage to do it. Nevertheless, by revealing our campsites, he proved important to the enemy.

At that period, Eutimio served us loyally; he was one of the many peasants who had fought for his land against the landlords, and who, in so doing, fought also against the Guardia Rural.

During that day's march we captured two *guajiros* (peasants). They turned out to be relatives of our guide; we released one of them, but kept the other as a precautionary measure. The following day, January 15, we sighted the half-constructed zinc-roofed barracks of La Plata. We saw a group of men who, although half-clothed, sported the enemy uniform. We saw that at six in the evening, just before sunset, a launch loaded with guards arrived. Some disembarked, others got on. Since we did not clearly understand these maneuvers, we decided to postpone the attack until the following day.

From dawn on the 16th the barracks was under constant surveillance. The coast guards had retired for the night; we sent out a few scouts who saw no soldiers anywhere. At three in the afternoon, in order to see more, we decided to move up the path leading to the barracks and bordering the river. At nightfall we crossed the shallow La Plata river and posted ourselves on the path. After five minutes two *guajiros* passed and we took them prisoner. One of them was a known informer. Once they knew who we were and believed our threats, they gave us vital information. We found out that there were about fifteen soldiers in the barracks; furthermore, we were told that in a while one of the three most infamous foremen in the region, Chicho Osorio, would pass along the road. These foremen worked on the Laviti plantation, an enormous fief run by means of terror with the help of individuals

like Chicho Osorio. After a while Chicho appeared, drunk and
mounted on a mule, which he was sharing with a little Negro
boy. Universo Sánchez called to him to halt in the name of the
Guardia Rural, and he immediately answered "mosquito," the pass-
word.

Despite our ragged appearance, we were able to trick Chicho
Osorio, maybe because he was so drunk. Fidel, in an indignant
manner, told him he was an Army colonel, that he had come to
find out why the rebels had not yet been destroyed, that *he* was
going into the mountains to find them (that was why he had a
beard), and that what the Army was doing was "garbage." All in
all he spoke quite contemptuously of the enemy's efficiency. With
great submissiveness, Chicho Osorio said that it was true, the
guards spent their time inside the barracks, eating and doing
nothing but carry out unimportant maneuvers; all the rebels, he
said strongly, should be destroyed. We began to ask Chicho dis-
creetly about friendly and unfriendly people in the region, naturally
reversing the roles: when Chicho said someone was bad, we then
had reason to believe he was good. In this way we collected about
twenty names, and the scoundrel continued jabbering. He told us
that he had killed two men, "but *mi general Batista* let me go
free immediately"; he told us how he had just beaten some peasants
who had "gotten a bit uppity" and that, in fact, the Guardia Rural
were incapable of doing anything like that; they allowed the
peasants to talk back with impunity. Fidel asked him what he
would do with Fidel Castro if he captured him, and Chicho
answered with an unmistakable gesture that he would cut off
his ———, as he would also do with Crescencio. Look, he said,
pointing to the Mexican-made boots he wore (and which we wore
also), "I got them off one of those sons of ——— we killed."
There, without knowing it, Chicho Osorio had signed his own
death sentence. In the end, on Fidel's suggestion, he agreed to
lead us to the barracks in order to surprise the soldiers and show

them that they were poorly prepared and were neglecting their duty.

We approached the barracks, with Chicho Osorio leading us; personally, I was not too sure that the man had not already caught on to our game. However, he continued in all innocence: he was so drunk his judgment was impaired. As we crossed the river once again in order to come closer to the barracks, Fidel told him that according to military regulations prisoners had to be bound; Chicho did not resist and he unknowingly continued as a real prisoner. He explained that the only guard post was between the partly constructed barracks and the house of one of the other overseers, Honorio, and he led us to a place near the barracks where the road to El Macío passed. Comrade Luis Crespo, today a major, was sent to reconnoiter and returned with the news that Chicho's information was correct, for Luis had seen the two buildings and the red point of the guard's cigarette between them.

We were about to move in when three guards passed by on horses, and we had to hide. Before them walked a prisoner whom they were driving like a mule. The prisoner passed near me and I remember the words of that poor peasant: "I am a man just like you," and the answer that one of the guards gave (we later identified him as Corporal Basól): "Shut up and move, or we'll whip you on." At the time we thought the peasant would be out of danger by not being in the barracks, and would escape the bullets at the moment of the attack; however, the following day, when they found out about the battle and its outcome, he was brutally murdered in El Macío.

We prepared to attack with the twenty-two available weapons. It was an important moment, for we had few bullets; we had to take the barracks no matter what, for otherwise we would spend all our ammunition and remain practically defenseless. Comrade Lieutenant Julito Díaz (who died heroically at El Uvero), with Camilo Cienfuegos, Benítez, and Calixto Morales, all with semi-

automatic rifles, were to surround the overseer's palm-thatched
house from the extreme right. Fidel, Universo Sánchez, Luis
Crespo, Calixto García, Fajardo (now a Major), and I would attack from the center. Raúl with his squad and Almeida with his
would attack the barracks from the left.

Thus, we slowly approached the enemy positions until we got
within forty meters. There was a full moon. Fidel started the shooting with two bursts of machine gun fire and was followed by all
the available guns. Immediately, we called on the soldiers to surrender, but with no result. The moment the shooting began, Chicho
Osorio, the murdering informer, was executed.

The attack began at 2:40 in the morning and the guards resisted
more than we had expected. In the barracks there was a sergeant
with an M-1, and each time we suggested surrender, he answered
with a volley of shots. We were ordered to throw our old Brazilian-
type grenades; Luis Crespo threw his, and I threw mine; neither
one exploded. Raúl Castro threw dynamite and this also had no
effect. So we then had to move in closer and set fire to the houses,
although it was at the risk of our lives. First Universo Sánchez
tried but failed, then Camilo Cienfuegos tried and also failed.
Finally Luis Crespo and I approached the building and set fire
to it. In the light of the fire we were able to see that it was simply
a coconut warehouse attached to a nearby coconut palm plantation;
but we had already intimidated the soldiers into abandoning the
fight. One of them, fleeing, almost collided with Luis Crespo's
rifle and was wounded in the chest; Luis took the soldier's weapon
and we continued firing at the house. Camilo Cienfuegos, sheltered
behind a tree, fired on the fleeing sergeant and used up his few
cartridges.

The soldiers, almost defenseless, were cut to pieces by our merci-
less fire. Camilo Cienfuegos was the first to enter the house and we
heard cries of surrender. We quickly counted the weapons with
which the battle had left us: eight Springfields, a Thompson submachine gun, and some thousand rounds; we had used about five

hundred rounds. In addition, we had cartridge belts, fuel, knives, clothing, and some food. The casualty list was as follows: they had two dead and five wounded, and three of them were our prisoners. Some, along with the wretched Honorio, had escaped. On our side, not even a scratch. We set the soldiers' houses on fire and withdrew, after attending to the wounded as best we could. There were three seriously wounded who subsequently died, as we found out after the final victory. We left them in the care of the captured soldiers. One of the soldiers later joined the troops of Major Raúl Castro and reached the rank of lieutenant, dying in an airplane crash after the end of the war.

Our attitude toward the wounded contrasted sharply with that of the Army. The Army not only murdered our wounded, but also abandoned their own. In time, this difference began having its effect, and constituted one of the factors in our victory. To my despair, Fidel ordered us to leave all our medicines with the prisoners who were to treat the wounded; I wanted to conserve our reserves for our fighting troops. We also freed the civilians and, at 4:30 on the morning of the 17th, we left for Palma Mocha, where we arrived at dawn, immediately seeking the most rugged and inaccessible regions of the Sierra Maestra.

We were met with a pitiful sight: the day before, a corporal and a foreman had informed all the local peasant families that the Air Force was going to bomb the whole region and this sparked an exodus to the coast. Since no one knew of our presence, this was clearly a maneuver among the overseers and the rural guards to rob the *guajiros* of their land and belongings. But their lie had coincided with our attack and now became a reality, so that real terror spread and it was impossible to stop the peasant exodus.

This was the Rebel Army's first victorious battle. This and the following battle were the only occasions in the life of our troop when we had more weapons than men. The peasants were not yet prepared to join the struggle and communication with urban bases was practically nonexistent.

# The Battle of El Arroyo del Infierno

El Arroyo del Infierno (Hell's Creek) is a narrow, shallow river flowing into the Palma Mocha. Walking along it, away from the Palma Mocha, and mounting the slopes of the bordering hills, we reached a small valley where we found two *bohíos* (peasant huts). Here we pitched camp, although we naturally did not use the huts.

Fidel was convinced that the Army would come after us and would probably find us. With this in mind, he planned an ambush during which we hoped to capture some enemy soldiers. To this end, he posted the men.

Fidel watched our lines closely, and checked and rechecked our defenses. On the morning of January 19 we were reviewing the troops when there was an accident which could have had serious consequences. As a trophy from the battle of La Plata, I had taken a corporal's cap, and I wore it with great pride; but when I went to inspect the troops, walking through the middle of the woods, the outposts heard us coming from afar and saw the group headed by someone wearing an Army cap. Fortunately at that moment they were cleaning their weapons and only Camilo Cienfuegos' rifle was working. He opened fire on us, and immediately realized his mistake. His first shot missed and then his automatic rifle jammed, preventing him from firing further. This incident was symptomatic of the state of high tension which prevailed as we waited for the relief which the battle would bring. At such times, even those with nerves of steel feel a certain gentle trembling in the knees and each man longs for the arrival of that luminous moment of battle. However, we none of us wanted to fight; we did it because it was necessary.

At dawn on the 22nd we heard a few isolated shots from the direction of the Palma Mocha river, and this forced us to maintain even stricter discipline in our lines, to be more cautious, and to await the now imminent appearance of the enemy.

Believing the soldiers to be nearby, we cooked neither breakfast nor lunch. Some time before, Crespo and I had found some hen's eggs and we rationed them, leaving one so the hen would continue to lay. That day, because of the shots we had heard during the night, Crespo decided we should eat the last egg, and we did so. At noon we saw a human figure in one of the *bohíos*. At first we thought that one of our comrades had disobeyed the order not to go near the houses. However, it turned out to be an enemy soldier.

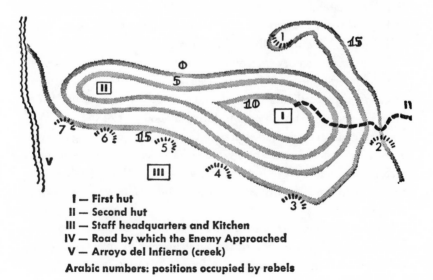

I — First hut
II — Second hut
III — Staff headquarters and Kitchen
IV — Road by which the Enemy Approached
V — Arroyo del Infierno (creek)
**Arabic numbers: positions occupied by rebels**

Then about six others appeared; some of them left, and three remained in view. We saw that the soldier on guard looked around him, picked a few weeds, put them behind his ears in an attempt at camouflage, and sat calmly in the shade, his face, clearly visible through the telescopic sight, showing no apprehension. Fidel's opening shot shattered him; he managed only to give a shout, something like "Ay, mi madre!" and fell over dead. The cross fire spread and the soldier's two companions also fell. Suddenly I noticed that in the closer *bohío* there was another soldier trying to hide from our fire. Only his legs were visible from my higher position, since the roof of the hut covered his body. I fired at him and missed; the second shot caught the man full in the chest and he fell, leaving his rifle stuck in the ground by the bayonet. Covered by Crespo, I reached the house where I saw the body, and I took his bullets, his rifle, and a few other belongings. The bullet had struck him full in the chest, probably piercing his heart, and his death had been instantaneous; he already showed the first signs of *rigor mortis,* perhaps because of the exhaustion of his last day's march.

The battle was extraordinarily fierce and soon, our plan successfully executed, we were all running for cover.

On taking inventory we found that we had used approximately nine hundred bullets and had retrieved seventy from a full cartridge case. We also acquired a rifle, a Garand, which was given to Major Efigenio Ameijeiras, who used it during a good part of the war. We counted four enemy dead, but months later, on capturing an informer, we learned that actually five had fallen. It was not a total victory, but neither was it a Pyrrhic victory. We had matched our forces against the enemy in a new situation, and we had passed the test.

This raised our spirits greatly, and enabled us to continue the whole day clambering toward the most inaccessible places in order to escape pursuit by larger enemy forces. In this way, we reached the other side of the mountain. We were walking parallel to Batista's troop, also withdrawing, both groups having crossed the same mountain peaks to reach the other side. For two days our troops and those of the enemy marched almost together without realizing it; once we slept in a *bohío* barely separated from the enemy by a small river and a couple of road bends. The lieutenant commanding the enemy patrol was Sánchez Mosquera, whose name had become infamous throughout the Sierra Maestra in the wake of his marauding. It is worth mentioning that the shots we had heard several hours before the battle had killed a peasant of Haitian descent who had refused to lead the troops to our hideout. If they had not committed this murder they would not have alerted us and found us waiting for them.

We were once again overburdened: many of us carried two rifles. Under these circumstances it was not easy to walk, but clearly there were motives other than personal which made it imperative to do so, motives different from those that obtained after the disaster of Alegría de Pío. A few days earlier we had defeated a smaller group, entrenched in a barracks; now we had defeated a column on the march, superior in numbers to our forces, and we all understood the importance of this type of battle which eliminates the vanguard, for without a vanguard an army is paralyzed.

# Air Attack

After the victory over Sánchez Mosquera's forces, we had walked along the banks of the La Plata river. Later, crossing the Magdalena river, we had returned to the already familiar region of Caracas. But the atmosphere there was different this time: the first time we were hidden there and all the people supported us; now Casillas' troops had passed through, sowing terror throughout the region. The peasants had gone, leaving only their empty huts and a few animals which we killed and ate. Experience had taught us that it was not safe to live in the houses, so after spending the night in one of the more isolated huts, we returned to the woods and pitched our camp beside a small waterfall almost at the top of Caracas hill.

Manuel Fajardo came to me and asked me if it were possible that we would lose the war. My reply, quite aside from the euphoria of victory, was always the same: the war would indisputably be won. He explained that he had asked me because "Gallego" Morán had claimed that it was no longer possible to win the war, that we were lost, and he had then invited Fajardo to abandon the campaign. I informed Fidel of this, but he told me that, very sensibly, Morán had already told him that he was covertly testing the morale of the troops. We agreed that this was not the most efficient system, and Fidel made a short speech urging greater discipline and explaining the dangers which might arise if this discipline were disregarded. He also announced the three crimes punishable by death: insubordination, desertion, and defeatism.

Our situation was not a happy one in those days. The column lacked cohesion. It had neither the spirit which comes from the experience of war nor a clear ideological consciousness. Now one comrade would leave us, now another; many requested assignments in the city which were sometimes much more dangerous but which meant an escape from the rugged conditions in the countryside. Nevertheless, our campaign continued on its course; Morán showed indefatigable activity looking for food and making contacts with the peasants of the region.

Such were our spirits on the morning of January 30. Eutimio Guerra, the traitor, had asked permission to visit his sick mother and Fidel had granted it, also giving him some money for the trip. According to Eutimio, the trip would last several weeks. We had not yet understood a series of incidents which were later clearly explained by this man's subsequent behavior. When he rejoined the troop, Eutimio said that he had almost reached Palma Mocha when he learned that the Government forces were on our trail. He had tried to warn us but he found only the corpses of the soldiers in the *bohío* belonging to Delfín, one of the *guajiros* on whose land we had fought the battle of El Arroyo del Infierno. Eutimio had followed our path across the Sierra until he finally found us. What had actually happened was that he had been captured and was now working as an enemy agent; he had been bribed with money and a military rank in exchange for murdering Fidel.

As part of this plan, Eutimio had left the camp the previous day and on the morning of the 30th, after a cold night, just as we were getting up, we heard the roar of planes which we could not locate exactly since we were in the brush. Our field kitchen was about two hundred meters below us near a small spring, in the same place as the advance guard. Suddenly we heard the dive of a bomber, the rattle of machine gun fire, and then the bombs. At the time our experience was very limited and we seemed to hear shots from all sides. Fifty-caliber bullets explode when they hit the ground and, although what we heard was the firing of machine guns from the air, as the bullets hit near us they gave the impression of coming from the woods. Because of this we thought we were being attacked by ground troops.

I was instructed to wait for the advance guard, and to collect some of the belongings we had abandoned during the air attack. I was to meet the rest of the troop at La Cueva del Humo. I was accompanied by Chao, a veteran of the Spanish Civil War. For a while we waited for some of the missing men, but no one came. We followed the column's tracks with difficulty since they were none too clear, and we both carried heavy loads. We came to a clearing and decided to rest. After a while, we heard sounds and saw movement. The column's tracks were also being followed by the present Major Guillermo García and Sergio Acuña, both from the advance guard. After some deliberation, Guillermo García and I returned to the camp to see what was happening since we no longer heard any noise: the planes had disappeared. We beheld a desolate spectacle: with a strange precision which fortunately was not repeated during the war, the field kitchen had been attacked. The hearth had been smashed to pieces by machine gun fire, and a bomb had exploded exactly in the middle of our advance guard camp, but, naturally, there was no one there. Morán and a comrade had gone to explore and Morán returned alone, announcing that he had seen the planes from afar, that there were five of them, and that there were no ground troops in the vicinity. The five of us, carrying heavy loads, continued walking past saddening scenes of the burned-out *bohíos* of our friends. The only living things remaining were a cat which miaowed at us pitifully and a pig which came out grunting on hearing us pass. We had heard of La Cueva del Humo, but we did not know exactly where it was. Thus we spent the night in uncertainty, waiting to see our comrades but fearing that we would meet the enemy instead.

On the 31st we took our positions on the top of a hill overlooking some cultivated fields. In what we thought was La Cueva del Humo we made various explorations without finding anything. Sergio, one of the five, thought he saw two men in baseball caps, but he delayed in telling us and we could not catch up with them. We went out with Guillermo to explore the bottom of the valley near the banks of the Ají where a friend of Guillermo's gave us something to eat, but all the people were very frightened. The friend told us that all Ciro Frías' merchandise had been taken by the guards and burned; the mules had been requisitioned and the muleteer killed. Ciro Frías' store was then burned down and his wife taken prisoner. The men who had passed in the morning were under the orders of Major Casillas, who had slept somewhere near the house.

On February 1 we stayed in our little camp, practically in the open, resting from the exhausting march of the previous day. At 11 in the morning we heard gunfire on the other side of the hill and soon, much closer to us, we heard the heart-rending cries of someone begging for help. With this, Sergio Acuña's nerves snapped. Silently, he left his cartridge belt and rifle, and deserted the guard post which he commanded. I noted in the field diary that he had taken with him a straw hat, a can of condensed milk and three sausages; at the time we were very sorry about the can of milk and the sausages. A few hours later we heard a noise and we prepared for an attack, not knowing whether the deserter had betrayed us or not. But Crescencio appeared with a large column of almost all our men, and also some new people from Manzanillo led by Roberto Pesant. Missing from our forces were Sergio Acuña, the deserter, and comrades Calixto Morales, Calixto García, and Manuel Acuña; also a new recruit who had been lost on this first day in the cross fire.

Once again we descended to the valley of the Ají, and on the way some of the supplies from Manzanillo were distributed, including a surgical kit for me and changes of clothing for everyone. We felt especially moved to change into clothing which sported initials embroidered by the girls of Manzanillo. The next day, February 2, two months after the landing of the "Granma," we were a reunited, homogeneous group; ten more men from Manzanillo had joined us and we felt stronger and in better spirits than ever. We had many discussions on how the surprise attack and the air attack had been managed, and we all agreed that our cooking by day and the smoke from the bonfire had guided the planes to our camp. For many months and perhaps for the duration of the war, the memories of that surprise attack weighed on the spirits of the troop and right to the end, fires were not built in the open air during the day, for we always feared some unfortunate consequence.

We would have found it impossible to believe, and I think it did not enter anyone's mind, that Eutimio Guerra, the traitor and informer, had been in the observation plane, pointing out to Casillas the place where we were. His mother's illness had been a pretext to leave us and look for the murderer Casillas.

For some time thereafter Eutimio played an important adverse role in the development of our war of liberation.

# Surprise Attack at Altos de Espinosa

After the surprise air attack we abandoned the hill of Caracas and attempted to return to familiar regions where we could establish direct contact with Manzanillo, receive more help from the outside, and better understand the situation in the rest of the country.

For this reason, we crossed the Ají and returned through territories familiar to all of us, until we reached the house of old Mendoza. We had to cut our way with machetes on the ridge of the hills, along paths unwalked by men for many years, and our progress was very slow. We spent the night on one of those hills, practically without eating. I still remember, as if it were one of the great banquets of my life, when Crespo arrived with a can containing four pork sausages, a result of his earlier frugality, saying that they were for his friends; Crespo, Fidel, and I along with a fourth man enjoyed that meager ration as if it were a sumptuous feast. The march continued until we reached the house, to the right of Caracas hill, where old Mendoza was to prepare us something to eat; despite his fear, his peasant loyalty led him to welcome us each time we passed by there; he was responding to the commitments of a friendship with Crescencio Pérez and the other peasants in the troop.

The march was particularly painful for me, for I was suffering from an attack of malaria. It was Crespo and that unforgettable comrade Julio Zenón Acosta who helped me finish that anguished march.

69

On reaching a hamlet we never slept in the *bohíos;* but my poor health and that of Morán, who always found an excuse to get sick, made it necessary for us to sleep under a roof while the rest of the troop kept watch in the vicinity, coming to the house only to eat.

We were forced to cut down the size of the troop, for there was a group of men with very low morale, and one or two seriously wounded; in this last group were the present Minister of the Interior, Ramiro Valdés, and Ignacio Pérez, a son of Crescencio, who later, as a captain, died heroically. Ramirito had been badly wounded in the knee, the same knee which had already been hit at the Moncada barracks, so we were forced to leave him behind. A few other boys left us, a fact which was to the advantage of the troop. I remember one of them had an attack of nerves, there in the solitude of mountains and guerrillas. He began to shout that he had been promised a camp with abundant food and anti-aircraft defenses, and that now the planes harassed him and he had neither permanent quarters, nor food, nor even water to drink. This was more or less the impression of the new guerrillas. Afterward, those who stayed and passed the first tests grew accustomed to dirt, to lack of water, food, shelter and security, and to continually relying only on a rifle and the cohesion and resistance of the small guerrilla nucleus.

Ciro Frías arrived with some recent recruits, bringing news which today makes us smile, but which at that time filled us with confusion: news that Díaz Tamayo was on the verge of switching allegiance and "dealing" with the revolutionary forces; news that Faustino had been able to collect many thousands of pesos; in one word, that sabotage was spreading through the country and the day of chaos for the government was approaching. In addition, we heard a sad but instructive piece of news. Sergio Acuña, the deserter, had gone to the home of some relatives. There, he began to brag to his cousins about his deeds as a guerrilla; a certain Pedro Herrera overheard and denounced him to the Guardia Rural. The infamous Corporal Roselló arrived (he has since been brought to justice by the people), tortured him, shot him four times and, apparently, hanged him. This clearly showed our men the value of unity and the uselessness of attempting individually to flee the collective destiny. But it also made it necessary for us to change camps, for presumably the boy might have talked before being murdered, and he knew we were at Florentino's house.

There was a curious incident at that time and it was only later that the full evidence made things clear to us: Eutimio Guerra told us that he had dreamed about Sergio Acuña's death, and furthermore, it had been Corporal Roselló who killed him. This sparked a long philosophical discussion about whether prediction of things to come was possible through dreams or not. It was part of my daily task to make explanations of a cultural or political type to the men, and I explained firmly that this was not possible, that it could be due to some great coincidence, that we had all believed that Sergio Acuña might end that way, and that Roselló was the man who was at that time devastating the region. Furthermore, Universo Sánchez gave the key by saying that Eutimio was a "storyteller," that someone had clearly told him about it the previous day when he had left the camp to go get some supplies.

One of the men who insisted most strongly on the theory of illumination was an illiterate *guajiro* of forty-five whom I have already mentioned: Julio Zenón Acosta. He was my first pupil in the Sierra; I was teaching him to read and write, and every time we stopped I would teach him a few letters; we were then learning the vowels. With great determination, looking ahead rather than back, Julio Zenón had set himself the task of becoming literate. Perhaps his example may be useful today to many peasants, comrades of his during the war, or to those who know his story. For Julio Zenón Acosta was another of our great supporters at that time; he was a tireless worker, familiar with the area, always ready to help a comrade in trouble, or a comrade from the city who did not yet have sufficient stamina to get out of tight spots. It was he who brought water from distant water holes, who could make a quick fire, who could find dry kindling even on a rainy day. He was, in fact, our jack-of-all-trades.

One night, shortly before his treachery became known, Eutimio complained that he did not have a blanket, and asked Fidel to lend him one. It was very cold in the hills in February. Fidel answered that both of them would be cold if he gave Eutimio his blanket. He suggested that they sleep under the same blanket and Fidel's two coats. So Eutimio Guerra spent the whole night next to Fidel; he had on him a .45 pistol with which to kill Fidel, and a pair of grenades to protect his retreat from the hilltop. He asked Universo Sánchez and me (at that time we were always close to Fidel) about our guards. He said: "I'm very interested in these guards; we have to be really careful." We explained that three men were posted nearby; we ourselves, veterans of the "Granma" and Fidel's right-hand men, relieved each other through the night to protect him personally. Thus, Eutimio spent the night beside the Revolution's leader, holding his life at the point of a gun, awaiting the chance to assassinate him. But he could not bring himself to do it. That night a good part of the Cuban Revolution depended on the uncharted and complex twists of a man's mind, on the balance of courage and fear, terror and, perhaps, scruple, on a traitor's lust for power and wealth. Luckily for us, Eutimio's inhibitions were stronger, and the day broke without incident.

We had left Florentino's house and were camped in a dry stream bed in a ravine. Ciro Frías had gone to his home, which was relatively near, and had brought back some hens and some other food, so that the long unsheltered night was compensated in the morning by hot soup and chicken. Somebody brought the news that Eutimio had been by there too. Eutimio came and went, for he was trusted by everyone, and he had found us at Florentino's house and explained that after he had left to see his sick mother he had seen what had happened at Caracas, and had followed after us to see what else happened. He also explained that his mother was now well. He was sometimes extraordinarily audacious; we were in a place called Altos de Espinosa, very close to a chain of hills—El Lomón, Loma del Burro, Caracas—which the planes strafed constantly. With the gravity of an oracle, Eutimio said: "Today they will strafe the Loma del Burro." The planes *did* in fact strafe the Loma del Burro, and Eutimio jumped for joy, exulting in his keen prediction.

On February 9, 1957, Ciro Frías and Luis Crespo left as usual, to scout for food, and all was quiet. At ten in the morning a peasant boy named Labrada, a recent recruit, captured someone nearby. He turned out to be a relative of Crescencio and an employee in Celestino's store where Casillas' soldiers were stationed. He informed us that there were a hundred and forty soldiers in the house; in fact, from our position we could see them in the distance in a clearing. Furthermore, the prisoner said he had talked with Eutimio and had been told that the following day the area would be bombarded. Casillas' troops had moved, but he could not say in what direction they were going. Fidel became suspicious; finally, Eutimio's strange behavior had come to our attention and speculations began.

At 1:30 P.M. Fidel decided to break camp and we climbed to the top of the hill, where we waited for our scouts. Soon Ciro Frías and Luis Crespo arrived; they had seen nothing unusual. We were talking about this when Ciro Redondo thought he saw a shadow moving. He called for silence and cocked his rifle. At that moment we heard a shot and then another. At once the air was full of shots and explosions provoked by the attack, which was concentrated on our previous camp. The new camp emptied rapidly; later I found out that Julio Zenón Acosta had died on the hilltop. That uneducated and illiterate *guajiro* who had understood the enormous tasks which the Revolution would face after its victory, and who was learning the alphabet to prepare himself for this, would never finish that task. The rest of us ran. I had to leave behind my knapsack— my pride and joy—full of medicines and some reserve rations, books, and blankets. However, I snatched up a blanket I had taken from the Batista Army as a trophy from La Plata, and ran.

Soon I met up with a group of our men: Almeida, Julito Díaz, Universo Sánchez, Camilo Cienfuegos, Guillermo García, Ciro Frías, Motolá, Pesant, Emilio Labrada, and Yayo. We followed a winding path trying to escape the shots and unaware of the fate of our other comrades. We heard isolated detonations behind us; we were easy to follow since the speed of our flight made it impossible to erase our traces. At 5:15 P.M., by my watch, we reached a craggy spot where the forest ended; after vacillating a while we decided it was better to wait there for nightfall, for if we crossed the clearing in daylight we would be spotted. If the enemy followed us, we were well placed to defend ourselves. However, the enemy did not appear and we were able to continue on our way, guided unsurely by Ciro Frías who knew the region vaguely. It had been suggested that we divide into two patrols in order to ease the march and leave fewer tracks. But Almeida and I were opposed to this because we wanted to preserve the unity of the group. We recognized where we were, at a place called Limones, and after a few hesitations, for some of the men wanted to move on, Almeida, who led the group because he was a captain, ordered us to continue to El Lomón, which Fidel had designated as our meeting place. Some of the men argued that El Lomón was a place known to Eutimio and that therefore the Army would be there waiting for us. Of course we no longer had any doubt that Eutimio was a traitor, but Almeida's decision was to comply with Fidel's order.

After three days of separation, on February 12 we met Fidel near El Lomón, in a place called Derecha de la Caridad. There it was confirmed for us that Eutimio Guerra was a traitor, and we heard the whole story. It began after the battle of La Plata, when he was captured by Casillas and, instead of being killed, was offered a certain amount for Fidel's life; we learned that it was he who had revealed our position in Caracas and that he had also given the order to attack the Loma del Burro, since that place had been on our itinerary (we had changed our plan at the last minute). He had also organized the attack on the small hollow in which we were sheltered in the Cañón del Arroyo, from which we saved ourselves with only one casualty because of the opportune retreat which Fidel ordered. We also had confirmation of the death of Julio Acosta; at least one rural guard was dead, and there were also a few wounded. I must confess that my rifle caused neither the death nor the wounds, for I did nothing more than beat a speedy "strategic retreat." Now we twelve (minus Labrada who had disappeared) were once again reunited with the rest of the group: Raúl, Ameijeiras, Ciro Redondo, Manuel Fajardo, Echeverría, "Gallego" Morán, and Fidel, a total of eighteen men. This was the Reunified Revolutionary Army of February 12, 1957. Some of our comrades had been scattered, some new recruits had abandoned us, and there was the desertion of a veteran of the "Granma." His name was Armando Rodríguez and he carried a Thompson submachine gun; toward the end, he had such a terrified and anguished face whenever he heard shots in the distance that we called that expression *cara de cerco,* "the face of one besieged." Each time a man showed the face of a terrified animal, possessed by the terror which our ex-comrade had shown in the days before Altos de Espinosa, we immediately predicted an unfortunate outcome, for that expression was incompatible with guerrilla life. "Cara de Cerco" went over the hill, as we said in our new guerrilla slang, and his machine gun showed up later in a *bohío* a great distance away: his legs had carried him well.

# Death of a Traitor

After this small army was reunited, we decided to leave the region of El Lomón and move on to new ground. On the way, we went on making contacts with peasants in the area and establishing the bases necessary for our subsistence. At the same time, we were leaving the Sierra Maestra and walking toward the plains, to places where we were to meet the people involved in organizing the cities.

We passed through a village called La Montería, and afterward camped in a small thicket near a little stream, on the property of a man named Epifanio Díaz, whose sons fought in the Revolution.

We moved closer in order to establish tighter contact with the [26th of July] Movement, for our nomadic and clandestine life made any exchange between the two parts of the 26th of July Movement impossible.* (Practically speaking, they were two separate groups, with different tactics and different strategy. The deep rift which in later months would endanger the unity of the Movement had not yet appeared, but we could already see that our concepts were different.)

It was on that farm that we met with the most important figures in the urban Movement; among them were three women known

---

* The "Sierra" (Mountain) and the "Llano" (Plain); the guerrilla and urban parts of the movement. See chapter called "One Year of Struggle."

today to all the Cuban people: Vilma Espín, now the President of the Federation of Cuban Women and Raúl's wife; Haydée Santamaría, President of the Casa de las Américas and Armando Hart's wife; and Celia Sánchez, our beloved comrade throughout the struggle, who some time later definitively joined us, for the duration. Another person who came to our camp was Faustino Pérez, an old acquaintance of ours from the "Granma," who had gone on some missions in the city and came to report to us, returning at once to the city. (A little later he was taken prisoner.)

We also met Armando Hart, and I had my only opportunity to meet that great leader from Santiago, Frank País.

Frank País was one of those men who command respect from the first meeting; he looked more or less as he appears in the photographs we see of him today, but his eyes had extraordinary depths.

It is difficult to speak of a dead comrade, whom I met only once and whose history belongs to the people. I can only say of him that his eyes immediately showed a man possessed by a cause, and that he was clearly a superior person. Today he is called "the unforgettable Frank País"; for me, who saw him only once, he *is* unforgettable. Frank is another of the many comrades who, had their lives not been cut short, would today be dedicating themselves to the common task of the socialist revolution. This loss is part of the heavy price which the people had to pay in order to gain their liberation.

Frank gave us a quiet lesson in order and discipline, cleaning our dirty rifles, counting bullets and packing them so that they would not be lost. From that day, I decided to take better care of my gun (and I carried through with this, although I cannot say that I was ever a model of meticulousness).

The thicket was also the scene of other events. For the first time we were visited by a journalist and a foreign journalist at that; this was the famous [Herbert L.] Matthews, who brought with him only a small box camera with which he took the pictures that were later so widely distributed and so hotly disputed in the stupid

speeches of a Batista Minister. At that time the interpreter was
Javier Pazos, who later joined the guerrillas and remained for some
time.

Matthews, according to Fidel (for I was not present at that interview) asked concrete questions, none of them tricky, and he obviously sympathized with the Revolution. I remember that Fidel said,
yes, he was anti-imperialist, and he publicly objected to the delivery
of arms to Batista, insisting that these arms would not be used for
inter-continental defense but rather to oppress the people.

Matthews' visit was naturally very brief. As soon as he left we
were ready to move on. However, we were advised to redouble our
guard since Eutimio was in the area; Almeida was immediately
ordered to find him and take him prisoner. The patrol was made up
of Julito Díaz, Ciro Frías, Camilo Cienfuegos, and Efigenio Ameijeiras. It was Ciro Frías who easily overcame Eutimio, and he was
brought to us. We found on him a .45 pistol, three grenades, and a
safe conduct pass from Casillas. Once captured and this incriminat-
ing evidence discovered, he could not doubt his fate. He fell on his
knees before Fidel and asked simply that we kill him. He said he
knew he deserved death. At that moment he seemed to have aged;
on his temple were a good many grey hairs we had never noticed
before.

The moment was one of extraordinary tension. Fidel upbraided
him harshly for his betrayal and Eutimio wanted only to be shot,
for he recognized his guilt. We can never forget the moment Ciro
Frías, a close friend of his, began to speak to him; he reminded
Eutimio of everything he had done for him, of the little favors he and
his brother had done for Eutimio's family, and of how Eutimio had
betrayed them, first by causing the death of Ciro's brother—whom
Eutimio had turned over to the Army—and then by trying to destroy the whole group. It was a long and moving speech, which
Eutimio listened to in silence, his head bent. We asked him if he

wanted anything and he answered yes, that he wanted the Revolution, or rather us, to take care of his children.

The Revolution has kept this promise. Eutimio Guerra's name reappears today in this book, but it has already been forgotten, perhaps even by his children. They now have new names and are attending one of our many new schools; they receive the same treatment as all the sons of the people, and are preparing themselves for a better life. But one day they will have to know that their father was executed by the revolutionary power because of his treachery. It is also just that they be told how their father—a peasant who had allowed himself to be tempted by corruption and had tried to commit a grave crime, moved by the desire for glory and wealth—had nevertheless recognized his error, and had not even hinted at a desire for clemency, which he knew he did not deserve. Finally, they should also know that in his last moments he remembered his children and asked that they be treated well.

Just then a heavy storm broke and the sky darkened; in the midst of a deluge, the sky crossed by lightning and the noise of thunder, as one of these strokes of lightning burst and was followed closely by a thunderbolt, Eutimio Guerra's life was ended and even those comrades standing near him did not hear the shot.

The following day, as we were burying him, there was a small incident which I remember. Manuel Fajardo wanted to put a cross on his grave, and I refused to let him because such evidence of the execution was very dangerous for the owners of the property where we were camped. So he cut a small cross into the trunk of a nearby tree. And this is the sign which marks the grave of the traitor.

Morán left us at that time; he knew how little we esteemed him by then, and we all considered him a potential deserter: he had disappeared once for three days on the pretext that he had been looking for Eutimio and had got lost in the forest.

As we prepared to leave, a shot sounded and we found Morán

with a bullet in the leg. The men who saw this had many heated discussions, for some said that the shot was accidental and others that he shot himself in order to stay behind.

Morán's subsequent history, his treachery and his death at the hands of revolutionaries in Guantánamo, seems to establish that he shot himself intentionally.

Then we left. Frank País had promised to send a group of men during the first days of the following month, March; they would join us at the house of Epifanio Díaz, in the vicinity of the Jíbaro.

# Bitter Days

The days following our departure from Epifanio Díaz' house were for me personally the most painful days of the war. These notes have attempted to give an idea of what the first part of our revolutionary struggle was like for all the men involved; if in this section, more than any other, I must refer to my personal participation, it is because it is connected to the later episodes and it was not possible to separate the two without losing the continuity of the narrative.

After leaving Epifanio's house, our revolutionary group consisted of seventeen men from the original army, and three new comrades: Gil, Sotolongo, and Raúl Díaz. These three comrades had arrived on the "Granma"; they had been hiding for some time near Manzanillo and, hearing of our presence, had decided to join us. Their stories were the same as all of ours; they had been able to evade the rural guards by seeking refuge in the house of one peasant after another, had reached Manzanillo, and had hidden there. Now they joined their fate to that of the whole column. In that period it was very difficult to enlarge our army; a few new men came, but others left; the physical conditions of the struggle were very hard, but the spiritual conditions were even more so, and we lived with the feeling of being continually under siege.

In those days we were walking slowly in no fixed direction, hiding in small thickets in a region where the foliage had been consumed by livestock, leaving only remnants of vegetation. One night on Fidel's small radio we heard that a comrade from the "Granma" who had left with Crescencio Pérez had been captured. We already knew from Eutimio about this, but the news had not yet been officially given; now we at least knew that he was alive. Prisoners did not always emerge alive from an interrogation by Batista's Army. Every now and then, from different directions, we heard machine gun fire; the rural guards were shooting into the wooded areas, which they often did, although they never actually entered them.

In my field diary I noted, on February 22, that I had the first symptoms of what might be a serious asthma attack, for I was without my anti-asthmatic medicine. The date of the new rendezvous was March 5, so we were forced to wait for a few days.

In that period, as I said, we were walking very slowly, aimlessly, and we were simply marking time until March 5, the day on which Frank País was to send us a group of armed men. We had already decided to first strengthen the fire power of our small front before increasing it in numbers, and therefore all available arms in Santiago were to be sent up to the Sierra Maestra.

One morning at dawn found us by the side of a small river where there was almost no vegetation; we spent a precarious day in that spot, in a valley near Las Mercedes, which I think is called La Majagua (names are now a little vague in my memory), and we arrived by night at the house of old Emiliano, another of the many peasants who in those days were frightened each time they saw us but who nevertheless valiantly risked their lives for us, and thus contributed to the development of the Revolution. It was the rainy season in the Sierra and each night we were soaked, which is why we went into *bohíos,* despite the danger, for the area was crawling with soldiers.

My asthma was so bad that I could not move rapidly, and we had to sleep in a little coffee grove near a *bohío* where we regrouped our forces. On the day I am talking about, February 27 or 28, censorship in the country had been lifted and the radio gave news of everything which had happened during the past months. They spoke of terrorist acts and of Matthews' interview with Fidel; it was then that the Minister of Defense made his famous statement that Matthews' interview was a lie and he issued the challenge that the photographs be published.

Hermes was a son of old Emiliano and it was he who helped us with meals and showed us the route we should take. But on the morning of the 28th he did not appear and Fidel ordered us to evacuate the spot immediately and post ourselves elsewhere, overlooking the roads, for we did not know what would happen. At about four in the afternoon, Luis Crespo and Universo Sánchez were watching the roads and the latter saw a large troop of soldiers preparing to occupy the road from Las Vegas. We had to run fast to the edge of the hill and cross to the other side before the troops could block our path; it was not difficult since we had seen them in time. The mortars and machine guns were beginning to sound nearby, which proved that the Batista Army knew that we were there. Everybody was able to reach the peak easily, and go over it; but for me it was a tremendous job. I made it to the top, but with such an asthma attack that, for all practical purposes, to take one more step would have been impossible. I remember how much Crespo helped me when I could not go any further and begged to be left behind. In the usual way of speaking of our troops he said to me: "You . . . Argentine! You'll walk or I'll hit you with my rifle butt!" He virtually carried both me and my pack, as we slogged over the hill through a heavy rainstorm.

We thus reached a small *bohío,* learning that we were in a place called Purgatorio. There Fidel passed himself off as Major González of the Federal Army, who was supposedly looking for the rebels. The peasant, coldly polite, offered us his house and waited on us. There was also a friend from a neighboring *bohío,* who was an extraordinary toady. Because I was ill I could not fully enjoy that delicious dialogue between Fidel in the role of Major González and the *guajiro* who gave him advice and wondered why that boy, Fidel Castro, was in the hills fighting.

We had to reach some decision, for it was impossible for me to continue. When the indiscreet neighbor had left, Fidel told the host who he really was. The man immediately embraced him, saying he was a member of the Orthodox Party, was a follower of Chibás, and was at our service. At that moment we had to send the man to Manzanillo to establish contact or at least to bring back medicines, and I had to be left near the house without even his wife's knowing I was there.

The last man to join our group, a man of doubtful repute but great strength, was assigned to stay with me. Fidel, in a generous gesture, gave me a Johnson repeater, one of the treasures of our group. We all pretended to leave in the same direction, and after a few steps my companion (whom we called El Maestro) and I disappeared into the forest to reach our hiding place. That day the radio reported that Matthews had been interviewed by telephone and had announced that the famous photographs would be published. Díaz Tamayo had countered that this was impossible since Matthews could not have crossed the Army lines surrounding the guerrillas. Armando Hart was in prison, accused of being the second in command of the Movement. It was February 28.

The peasant carried out his job and brought me a good amount of adrenalin. Then came  ten of the most bitter days of the struggle in the Sierra: walking along, supporting myself on trees and leaning on the barrel of my rifle, accompanied by a frightened soldier who trembled each time we heard shots and who got nervous each time I coughed in some dangerous spot. It took us ten long days to reach Epifanio's house once again, when normally it took little more than one day. The date for the meeting had been March 5, but it had been impossible for us to arrive by then. Because of the soldiers in the region and our slow movement, we arrived on March 11.

The inhabitants of the house informed us of what had happened. Fidel's group of eighteen men had accidentally split up at a moment when they thought they were going to be attacked by the Army, in a place called Altos de Meriño; twelve men had gone on with Fidel and six with Ciro Frías. Later, Ciro Frías' group had fallen into an ambush, but they all came out of it unhurt and they met up again nearby. One of them, Yayo, who came back without his rifle, had passed by Epifanio Díaz' house going toward Manzanillo; from him we learned everything. The troop which Frank was to send was ready, although he himself was in prison in Santiago. We met with the troop's leader; he was Captain Jorge Sotús. He had been unable to come on the 5th, for news of the new group had gotten around and the roads were heavily guarded. We made all the necessary arrangements for the speedy arrival of the fifty new recruits.

# Reinforcements

On March 13, as we awaited the new revolutionary troop, we heard on the radio that there had been an attempt made on Batista's life, and they gave the names of the people who died as a result. First, there was José Antonio Echeverría, the student leader; then there were others, like Menelao Mora. People who were not involved in the attempt also died. The following day we learned that Pelayo Cuervo Navarro, a fighter from the Orthodox Party who had always maintained a firm position against Batista, had been assassinated and his body left in the aristocratic residential section of the Country Club known as El Laguito. It is interesting to note that, paradoxically, the murderers of Pelayo Cuervo Navarro and the sons of the dead man joined together in the unsuccessful invasion of the Bay of Pigs sent to "liberate" Cuba from "Communist ignominy."

Despite the curtain of censorship, some details of this memorable though unsuccessful attempt on Batista's life came through. Personally, I had not known the student leader, but I had known his friends in Mexico, when the 26th of July Movement and the Directorio Estudiantil [Student Directorate] had agreed to concentrated action. These friends were: Major Faure Chomón, who became Ambassador to the USSR, Fructuoso Rodríguez, and Joe Westbrook, all of whom participated in the attempt on Batista's life.

The men had almost penetrated to the third floor where the dictator was, but what could have been a successful blow was converted into a massacre of all those who could not get out of the trap which the Presidential Palace had become.

The arrival of our reinforcements was scheduled for the 15th; we waited for hours in the agreed-upon place, in a river-canyon where the river bends, and it was easy to wait there secretly; but no one arrived. Later they explained to us that there had been some sort of contretemps. Subsequently they arrived, at dawn on the 16th. The men were so tired they could hardly walk the few necessary steps to the wooded area where they would rest until day. They came in trucks owned by a rice farmer from the area who, frightened by the implications of his act, went into exile in Costa Rica, from where he later returned as a hero by flying arms into Cuba from that country; his name was Hubert Matos.

The new troop consisted of about fifty men, only thirty of whom were armed. They brought two automatic rifles, one Madzen and one Johnson. After a few months of living in the Sierra, we had become veterans, and we saw in the new troop all the defects which those who had landed on the "Granma" had had: lack of discipline, the inability to adjust to major difficulties, lack of decision, the incapacity to adapt to this life. The group of fifty was led by Captain Jorge Sotús, and was divided into five squads of ten men, each of whose leaders were lieutenants (they had been given these ranks, which still awaited ratification, by the Movement in the plains). The squads were directed by: Comrade Domínguez, I believe, who was killed in Pino del Agua a little while later; Comrade René Ramos Latour, a guerrilla organizer in the plains who died heroically in battle during the last days of the final government offensive; "Pedrín" Soto, our old friend from the "Granma," who finally managed to join us and was also killed in battle and posthumously promoted to major by Raúl Castro, on the Second Eastern Front named after Frank País; also, comrade Pena, a student from Santiago who reached the rank of major and killed himself after the Revolution; finally, Lieutenant Hermo, the only group leader to survive the two years of the war.

Of all the problems which the new troop had, one of the major ones was the difficulty in marching; their leader, Jorge Sotús, was the worst marcher, and he constantly lagged behind, setting a bad example for the men. I had been ordered to take charge of the troop, but when I mentioned this to Sotús he told me that he had orders to turn the men over to Fidel and that he could not therefore turn them over to anyone else as long as he continued as the leader, etc., etc. In that period I still had a complex about being a foreigner, and I did not want to go to extremes, although I noticed a great uneasiness in the troop. After several short marches, which took a very long time because of the men's poor preparation, we reached the place where we were to wait for Fidel Castro. There we met the small group of men who had been separated from Fidel earlier: Manuel Fajardo, Guillermo García, Juventino, Pesant, the three Sotomayor brothers, and Ciro Frías.

In those days the enormous difference between the two groups was easily noticed: ours was disciplined, compact, inured to warfare; that of the novices was still suffering the sickness of the first days: they were not used to eating only once a day, and if the ration did not taste good they would not eat it. The novices had their packs full of useless items, and if the packs were too heavy they would rather, for example, give up a can of condensed milk than a towel (a crime of "lèse guerrilla"!). We took advantage of this by collecting all the cans and food they left behind. After we were installed in La Derecha the situation became tense because of constant friction between Jorge Sotús, a man of authoritarian spirit who could not get on with the men, and the troop in general; we had to take special precautions and René Ramos, whose nom-de-guerre was Daniel, was put in charge of the machine gun squad at the mouth of our refuge so that we had a guarantee that nothing would happen.

Some time later, Jorge Sotús was sent on a special mission to Miami. There he betrayed the Revolution by meeting with Felipe Pazos, whose immeasurable ambition for power made him forget his obligations and set himself up as the provisional president in a shoddy maneuver in which the State Department played an important role.

With time, Captain Sotús showed signs of wanting to redeem himself and Raúl Castro gave him the opportunity which the Revolution has denied no one. However, he began to conspire against the Revolutionary Government and he was condemned to twenty years in prison, escaping thanks to the complicity of one of his guards who fled with him to the usual shelter of *gusanos*: the United States.

At the time of our story, however, we tried to help him as much as possible, to smooth his disagreements with the new comrades, and to explain to him the necessity for discipline. Guillermo García went to fetch Fidel from the region of Caracas, while I made a little trip to pick up Ramiro Valdés, who had more or less recovered from the wound in his leg. On the night of March 24, Fidel arrived; his arrival with the twelve comrades who at that time stuck firmly by his side was impressive. There was a notable difference between the bearded men, with packs made of any available material and tied with whatever could be found, and the new soldiers with clean-shaven faces, clean uniforms, and pretty knapsacks. I explained to Fidel the problems which we had encountered and a small council was established to decide on these questions. The council was made up of Fidel himself, Raúl, Almeida, Jorge Sotús, Ciro Frías, Guillermo García, Camilo Cienfuegos, Manuel Fajardo, and myself. Fidel criticized my attitude in not exercising the authority which had been conferred on me, and leaving it in the hands of the recently arrived Sotús, against whom there was no personal animosity but whose attitude, in Fidel's opinion, should not have been tolerated at that moment. The new platoons were also organized, uniting the whole to form three groups under the direction of Captains Raúl Castro, Juan Almeida, and Jorge Sotús; Camilo Cienfuegos would lead the advance guard and Efigenio Ameijeiras the rear guard; I was General Staff physician and Universo Sánchez functioned as General Staff squad leader.

Our troop reached a new excellence with these additional men and two more automatic rifles. These weapons, although of doubtful efficiency since they were old and badly worn, nevertheless helped to strengthen our force. We discussed what we could immediately do; it was my opinion that we should attack the first possible enemy post in order to temper the new men in battle. But Fidel and all the other members of the council thought it better to march for some time so they could get used to the rigors of life in the forest and the mountains, and the long marches from hill to hill. So we decided to move toward the east and walk as much as possible, seeking the opportunity to attack some group of soldiers after having some elementary practical lessons in guerrilla warfare.

The troop prepared itself enthusiastically and left to fulfil its tasks. Its blood-baptism was to be the battle of El Uvero.

# Our Men Are Toughened

The months of March and April, 1957, were months of restructuring and apprenticeship for the rebel troops. After being reinforced at La Derecha, our army consisted of about eighty men and was organized as follows:

The advance guard, directed by Camilo, had four men. The platoon which followed was led by Raúl Castro and had three lieutenants, Julito Díaz, Ramiro Valdés, and Nano Díaz, each with a squad. (The two comrades named Díaz, both of whom died heroically in El Uvero, were not related. One of them was from Santiago: the refinery "Hermanos Díaz" in that city is honored with his name in memory of Nano and his brother who fell in Santiago de Cuba. The other, a comrade from Artemisa, was a veteran of Moncada and of the "Granma"). With Captain Jorge Sotús were Lieutenants Ciro Frías (later killed on the Frank País Front), Guillermo García (today Chief of the Army of the Western Sector), and René Ramos Latour (killed after attaining the rank of major in the Sierra Maestra). Then came the General Staff or "Comandancia," which was made up of Fidel as Commander-in-Chief, Ciro Redondo, Manuel Fajardo (today major), Crespo (major), Universo Sánchez (major), and myself as the doctor.

The platoon which customarily followed was that of Almeida, whose Lieutenants were Hermo, Guillermo Domínguez (killed in

Pino del Agua), and Pena. Efigenio Ameijeiras, a lieutenant, and three men made up the rear guard.

Because of the size of our group, our cooking now had to be done separately by each squad. Food, medicines, and ammunition were distributed by squads. In almost all the squads, and certainly in all the platoons, there were veterans who showed the new men how to cook, how best to use the food; they also taught them how to pack their knapsacks, and how best to march through the Sierra.

The road between La Derecha, El Lomón, and El Uvero can be covered in a few hours by car, but for us it meant months of cautious walking, and all the while we pursued our principal mission of preparing the men for combat and life after a battle. It was thus that we again passed through Altos de Espinosa, where we veterans formed an honor guard around the grave of Julio Zenón, who had fallen there some time before. There I found a piece of my blanket, tangled in the brambles as a reminder of my speedy "strategic retreat." I put it in my pack, firmly resolving never again to lose my equipment in that manner.

I was assigned a new recruit, Paulino, as an assistant to carry the medical supplies. This eased my task a little so that I could attend to the men's medical problems for a few minutes each day after our long marches. We again passed by the Loma de Caracas where we had had such a disagreeable encounter with enemy planes, thanks to Guerra's betrayal. There we found one of the extra rifles which one of our men had left behind in order to retreat more easily. By now we had no extra weapons; on the contrary, we were short. We had entered a new phase. There had been a qualitative change; there was now a whole area which the enemy avoided for fear of meeting us, although we also showed little interest in encountering them.

The political situation in those days was full of the nuances of opportunism. The well-known voices of Pardo Llada, Conte Agüero, and other vultures of the same ilk specialized in demagogic outbursts calling for harmony and peace, and timidly criticizing the government. The government had spoken of peace; the new Prime

Minister, Rivero Agüero, indicated that if necessary he would go to the Sierra Maestra to pacify the countryside. Nevertheless, a few days later, Batista stated that it was no longer necessary to speak to Fidel or the rebels, that Fidel Castro was not in the Sierra, and that, therefore, there was no reason to talk with "a bunch of bandits."

In this way the Batista group showed its willingness to continue the fight, the only thing on which both sides agreed, for it was also our intent to continue to fight at any price. In those days a new Chief of Operations was named: Colonel Barrera, well known for embezzling Army ration funds. He later calmly watched the destruction of the Batista entity from Caracas, Venezuela, where he was military attaché.

At that moment we had with us some engaging characters, who were helpful as propagandizers of our movement in the United States. Two of them in particular brought us a few problems as well. There were three North American boys who had left their parents at the Naval Base at Guantánamo, and had joined our fight. Two of them never heard a shot in the Sierra, and, exhausted by the climate and the many privations they left, taken back by the journalist Bob Taber. The third participated in the battle of El Uvero and later he too left, sick but having fought in a battle. The boys were not ideologically prepared for revolution and were simply satisfying their thirst for adventure in our company. We were sorry, but also glad to see them go. Personally, I was especially pleased, for they frequently came to me in my capacity as doctor because they could not stand the rigors of our life.

At that same period, the government took some journalists up several thousand meters in military planes to prove to them that there was no one in the Sierra Maestra. It was a strange operation which did not convince anyone; it also demonstrated the manner in which the Batista government deceived public opinion with the help of Conte Agüero and men like him, men disguised as revolutionaries who daily lied to the people.

During the days of trial I finally got a canvas hammock. The hammock is a precious belonging which I had not received before because of the rigorous guerrilla axiom according to which canvas hammocks had to be given only to those men who had already made hammocks of sacking. This was done in order to combat laziness. Anyone could make himself a hammock of sacking, and having it gave him the right to the next canvas one. However, I could not use the sacking hammock because of my allergies: the lint greatly affected me, and I had to sleep on the ground. Since I did not have a hammock of sacking, I was not entitled to a canvas one. These homely details are part of the everyday annoyances we all faced. But Fidel noticed, broke the rule, and gave me a hammock. I shall always remember that it was on the banks of the La Plata, in the last foothills before reaching Palma Mocha, and it was a day after we ate our first horse.

The horse was more than a luxury meal; it was also a kind of trial by fire, testing the men's capacity to adapt. The peasants in our group were indignant and they refused to eat their ration of horse meat; some of them considered Manuel Fajardo a virtual murderer, for he was the man chosen to slaughter the animal since he had been a butcher in peacetime.

This first horse belonged to a peasant named Popa, from the other side of the La Plata. Popa must now know how to read, and if he sees the magazine *Verde Olivo** he will remember that night when three sinister-looking rebels banged on the door of his *bohío*, mistaking him for an informer, and took that tired old horse from him. This animal was to be our ration hours later and its meat would constitute an exquisite feast for some and a test for the prejudiced stomachs of the peasants, who believed they were committing an act of cannibalism as they chewed up man's old friend.

---

* These pages were originally published in *Verde Olivo*, the Revolutionary Army magazine.

# A Famous Interview

In mid-April 1957 we returned with our apprentice army to the region of Palma Mocha, near El Turquino. During that period our most valiant mountaineer-fighters were those of peasant stock.

Guillermo García and Ciro Frías, with patrols of peasants, came and went from place to place in the Sierra, bringing news, scouting, getting food; in fact, they constituted the real mobile vanguard of our column. In those days, we were once again in El Arroyo del In-fierno, the site of one of our battles. The peasants who came to greet us filled us in on the details of that attack: who had led the guards directly to our camp, who had died there. In fact the peasants, skill-ful in the art of the grapevine, informed us of all the life of the re-gion.

Fidel, who in those days did not have a radio, asked to borrow one from a local peasant, who lent him his, and thus on a large radio carried in a soldier's knapsack we were able to hear the news direct from Havana. They were once again speaking more freely because of the re-establishment of so-called guarantees.

Guillermo García, in the uniform of an Army corporal, accom-panied by two comrades disguised as Army soldiers, went to look for the informer who had led the Army to us. They brought him back the following day "on the order of the colonel." The man had come innocently, but when he saw the ragged army he knew what

95

awaited him. With great cynicism he told us everything about his relations with the Army and how he had told "that bastard Casillas" that he would be perfectly willing to take the Army to where we were, for he had seen us, and that they could then capture us; however, they had not listened to him.

Some days later, on one of the hills nearby, the informer was executed and buried. We received a message from Celia announcing that she would be coming with two North American journalists who wanted to interview Fidel, under the pretext of seeing the three North American boys. She also sent some money collected from among sympathizers of the Movement.

It was decided that Lalo Sardiñas would bring the North Americans through the region of Estrada Palma which, as an ex-merchant in the region, he knew well. We were devoting our time to making contact with peasants who could serve as links and who could maintain permanent encampments as centers of contact with the whole region, which was growing in size. Thus we located houses which we used as supply centers for our troops, and there we installed warehouses from which we drew supplies according to our needs. These places also served as rest stops for the fast human stage coaches who moved along the edge of the Maestra from one place to another carrying messages and news.

These messengers showed an extraordinary capacity for covering very long distances in a short time. We were constantly fooled by their version of "a half-hour's walk" or "just over there." For the peasants this almost always turned out to be exact, even though their concept of time and distance was quite different from that of a city dweller.

Three days after Lalo Sardiñas left, we heard that six people were coming up through the region of Santo Domingo; there were two women, two "gringos" (the journalists), and two others whom nobody knew. However, we also received some contradictory news to the effect that the rural guards, having learned of their presence from an informer, had surrounded the house where they were.

In the Sierra news travels with remarkable speed, but it is also distorted. Camilo went out with a platoon to liberate Celia Sánchez and the North Americans at all costs. However, they arrived safe and sound; the false alarm was due to troop movements provoked by a denunciation which in those days was easy to produce among backward peasants.

On April 23, the journalist Bob Taber and a photographer arrived at our camp. With them came comrades Celia Sánchez and Haydée Santamaría and the men sent by the Movement in the plains: "Marcos" or "Nicaragua," Major Iglesias, today Governor of Las Villas and in those days in charge of maneuvers in Santiago, and Marcelo Fernández who was coordinator of the Movement, later Vice President of the National Bank. He acted as interpreter.

The days went according to schedule, as we tried to show the North Americans our strength, and tried to evade their more indiscreet questions. We did not know anything about these journalists; however, they interviewed the three boys who answered all the questions well, showing the new spirit which they had developed in that primitive life among us, despite the difficulties of adjusting to it and to us.

We were soon joined by one of the most "simpático" and beloved figures of our revolutionary war, Vaquerito. Vaquerito, together with another comrade, found us one day and said that he had spent over a month looking for us. He was from Morón in Camagüey. As always in those cases, we subjected him to interrogation and gave him the rudiments of a political orientation, a task which frequently fell to me. Vaquerito did not have a political idea in his head, nor did he seem to be anything other than a happy, healthy boy, who saw all of this as a marvelous adventure. He came barefoot and Celia lent him some Mexican tooled-leather shoes. She had an extra pair and since his feet were so small they were the only shoes which fit him. With the new shoes and a large straw hat, Vaquerito looked like a Mexican cowboy or "vaquero," and that is why we nicknamed him Vaquerito.

As is well known, Vaquerito did not see the end of the revolutionary struggle, for as chief of the suicide squad of the 8th Column, he died a day before Santa Clara was taken. We all remember his extraordinary gaiety, his continual joviality, and the strange and romantic manner he had of confronting danger. Vaquerito was an amazing liar; I wonder if he ever had a conversation where he did not so adorn the truth that it was unrecognizable. But in his activities as a messenger in the early days, and later as a soldier or as chief of the suicide squad, Vaquerito demonstrated that reality and fantasy had for him no exact boundaries and the same feats which his agile mind invented he was able to carry out on the battlefield. His extreme bravery had become legend by the time our epic war was over.

Sometime after he had joined us, I decided to question Vaquerito about his life. A group was sitting around after one of the nightly reading sessions. Vaquerito began to tell us about himself, and we all began surreptitiously calculating his age. When he finished, after many sparkling anecdotes, we asked him how old he was. Vaquerito at that time was a little over 20, but according to all of his deeds and the jobs he had held, it worked out that he had begun to work five years before he was born.

Comrade "Nicaragua" brought news of more weapons in Santiago, remnants of the assault on the Palace. There were ten machine guns, eleven Johnson rifles, and six short carbines, according to him. There were a few more but another front was going to be opened in the region of the Miranda sugar mill. Fidel opposed this idea and only allowed a few arms for the second front, giving orders that all possible weapons be brought up to reinforce us. We continued the march, withdrawing from the uncomfortable company of some rural guards who were marauding nearby. But first we decided to go up El Turquino. The ascent of our highest mountain had an almost mystical meaning for us. And anyway, we were already quite near the peak.

El Turquino was climbed by the entire column and up there we finished the interview with Bob Taber. He was preparing a film which was later televised in the United States, at a time when we were not feared so much. An enlightening note: a *guajiro* who joined us told us that Casillas had offered him 300 pesos and a pregnant cow if he would kill Fidel. The North Americans were not the only ones who were wrong about the price of our highest commander.

According to an altimeter which we had, the mountain of El Turquino was 1,850 meters above sea level. I note this as an incidental point, for we never tested the instrument; but at sea level it worked well, and this figure differs quite a bit from that given in official records.

Since an Army company was on our heels, Guillermo was sent with a group of comrades to snipe at them. Because of my asthmatic condition which obliged me to walk at the end of the column and did not permit any special efforts, I was relieved of the Thompson submachine gun which I was carrying. About three days passed before I got it back. These were some of the tensest days in the Sierra for me, for I was unarmed while every day there was the possibility of encounters with the enemy.

In May 1957, two of the North American boys left the column with Bob Taber, who had finished his story, and they reached Guantánamo safe and sound. We continued to march slowly along the crest of the Maestra and its slopes. We were making contacts, exploring new regions, and spreading the revolutionary flame and the legend of our troop of *barbudos* across the Sierra. The new spirit was communicated far and wide. Peasants came to greet us with less fear, and we in turn had more confidence in them. Our relative strength had increased considerably and we felt more secure against any surprise attack by the Batista Army. In general, we were a great deal closer now to the *guajiros*.

# On the March

The first fifteen days of May were days of continual marching. At the beginning of the month, we were on a hill close to El Turquino; we crossed regions which later were the scenes of many revolutionary victories. We passed through Santa Ana and El Hombrito; later on, at Pico Verde, we found Escudero's house and we continued until we reached the Loma del Burro. We were moving eastward, looking for the weapons which were supposed to be sent from Santiago and would be hidden in the region of Loma del Burro, close to Oro de Guisa. One night during this two-week journey, while going to carry out a private necessity, I confused the paths and was lost for three days until I found the troop again in a spot called El Hombrito. At that time I realized that luckily we were each carrying on our backs everything necessary for individual survival: salt, oil, canned foods, canned milk, everything required for sleeping, making fire, and cooking, and also a compass, on which I had relied very heavily until then.

Finding myself lost, the next morning I took out the compass and, guiding myself with it, I continued for a day and a half until I realized that I was even more lost. I approached a peasant hut and the people directed me to the rebel encampment. Later we found that in such rugged territory a compass can only give a general orientation, never a definite course; one has either to be led by guides or to know the area oneself, as we later knew it when I was operating in that same region.

I was very moved by the warm reception which greeted me when I rejoined the column. When I arrived they had just held a people's trial in which three informers were judged, and one of them, Nápoles, was condemned to death. Camilo was the president of that tribunal.

At that period I had to perform my duties as a doctor and in each little village I set up my consulting station. It was monotonous, for I had few medicines to offer and the clinical cases in the Sierra were all more or less the same: prematurely aged and toothless women, children with distended bellies, parasitism, rickets, general avitaminosis—these were the marks of the Sierra Maestra. Even today they continue, but in much smaller proportion. The sons of those mothers of the Sierra have gone to study at the Camilo Cienfuegos School City; they are grown up and healthy, they are different boys from the first undernourished inhabitants of our pioneer School City.

I remember that a little girl was watching the consultations which I gave to the women of the region. They came in with an almost religious air to find out the reasons for their sufferings. When her mother arrived, the little girl, after attentively watching several previous examinations in the *bohío* which served me as a clinic, chattered gaily: "Mamá, this doctor says the same thing to all of them."

And it was absolutely true; my knowledge was good for little else. But, in addition, they all had the same clinical case history, and without knowing it they each told the same heart-rending story. What would have happened if the doctor had diagnosed the strange tiredness which the young mother of several children suffered when she carried a can of water up from the river to the house as being simply due to too much work on such a meager diet? Her exhaustion is something inexplicable to her, since all her life the woman the same cans of water to the same place and only now eel tired. The people in the Sierra grow like wild flowers, untended and without care, and they wear themselves out rapidly, working without reward. During those consultations we began to grow more conscious of the necessity for a definitive change in the life of the people. The idea of agrarian reform became clear and oneness with the people ceased being theory and was converted into a fundamental part of our being.

The guerrilla group and the peasantry began to merge into one single mass, without our being able to say at which moment on the long revolutionary road this happened, nor at which moment the words became profoundly real and we became a part of the peasantry. As far as I'm concerned, those consultations with the *guajiros* of the Sierra converted my spontaneous and somewhat lyrical resolve into a force of greater value and more serenity. Those suffering and loyal inhabitants of the Sierra Maestra have never suspected the role they played as forgers of our revolutionary ideology.

It was there that Guillermo García was promoted to captain and took charge of all the peasants who joined the column. Perhaps Comrade Guillermo does not remember the date: it is noted in my diary as May 6, 1957.

The following day, Haydée Santamaría left with precise instructions from Fidel, to make the necessary contacts. But a day later we got the news of "Nicaragua's" arrest. He was in charge of bringing us the weapons. This caused a great deal of confusion among us, for we could not imagine what we would do now in order to get the arms; nevertheless, we decided to continue walking in the same direction.

We reached a place near Pino del Agua, a small ravine with an abandoned lumber camp on the very edge of the Sierra Maestra; there were also two uninhabited *bohíos*. Near a highway, one of our patrols captured an Army corporal. This corporal was an individual well known for his crimes since the time of Machado. For this reason some of us proposed that he be executed, but Fidel refused; we simply left him guarded by the new recruits who did not yet have rifles, but only small arms. He was warned that any attempt to escape would cost him his life.

Most of us continued on our way to see if the weapons had arrived at the agreed spot, and if so, to transport them. It was a long walk, although easier than usual since our full packs had been left in the camp where the prisoner was. The walk, however, brought no results: the equipment had not arrived and naturally we attributed this to the arrest of "Nicaragua." We were able to buy food in a store, and returned with a different but welcome load to the camp.

We were returning by the same road, slowly and tiredly, going along the ridges of the Sierra Maestra and crossing the open spaces carefully. Suddenly we heard shots ahead of us. We were worried because one of our men had gone before us in order to reach the camp as soon as possible; he was Guillermo Domínguez, lieutenant of our troop and one of the men who had arrived with the reinforcements from Santiago. We prepared for whatever contingency might arise while we sent out some scouts. After a reasonable length of time, the scouts appeared and with them came Comrade

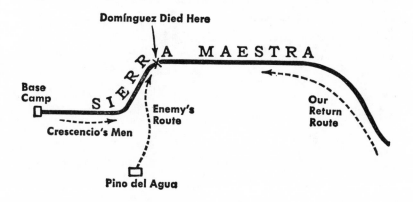

Fiallo, who belonged to Crescencio's group and had joined the guerrillas during our absence. He came from our camp and explained that there was a body on the road, and that there had been an encounter with some guards, who had retreated in the direction of Pino del Agua where there was a larger detachment. We advanced cautiously, and came upon the body, which I recognized.

It was Guillermo Domínguez; he was naked from the waist up and had a bullet hole in the left elbow, and a bayonet wound in the upper chest, over his heart; his head was literally shattered by a shot, apparently from his own shotgun. Some buckshot pellets remained in his lacerated flesh as testimony.

We were able to reconstruct the facts by analyzing various data: the guards were probably scouting for their friend, the corporal, whom we had captured. They had heard Domínguez coming ahead of us: he must have been confident, for he had walked the same path the day before. They had taken him prisoner as some of Crescencio's men were coming to meet us from the other direction. On surprising the guards from the rear, Crescencio's men had fired and the guards had retreated, murdering our comrade Domínguez before fleeing.

Pino del Agua is a sawmill camp in the middle of the Sierra and the path the guards took is an old cross path for transporting lumber. We had to follow this path for a hundred meters, in order to reach our narrow path. Our comrade had not taken the most elementary precautions in this case, and was unlucky enough to bump into the guards. His bitter fate served us as an example for the future.

# The Weapons Arrive

It was near the lumber camp of Pino del Agua that we killed the magnificent horse which the imprisoned corporal had been riding. The animal was useless to us in such craggy terrain, and we were low on food. In any case, our customary diet was such that we could not afford to disdain fresh meat, horse or otherwise. An amusing touch was provided by our prisoner. As, unaware, he drank his horse soup and ate his portion of horse meat, he explained that the animal had been lent him by a friend whose name and address he gave us, urging us to return it to him as soon as possible.

That day on the radio we learned of the sentencing of our comrades from the "Granma." In addition, we learned that a magistrate had cast his personal vote against the sentence. This was Magistrate Urrutia, whose honorable gesture later brought him the nomination as provisional President of the Republic. The personal vote of a magistrate was no more than a worthy gesture—as it clearly was at that time—but its subsequent consequences were more serious: it led to the appointment of a bad president, a man incapable of understanding the revolutionary process, incapable of digesting the profundity of a revolution which was not made for his reactionary mentality. His character and his reluctance to take a definite stand brought many conflicts. Finally, in the days celebrating the first post-revolutionary July 26, it culminated in his resignation as President when faced with unanimous rejection by the people.

On one of those days a contact from Santiago arrived. His name was Andrés, and he had exact information about the weapons: they were safe, and would be moved shortly. A delivery point was fixed in the region of a coastal lumber camp operated by the Babún brothers. The arms would be delivered with the full knowledge of these men who felt they could do a lucrative business by helping the Revolution. (Subsequent developments divided the family, and three of the Babún sons have the questionable privilege of being among those captured at the Bay of Pigs.)

It is curious to note that in that period many people tried to use the Revolution for their own ends by doing small favors for us in order later to reap rewards from the new government. The Babún brothers hoped later to have a free hand in the commercial exploitation of the forests, all the while pitilessly expelling the peasants, thereby increasing the size of their latifundia. It was around that time that we were joined by a North American journalist, the same type as the Babún family. He was Hungarian by birth, and his name was Andrew Saint George.

At first he only showed one of his faces, the better one, which was simply that of a Yankee journalist. But in addition to that he was an FBI agent. Since I was the only person in the troop who spoke French (in those days nobody spoke English), I was chosen to take care of him. Quite frankly, he did not seem to me as dangerous as he turned out to be in our second interview, when he was already openly showing himself as an agent. We were walking on the edge of Pino del Agua toward the source of the Peladero river. These were rugged areas and we all carried heavy packs. On the Peladero river there is a tributary, the Arroyo del Indio. Here we spent a couple of days, getting food and moving the arms we had received. We passed through a few peasant settlements and established a kind of extra-legal revolutionary state, leaving sympathizers who were to inform us of anything that happened and to tell us of the Army's movements. But we always lived in the wooded mountains; only occasionally, at night, did we unexpectedly reach a group of houses and then some of us slept in them. But the majority always slept under the protection of the mountains, and during the day all of us were on guard, protected by a roof of trees.

Our worst enemy at that time of year was the *macagüera,* a species of horsefly which hatches and lays its eggs in the tree called Macagua or Macaw tree. At a certain time of year it reproduces prolifically in the mountains. The *macagüera* bites exposed areas of the body; as we scratched, what with all the dirt on our bodies, the bites were easily infected and caused abscesses. The uncovered parts of our legs, our wrists, and our necks always bore proof of the presence of the *macagüera.*

Finally, on May 18, we received news of the weapons and also a tentative inventory. This news caused great excitement in the camp, for all the men wanted better weapons. We also heard that the film made by Bob Taber had been shown in the United States with great success. This news cheered everyone but Andrew Saint George, who, in addition to being an FBI agent, had his petty journalist's pride, and he felt somewhat cheated of glory. The next day he left in a yacht for Santiago de Cuba.

That day we also found out that one of our men had deserted. Since everyone at the camp knew of the arrival of the weapons, this was especially dangerous. Scouts were sent to look for him. They returned with the news that he had managed to take a boat to Santiago. We assumed that it was to inform the authorities, although later it came out that the desertion was simply brought about by the man's physical and moral inability to endure the hardships of our life. In any case, we had to double our precautions. Our struggle against the lack of physical, ideological, and moral preparation among the men was a daily one; the results were not always encouraging. The weaker men often asked permission to leave for the most petty reasons, and if they were refused, they would usually desert. We must remember that desertion was punishable by death directly upon capture.

That night the weapons arrived. For us it was the most marvelous spectacle in the world: the instruments of death were on exhibition before the covetous eyes of all the men. Three tripod machine guns, three Madzen automatic rifles, nine M-1 carbines, ten Johnson automatic rifles, and a total of six thousand rounds were delivered. Although the M-1 carbines had only forty-five rounds apiece, they were highly prized weapons, and they were distributed according to the acquired merits of the men and their time in the Sierra. One of the M-1's was given to the present-day Major Ramiro Valdés, and two went to the advance guard which Camilo commanded. The other four were to be used to cover the tripod machine guns. One of the automatics went to Captain Jorge Sotús' platoon, another to Almeida's and the third to the General Staff (I had the responsibility for operating it). The tripods were distributed as follows: one for Raúl, another for Guillermo García, and the third for Crescencio Pérez. In this way, I made my debut as a fighting guerrilla, for until then I had been the troop's doctor, knowing only occasional combat. I had entered a new stage.

I shall always remember the moment I was given the automatic rifle. It was old and of poor quality, but to me it was an important acquisition. Four men were assigned to help me with this weapon. These four guerrillas have subsequently followed very different paths: two of them were the brothers Pupo and Manolo Beatón, executed by the Revolution after they murdered Major Cristino Naranjo and fled to the Sierras de Oriente, where a peasant captured them. Another was a boy of fifteen who was almost always to carry the enormous weight of the equipment for the automatic. He was Joel Iglesias, and today is the President of the *Jóvenes Rebeldes* and a major in the Rebel Army. The fourth man, today a lieutenant, was named Oñate, but we affectionately labeled him Cantinflas.

The arrival of the weapons did not mean an end to our attempt at instilling greater ideological and fighting force in the troop. A few days later, on May 23, Fidel ordered new discharges, among them an entire squad, and our force was reduced to 127 men, the majority of them armed and about eighty of them well armed.

From the squad which, along with its leader, was dismissed, there remained one man named Crucito who later became one of our best-loved fighters. Crucito was a natural poet and he had long rhyming matches with the city-poet, Calixto Morales. Morales had arrived on the "Granma" and had nicknamed himself "nightingale of the plains," to which Crucito in his *guajiro* ballads always answered with a refrain, directed in mock derision at Calixto: *Soy guacaico de la Sierra:* "I'm an old Sierra buzzard."

This magnificent comrade had written the whole history of the Revolution in ballads which he composed at every rest stop as he puffed on his pipe. Since there was very little paper in the Sierra, he composed the ballads in his head, so that none of them remained when a bullet put an end to his life in the battle of Pino del Agua.

In the timber belt we received the invaluable help of Enrique López, an old childhood friend of Fidel and Raúl, who was at that time employed by the Babúns and served as a supply contact. He also made it possible for us to move through the entire area without danger. This region was full of roads used by army trucks; several times we prepared unsuccessful ambushes aimed at capturing some trucks. Perhaps these failures contributed to the success of the approaching operation. This victorious battle was to have greater psychological impact than any other in the history of the war. I refer to the battle of El Uvero.

On May 25, we heard that an expeditionary force led by Calixto Sánchez had arrived in the boat "El Corintia" and had landed at Mayarí; a few days later we were to learn of the disastrous result of this expedition: Prío [Socarrás] sent his men to die without ever bothering to accompany them. The news of this landing showed us the absolute necessity for diverting the enemy forces in order to allow those men to reach some place where they could reorganize and begin their actions. We did all this out of solidarity with the other group, although we did not even know its social composition or its true goals.

At this point we had an interesting discussion, led principally by myself and Fidel. I was of the opinion that we ought not lose the opportunity of capturing a truck and that we should devote ourselves to ambushing them on the roads where they passed unconcernedly. But Fidel had already planned the action at El Uvero, and he thought that it would be much more important and would bring us a more resounding success if we captured the Army post at El Uvero. If we succeeded, it would have a tremendous moral impact and would be spoken of throughout the country; this would not happen with the capture of a truck, which could be reported as a highway accident with a few casualties and, although people would suspect the truth, our effective fighting presence in the Sierra would never be known. This did not mean that we would totally reject the idea of capturing a truck, under optimum conditions; but we should not convert this into the focal point of our activities.

Today, several years after that discussion (which at the time did not convince me) I must recognize that Fidel's judgment was correct. It would have been much less productive for us to carry out an isolated action against one of the patrols which travelled in the trucks. At that period, our eagerness to fight always led us impatiently to adopt drastic attitudes; perhaps we could not yet see the more distant objectives. In any case, we began the final preparations for the battle of El Uvero.

# The Battle of El Uvero

Having decided on the point of attack, we then had to work out exactly the form it would take; we had to solve such important problems as ascertaining the number of soldiers present, the number of guard posts, the type of communications they used, the access roads, the civilian population and its distribution, etc. In all of this we were admirably served by Comrade Caldero, today a major, who was, I believe, the son-in-law of the administrator of the lumber camp.

We assumed that the Army had more or less exact data on our presence in the area, for two informers had been captured and they carried Army identification documents and confessed to being sent by Casillas to ascertain our position and our customary meeting places. The spectacle of the two men begging for mercy was truly repugnant, but at the same time pathetic. However, the laws of war, in those difficult times, could not be ignored, and both spies were executed the following day.

That same day, May 27, the General Staff met with all the officers and Fidel announced that within the next forty-eight hours we would be fighting. He ordered us to have our men and their weapons ready for the march. We were not given details at that point.

Caldero would be the guide, for he knew the post of El Uvero well: its entrances and exits, and its roads of access. That night we started walking; it was a long march of some sixteen kilometers, but all downhill on the roads which had been specially constructed by the Babún Company to reach its sawmills. However, we took about eight hours to walk it, for we were slowed by the extra precautions which we had to take, especially as we got nearer the danger zone. Finally we were given our orders, which were very simple: we were to take the guard posts and riddle the wooden barracks with bullets.

We knew that the barracks had no major defenses apart from some logs scattered in the immediate vicinity. Its strong points were the guard posts, each with three or four soldiers and strategically placed around the outside of the building. Overlooking the barracks was a hill from which our General Staff would direct

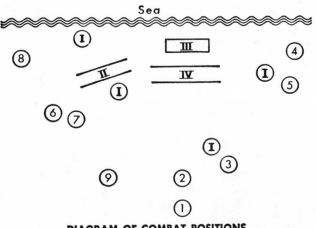

**DIAGRAM OF COMBAT POSITIONS**

I — Enemy Posts
II — Sugar Plant
III — Barracks
IV — Lumber Company Installations

1. Rebel Staff Headquarters
2. Raúl Castro
3. Juan Almeida
4. Jorge Sotús
5. Guillermo García
6. Camilo Cienfuegos
7. Efigenio Ameijeiras
8. Crescencio Pérez
9. Che Guevara

the battle. We were to approach the building through the thickets and station ourselves a few meters away. We were carefully instructed not to fire on the outlying buildings since they sheltered women and children, including the administrator's wife who knew about the attack but preferred to stay there in order to avoid suspicion later. As we left to occupy our attack positions, we were most of all concerned about the civilians.

The barracks of El Uvero was located close to the sea, so that we needed only to attack it from three sides in order to surround it completely.

The coastal road from Peladero was commanded by one guard post in the barracks; the platoons led by Jorge Sotús and Guillermo García were sent to attack that post. Almeida was to take charge of liquidating a post located in front of the mountain, more or less to the north. Fidel would be on the hill overlooking the barracks and Raúl would advance from the front with his platoon. I was assigned an intermediate post with my automatic rifle and my adjutants. Camilo and Ameijeiras were to advance from the front, between my position and Raúl's. But they miscalculated because it was dark and they began shooting from my left instead of my right. Crescencio Pérez' platoon was to advance along the road to Chivirico and hold back whatever Army reinforcements were sent.

We expected the element of surprise to make the battle quite short. However, the minutes passed and we were not able to place our men in the ideal positions we had hoped for. Our guides, Caldero and another from the region named Eligio Mendoza, brought whatever news there was. The night would soon end and the dawn would creep in before we could surprise the soldiers in the manner we had planned. Jorge Sotús advised us that he was not at his assigned position but that it was too late now to move. When Fidel opened fire with his telescopic rifle, we were able to locate the barracks from the answering shots which came from it. I was on a small elevation and I had a perfect view of the barracks;

but I was very far from it and my men and I advanced to find better positions.

Everyone advanced. Almeida moved toward the post which defended the entrance to the little barracks. To my left I could see Camilo wearing his beret with a handkerchief on his neck like the hats of the French Foreign Legion, but his of course sported the Movement insignias. We advanced cautiously amidst the general exchange of fire.

The small squad was joined by men who had been separated from their own units; a comrade from Pilón named Bomba, Comrade Mario Leal, and Acuña joined what already constituted a small combat unit. The resistance had been great and we had arrived at a flat open space where we were forced to advance with infinite precautions, for the enemy fired continuously and accurately. From my position, hardly fifty or sixty meters from the enemy outpost, I saw two soldiers run out of the foremost trench, and I fired at both of them, but they hid in the nearby buildings and these were of course sacred to us. We continued advancing, although there was now nothing more than a narrow, sparsely grown strip of land between us and the enemy, whose bullets whistled dangerously near. At that moment I heard a groan near me, and then some shouts. I thought it must be a wounded enemy soldier, and I dragged myself forward, shouting to him to surrender. It turned out to be Comrade Leal, who was wounded in the head. I hastily examined him and found that both entrance and exit wounds were in the parietal region. Leal was losing consciousness, and the limbs on one side of his body were becoming paralyzed. The only bandage I had on hand was a piece of paper which I put on the wounds. Later, Joel Iglesias went to watch over him, while we continued the attack. Then Acuña was wounded also. We advanced no more, and continued to shoot at the trench in front of us. Our fire was efficiently answered. We were just mustering our courage again, and had decided to capture the warehouse and end the resistance, when the barracks surrendered.

This description has taken only a few minutes, but the actual battle lasted about two hours and forty-five minutes from the first shot until the barracks surrendered. At my left, some of the men from the vanguard, Victor Mora and three others I believe, took the last resisters prisoner. From the trench emerged a soldier holding his gun above his head. From all sides came shouts of surrender. We advanced rapidly on the barracks and we heard one last rattle of machine gun fire which I later found had killed Lieutenant Nano Díaz.

We reached the warehouse where we made prisoners of the two soldiers who had escaped my shots, and also the post doctor and his adjutant. The doctor was a quiet, grey-haired man; I do not know whether he is part of the Revolution today. A strange thing happened with this man: my knowledge of medicine had never been very extensive; the number of wounded was enormous and at that moment I was not able to attend to them. When I brought the wounded to the Army doctor, he asked me how old I was and when I had finished my training. I explained that it had been some years ago, and then he said frankly: "Look, kid, you'd better take charge of all this because I've just graduated and have had very little experience." What with his lack of experience and his fright on finding himself a prisoner, he had forgotten all his medical training. So I had once again to change from soldier to doctor, which in fact involved little more than a handwashing.

After the battle, which was one of the bloodiest of the revolutionary war, we pooled our experiences, and I can now give a more general picture of the action. The battle proceeded more or less as follows: When Fidel's shot gave the signal to open fire, everyone began to advance on the barracks. The Army responded with full fire, in many cases against the hill from where our leader directed the battle. After a few minutes, Julito Díaz died at Fidel's side when he was hit in the head by a bullet. The minutes passed and the resistance continued; we were unable to frighten the soldiers to the point of surrender. The most important task in the center was Almeida's: he was in charge of liquidating the post at all costs in order to allow his and Raúl's troops to march on the barracks.

The men later recounted how Eligio Mendoza, the guide, had taken his rifle and flung himself into the battle; a superstitious man, he had a "Santo" who protected him, and when he was told to take care, he had answered contemptuously that his "Santo" would defend him from anything; a few minutes later he fell, hit by a bullet which literally shattered his body.

The well-entrenched enemy troops drove us back, causing us several casualties. It was very difficult to advance through the central area; from the road to Peladero, Jorge Sotús attempted to flank the position with an adjutant nicknamed "El Policía," but the latter was immediately killed by the enemy and Sotús had to throw himself into the sea in order to avoid being killed also. From that moment he was practically useless in the battle. Other members of his platoon attempted to advance, but they too were forced back. A peasant named Vega, I believe, was killed; Manals was wounded in the lung; Quike Escalona received wounds in the arm, the buttock, and the hand. The post, well-protected by a wooden palisade, fired automatic and semi-automatic rifles, devastating our small troop.

Almeida ordered a final assault in which he would attempt by any means to reduce the enemy he faced; Cilleros, Maceo, Hermes Leyva, Pena, and Almeida himself were wounded (the latter in the shoulder and the left leg), and Comrade Moll was killed. Nevertheless, this push forward overcame the post and a path to the barracks was opened. From the other side, Guillermo García's sure machine gun shots had liquidated three of the defenders; the fourth came out running and was killed in flight. Raúl, with his platoon divided into two units, advanced rapidly on the barracks. It was the action of Captains García and Almeida which decided the battle; each one destroyed the assigned guard post and thus made the final assault possible. Another individual who deserves special mention is Luis Crespo, who came down from the General Staff position to participate in the battle.

Enemy resistance was crumbling. A white handkerchief had been shown and we took the barracks. At that moment someone, probably one of our men, fired again and from the barracks came a burst of fire which took Nano Díaz through the head. To the very end, Nano's machine gun caused many enemy casualties. Crescencio's platoon hardly participated in the battle, because his machine gun had jammed; so he guarded the road from Chivirico. There he stopped some fleeing soldiers. The battle had lasted two hours and forty-five minutes and no civilian had been wounded, despite the great number of shots which had been fired.

When we took inventory we found the following situation: On our side there were six dead: Moll, Nano Díaz, Vega, "El Policía," Julito Díaz, and Eligio Mendoza. Badly wounded were Leal and Cilleros. Wounded more or less seriously were Maceo in the shoulder, Hermes Leyva with a surface wound on the chest, Almeida in the left arm and left leg, Quike Escalona in the right arm and hand, Manals in the lung, Pena in the knee, Manuel Acuña in the right arm. In all, fifteen comrades *hors de combat*. The enemy had nineteen wounded, fourteen dead, another fourteen prisoners, and six escapees, which made a total of fifty-three men, under the command of a second lieutenant who had shown the white flag when he was wounded.

If you consider that we were about eighty men and they were fifty-three, a total of a hundred and thirty-three men, of whom thirty-eight, that is to say more than a quarter, were *hors de combat* in a little over two and a half hours of fighting, you will understand what kind of battle it was. It was an assault by men who had advanced bare-chested against an enemy which was protected by very poor defenses. It should be recognized that on both sides great courage was shown. For us this was the victory which marked our coming of age. From this battle on, our morale grew tremendously, our decisiveness and our hopes for triumph increased also.

Although the months which followed were difficult ones, we were already in possession of the secret of victory. This action at El Uvero sealed the fate of all small barracks situated far from major clusters of enemy forces, and they were all closed soon after.

One of the first shots of the battle hit the barracks telephone, cutting communication with Santiago. Only a couple of small planes flew over the battlefield, but the Air Force did not send reconnaissance planes until hours later, when we were already high in the mountains. We have been told that, apart from the fourteen dead soldiers, three of the five parrots which the guards had in the barracks had been killed. One has only to remember the small size of this bird to be able to picture what kind of attack the building underwent.

My return to the medical profession had a few moving moments. My first patient was Comrade Cilleros. A bullet had severed his right arm and, after piercing a lung, had apparently embedded itself in his spine, paralyzing both legs. His condition was critical, and I was only able to give him a sedative and bind his chest tightly so that he could breathe more easily. We tried to save him in the only way possible at that time: we took the fourteen prisoners with us and left the two wounded guerrillas, Leal and Cilleros, with the enemy, having received the doctor's word of honor that they would be cared for. When I told this to Cilleros, mouthing the usual words of comfort, he answered me with a sad smile that said more than any words could have, and expressed his conviction that it was all over for him. We knew this too and I was tempted at that moment to place a farewell kiss on his forehead; but such an action on my part would have signified our comrade's death sentence, and duty told me that I must not further spoil his last minutes by confirming something which he already knew. I said good-bye, as affectionately as possible and with great pain, to the two men who remained in the hands of the enemy. They cried out that they would prefer to die among their comrades; but we also had the duty to fight to the end for their lives. There they remained, with the nineteen wounded Batista soldiers who had also been cared for as well as conditions allowed. Our two comrades were decently treated by the enemy Army, but Cilleros did not reach Santiago. Leal survived his wound, was imprisoned on the Isle of Pines for the rest of the war, and today still bears the indelible marks of that important episode in our revolutionary war.

In one of Babún's trucks we carried the largest possible quantity of every kind of equipment, especially medical. We left last, moving toward our hideout in the mountains which we reached in time to care for the wounded and take leave of the dead, who were buried by a bend in the road. We realized that persecution would now be great, and we decided that those men who could walk ought to move on quickly, leaving the wounded behind in my care. Enrique López would undertake to furnish me with transportation for the wounded, a hiding place, some adjutants, and all the necessary contacts through whom we could receive medicines and cure the men properly.

Almost no one slept that night as we heard from each man about the incidents which he had seen during the battle. Out of curiosity I took note of all the enemy soldiers supposedly killed during the battle. There were more enemy corpses than there had been enemy soldiers. This kind of experience taught us that all facts *must* be validated by several persons; being exaggeratedly careful, we even demanded physical proof, such as items taken from a fallen soldier, before we accepted an enemy casualty. Preoccupation with the truth was always a central theme in reports from the Rebel Army, and we attempted to imbue our men with a profound respect for truth and a feeling of how necessary it was to place truth above any transitory advantage.

In the morning, we watched the victorious troop leave us, bidding farewell sadly. My adjutants Joel Iglesias and Oñate stayed with me, as well as a guide named Sinecio Torres and Vilo Acuña, today a major, who stayed to be with his wounded uncle.

# Caring for the Wounded

The day after the battle of El Uvero, planes circled above from dawn. Our farewells to the departing column were over, and we devoted ourselves to effacing the traces of our entry into the forest. We were a mere hundred meters from a truck road and we waited for Enrique López and the trucks which would take us to our hideout.

Almeida, Pena, and Quike Escalona could not walk; I had to urge Manals not to walk either because of the wound in his lung; Manuel Acuña, Hermes Leyva, and Maceo could all walk on their own. To protect, nurse, and transport them, there were Vilo Acuña, Sinecio Torres, Joel Iglesias, Alejandro Oñate, and myself. The morning was well advanced when a messenger came to tell us that Enrique López could not help us because his daughter was ill and he had to leave for Santiago; he left word for us saying he would send us some volunteers to help, but they never arrived.

The situation was difficult, for Quike Escalona's wounds were infected and I could not determine exactly how serious Manals' wound was. We explored the nearby roads and found no enemy soldiers, so we decided to move the wounded to a *bohío* three or four kilometers away. The *bohío* had been abandoned but the owner had left behind several chickens.

On the first day two workers from the lumber camp helped us

with the tiring job of carrying the wounded in hammocks. At
dawn the next day, after eating well, we quickly left the place, for
we had stayed there a whole day immediately after the attack, close
to highways on which soldiers could arrive. The place where we
were was at the end of one of those roads constructed by the Babún
Company to reach deeper into the forest. With the few available
men we started on a short but difficult trek down to the small
ravine called Del Indio. Then we climbed a narrow path to a small
shack where a peasant named Israel lived with his wife and brother-
in-law. It was exceedingly difficult moving our wounded comrades
over such rugged terrain, but we did it. The two peasants even
gave us their own double bed for the wounded to sleep in.

We had left behind some of our older weapons and a variety of
equipment constituting minor war booty, for the weight of the
wounded increased with each step. Evidence of our presence always
remained in some *bohío;* because of this and since we had the time,
we decided to return to each campsite and efface all these traces,
since our security depended on it. At the same time Sinecio left
to find some friends of his in the region of Peladero.

After a short time Acuña and Joel Iglesias told me that they had
heard strange voices on the other slope. We really thought that the
time had come when we would be forced to fight under the most
difficult circumstances, for our obligation was to defend to the
death the precious burden of wounded men with which we had
been entrusted. We advanced so that the encounter would take
place as far as possible from the *bohío;* some prints of bare feet on
the path indicated that the intruders had gone along the same way.
Approaching warily, we heard an unconcerned conversation among
several persons; loading my Tommy gun and counting on the assistance of Vilo and Joel, I advanced and surprised the speakers.
They turned out to be the prisoners from El Uvero whom Fidel
had freed and who were simply looking for a way out of the
forest. Some of them were barefoot; an old corporal, almost un-

conscious, hoarsely expressed his admiration for us and our familiarity with the forest. They were without a guide, and had only a
safe-conduct signed by Fidel. Taking advantage of the impression
our surprise appearance had made on them, we warned them not
to enter the forest again for any reason.

They were all from the city and they were not used to the hardships of the mountains and the means of coping with them. We
came into the clearing where the *bohío* was and we showed them
the way to the coast, not without first reminding them that from
the forest inward was our territory and that our patrol—for we
looked like a simple patrol—would immediately notify the forces
of that sector of any foreign presence. Despite these warnings, which
they heeded carefully, we felt it prudent to move on as soon as
possible.

We spent that night in the sheltering *bohío,* but at dawn we
moved into the forest, first asking the owners of the house to bring
some chickens for the wounded. We spent the whole day waiting
for them, but they did not return. Some time later we found out
that they had been captured in the little house and that the next
day the enemy soldiers had used them as guides and had passed
by our camp of the day before.

We kept a careful watch and no one could have surprised us, but
the outcome of a skirmish under those conditions was not difficult
to foresee. Near nightfall Sinecio arrived with three volunteers: an
old man named Feliciano, and two men who would later become
members of the Rebel Army: Banderas, a lieutenant killed in the
battle of El Jigüe, and Israel Pardo, the oldest of a family of revolutionaries, who today holds the rank of captain. These comrades
helped us to move the wounded speedily to a *bohío* on the other side
of the danger zone, while Sinecio and I waited for the peasant
couple until nightfall. Naturally, they couldn't come because they
were already prisoners. Suspecting a betrayal, we decided to leave
the new house early the next day. Our frugal meal consisted of some

fruits and vegetables picked in the vicinity of the *bohío*. The following day, six months after the landing of the "Granma," we began our march early. These treks were tiring and incredibly short for anyone accustomed to long marches in the mountains. We could carry only one wounded comrade at a time, for we had to carry them in hammocks hanging from strong branches which literally ruined the shoulders of the carriers. They had to spell each other every ten or fifteen minutes, so that under those conditions we needed six or eight men to carry each wounded man. I accompanied Almeida, who was half dragging himself along. We walked very slowly, almost from tree to tree, until Israel found a short-cut through the forest and the carriers came back for Almeida.

Afterward, a tremendous rainstorm prevented us from reaching the Pardos' house immediately, but we finally got there close to nightfall. The short distance of four kilometers had been covered in twelve hours, in other words at three hours per kilometer.

At that time Sinecio Torres was the most important man in the small group, for he knew the roads and the people of the region and he helped us in everything. It was he who two days later arranged for Manals to go to Santiago to be cured; we were also preparing to send Quike Escalona whose wounds were infected. In those days contradictory news would arrive, sometimes telling us that Celia Sánchez was in prison, other times that she had been killed. Rumors also circulated to the effect that an Army patrol had taken Hermes Caldero prisoner. We did not know whether or not to believe these at times hair-raising things. Celia, for example, was our only known and secure contact. Her arrest would mean complete isolation for us. Fortunately it was not true that Celia had been arrested, although Hermes Caldero *had* been captured, but he miraculously stayed alive while passing through the dungeons of the tyranny.

On the banks of the Peladero river lived David, the overseer of a latifundio. He cooperated greatly with us. Once, David killed a

cow for us and we had to go out and get it. The animal had been
slaughtered on the river bank and cut into pieces; we had to move
the meat by night. I sent the first group with Israel Pardo in front,
and then the second led by Banderas. Banderas was quite undisciplined, and he let the others carry the full weight of the carcass,
so that it took all night to move it. A small troop was now being
formed under my command, since Almeida was wounded; conscious of my responsibility, I told Banderas that he was no longer
a fighter, but was now merely a sympathizer, unless he changed his
attitude. He really changed then; he was never a model fighter
when it came to discipline, but he was one of those enterprising and
broad-minded men, simple and ingenuous, whose eyes were opened
to reality through the shock of the Revolution. He had been cultivat-
ing his small, isolated parcel of land in the mountains, and he had
a true passion for trees and for agriculture. He lived in a small
shack with two little pigs, each with its name, and a dog. One day
he showed me a picture of his two sons who lived with his es-
tranged wife in Santiago. He also explained that some day, when
the Revolution triumphed, he would be able to go some place where
he could really grow something, not like that inhospitable piece of
land almost hanging from the mountain top.

I spoke to him of cooperatives and he did not understand too
well. He wanted to work the land on his own, by his own efforts;
nevertheless, little by little, I convinced him that it was better to
cultivate collectively, that machinery would also increase his pro-
ductivity. Banderas would today have been a vanguard fighter in
the area of agricultural production; there in the Sierra he taught
himself to read and write and was preparing for the future. He was
a diligent peasant who understood the value of contributing with
his own efforts to writing a page of history.

I had a long conversation with the overseer David, who asked me
for a list of all the important things we needed, for he was going
to Santiago and would pick them up there. He was a typical over-

seer, loyal to his boss, contemptuous of the peasants, racist. However, when the Army took him prisoner and tortured him barbarously on learning of his relations with us, his first concern on returning was to convince us that he had not talked. I do not know if David is in Cuba today, or if he followed his old bosses whose land was confiscated by the Revolution, but he was a man who in those days felt the need for a change. However, he never imagined that the change would also reach him and his world. The history of the Revolution is made up of many sincere efforts on the part of simple men. Our mission is to develop the goodness and nobility in each man, to convert *every* man into a revolutionary, from the Davids who did not understand well to the Banderas who died without seeing the dawn. The Revolution was also made by blind and unrewarded sacrifices. Those of us who today see its accomplishments have the responsibility to remember those who fell by the wayside, and to work for a future where there will be fewer stragglers.

# Our Return

We spent the whole month of June 1957 nursing our wounded comrades and organizing the small troop that would return with us to Fidel's column.

Contacts with the outside world were made through the overseer David, whose advice and opportune information, as well as the food he brought us, greatly alleviated our situation. In those first days we did not have the invaluable help of Pancho Tamayo, a man who was murdered by the Beatón brothers after the war. Pancho Tamayo, an old peasant from the area, later got in touch with us and also served as a contact.

Sinecio began showing signs of a loss of revolutionary morale; he got drunk on the Movement's money and committed indiscretions. He also neglected to carry out the orders he received and, after one of his binges, he brought us eleven new recruits, all of them unarmed. We generally tried to prevent the enlistment of unarmed men, but nevertheless, new people joined the young guerrilla force by every means and under all conditions, and the peasants, knowing where we were, often brought us new comrades. No fewer than forty persons passed through our ranks, but desertions were continual, sometimes with our consent, other times without, so the troop never had more than twenty-five or thirty effective members.

My asthma had gotten somewhat worse and the shortage of medicine immobilized me almost as much as the wounded. I was able to relieve the illness somewhat by smoking dried *clarín* leaves, a local remedy, until medication arrived from Santiago. This helped me to restore my health in preparation for our leaving. But departure was delayed several days. Finally we organized a patrol to look for all the weapons we had left behind as unusable after the attack on El Uvero; we needed to have them, despite their poor condition.

In our position, all those old weapons, including a .30-caliber machine gun, were potential treasures and we spent a whole night looking for them. We finally fixed the date for our departure for June 24. Our army was made up of twenty-six men: five recuperating wounded, five helpers, ten recruits from Bayamo, four recruits from the vicinity, and two other individual recruits. The march was organized with Vilo Acuña in the advance guard, then what could be called the General Staff, which I led since Almeida had enough work just walking, and two other small squads led by Maceo and Pena.

Pena was a lieutenant at that time. Maceo and Vilo were soldiers, and Almeida, as captain, held the highest rank. We did not leave on June 24 because of some incidents. First it was announced that one of the guides was arriving with a new recruit, and we had to wait for them; then we heard that the guide was coming with a new supply of medicines and food. Old Tamayo came and went constantly, bringing news and some supplies. At one point we had to find a cave in which to leave some of our supplies, because our contacts in Santiago had finally come through and David brought us an important shipment which was impossible to transport, given the fact that we were travelling with convalescents and new recruits.

On June 26 I made my debut as an odontologist, although in the Sierra I was given the more modest title of "tooth-yanker." My first victim was Israel Pardo, today a captain, who came out of it pretty well. The second was Joel Iglesias; all he would have needed to remove the tooth was a stick of dynamite in the canine, and in fact he saw the end of the war with the tooth still in place since my efforts to extract it had been fruitless. Besides the meagerness of my skill, we had no anesthetics, so I frequently used "psychological anesthesia"—a few harsh epithets when my patients complained too much.

A loathing for the marches caused some of the men to leave us, but new ones replaced them. Tamayo brought us a group of four men. Among them was Félix Mendoza, who came with a rifle. He explained that an Army troop had surprised him and his companion, and while the other man was being arrested, he had thrown himself over a precipitous cliff and escaped without harm. We later learned that the "Army" was a patrol led by our comrade Lalo Sardiñas who had not captured the companion but had taken him to Fidel's troop. We were also joined by Evelio Saborit, today a major in the Rebel Army.

With the arrival of Felix Mendoza and his men, we were now thirty-six in number, but the following day three left, then we were joined by two others, and we numbered thirty-five in all. Naturally, when the march started, our number once again diminished. We were climbing the slopes of Peladero, making but a little progress each day.

The radio informed us of generalized violence throughout the island. On July 1 we heard the news of the death of Josué País, Frank's brother, along with other comrades, all of them in the continuing struggle in Santiago. Despite the short marches our troops felt demoralized and some of the new recruits asked to leave in order to "carry out more useful missions in the city." On the way down La Botella hill we passed the house of Benito Mora, who entertained us in his humble abode which clung to the steep rocks of this part of the Sierra. Shortly before arriving, I called the little troop together, telling the men that moments of great danger were approaching, that the enemy was close by, that probably we would have to pass many days without food, walking almost continually. I urged whoever did not feel up to it to say so now;

some of the men had the frankness to speak their fears and they left; another, named Chicho, spokesman for a small group, swore they would all follow us till death. He spoke with such conviction and decisiveness that we were truly surprised when, after passing Benito Mora's house and camping in a small valley for the night, this same group communicated to us its desire to leave the guerrillas. We agreed to this, and we jokingly baptized the place "the river of death," for Chicho's tremendous determination and that of his friends had lasted only until that point. That name stuck until we left the Sierra.

We were now twenty-eight men, but on leaving the next day, we were joined by two new recruits; they were ex-soldiers who came to fight for freedom in the Sierra. They were Gilberto Capote and Nicolás. Arístides Guerra brought them. He was another of the local contacts who later became an invaluable asset to our column and whom we called "El Rey del Condumio" or "Chow King." During the whole war, Chow King did us innumerable services— and many times they were more dangerous than actually fighting against the enemy—such as moving mule teams from Bayamo to our field of operations.

As we marched we tried to familiarize the recruits with their weapons. We had the two ex-soldiers teach them how to handle a rifle, how to load, unload, dry-run shooting, etc. No sooner had the lessons begun than one of the instructors fired a shot; we had to remove him from that job and we eyed him suspiciously, although the consternation on his face was such that great talent for acting would have been necessary to simulate it. The two ex-soldiers could not endure the march and they left again with Arístides, but Gilberto Capote returned to us later, dying heroically in Pino del Agua.

We left our camp, the house of Polo Torres at La Mesa, which later became one of our operations centers. We were led now by a peasant named Tuto Almeida. Our aim was to reach La Nevada and afterward go to Fidel by crossing over the northern slopes of

El Turquino. We were walking in that direction when we saw in the distance two peasants who tried to flee when they saw us. We ran after them and they turned out to be two Negro girls with the last name of Moya. They were Adventists who, even though they were against violence of any kind because of their beliefs, gave us their full support at that time and for the duration of the war.

We ate heartily and rested there, but when we passed through Malverde (we had to in order to reach La Nevada), we found out that there were Army troops in the region. After brief deliberation, our small General Staff and the guides decided we should fall back and go directly across El Turquino, a rougher route but less dangerous under those circumstances.

On our small transistor radio we heard disquieting news; they said that there were heavy battles being fought in Estrada Palma, and that Raúl was badly wounded. (Today, after the passage of time, I cannot say whether we heard this from the grapevine or the radio.) We did not know whether to believe this or not, for we had learned to mistrust all such reports. But we hurried our men on in order to reach Fidel as soon as possible. We marched through the night, spending part of it in the house of a lone peasant, called El Vizcaíno because of his Spanish origins. He lived on the foothills of El Turquino, all alone in a small *bohío,* and his only friends were some Marxist texts, which he kept carefully hidden in a small hole beneath a stone, far from his *bohío.* He proudly displayed his Marxist militancy, which few people in the zone knew about. El Vizcaíno showed us which path to follow and we continued our slow march. Sinecio was getting further and further from his own district, and for a peasant like him, now practically an outlaw, this situation brought only anguish. One fine day, during a rest stop, while a recruit named Cuervo was on guard with his Remington, Sinecio Torres joined him at the post with another rifle. When I heard of this, about half an hour later, I went to find them, for I did not trust Sinecio and rifles were rather precious at that time. Both of them had already deserted. Banderas and Israel Pardo went after them, aware that the fugitives were armed with heavy weapons while they had only revolvers. They did not meet up with the deserters.

It was very difficult to maintain troop morale. We were short of weapons, lacked direct contact with the Commander of the Revolution; we were practically feeling our way, inexperienced and surrounded by enemies who loomed as giants in our imagination and in the stories of the *guajiros*. The reluctance of the recruits from the cities, and their unfamiliarity with the thousand and one difficulties of the Sierra, provoked continual crises in the morale of our small band. There was an attempted desertion led by an individual named "El Mexicano," who had reached the rank of captain and today is in Miami as a traitor to the Revolution.

I found out about the deserters when Comrade Hermes Leyva denounced them. He is a cousin of Joel Iglesias. I called a meeting to resolve this problem. El Mexicano swore on all his ancestors that even when he had thought of leaving, he had no intention of deserting the struggle; he had meant to form a small guerrilla band which would assault and kill informers, for there was not enough action in our forces. The truth is that he wanted to devote himself to killing informers for their money, a typical banditlike action. In a subsequent battle, at El Hombrito, Hermes was our only casualty, and we were always left with the suspicion that it could have been El Mexicano who had killed him, since Hermes had turned him in earlier. However, no one could prove this.

El Mexicano remained in the column, giving his word as a man, a revolutionary, etc., etc., that he would not leave and would not attempt to leave, nor would he incite anyone else to do so. After short but difficult marches, we reached the region of Palma Mocha, on the western slope of El Turquino, near Las Cuevas. The *guajiros* received us very well and we established a direct contact through my new profession as "tooth-yanker" which I now exercised with great enthusiasm.

We ate and recuperated strength to continue rapidly to the familiar regions of Palma Mocha and El Infierno. We arrived on June 15. There, Emilio Carrera, a local peasant, informed us that Lalo Sardiñas had set up an ambush nearby. He was concerned, for, in case of an attack on an enemy patrol, his house would be endangered.

On June 16 the small new column met the platoon from Fidel's column which was led by Lalo Sardiñas. Lalo told us why he had felt it necessary to join the revolution, although he had been no more than a merchant who used to bring us supplies from the city: he had been surprised once and had had to kill a man, which virtually forced him to become a guerrilla. Lalo had received instructions to wait there for the arrival of the vanguard of Sánchez Mosquera's enemy column. We learned that once again the obstinate Sánchez Mosquera had penetrated the region of the Palma Mocha river and was almost surrounded by Fidel's men, but had managed to elude them by crossing El Turquino on forced marches, reaching the other side of the mountain.

We already knew of the proximity of the troops; a few days before, on reaching a *bohío,* we had seen the trenches which the soldiers had occupied until the previous day. We did not suspect that this apparent proof of a sustained offensive against us was in reality a sign of the retreat of the repressive column, marking a total qualitative change in operations in the Sierra. We now had sufficient strength to surround the enemy and oblige him, under the threat of annihilation, to withdraw.

The enemy understood this lesson well and made only sporadic incursions into the Sierra. But one of the most tenacious, aggressive and bloody enemy officers was Sánchez Mosquera, who rose from simple lieutenant in 1957 to colonel, a rank which was awarded him after the final defeat in the general Army offensive, in June of the following year. His career was meteoric—and fruitful in his personal enrichment, for he robbed the peasants mercilessly each time he and his troops penetrated the maze of the Sierra Maestra.

# A Betrayal in the Making

It was a great pleasure to see our entire troop again. We now had greater discipline, higher morale, close to two hundred men, and some new weapons. It was obvious that the qualitative change which I have already mentioned was showing itself in the Sierra Maestra. A truly liberated zone existed; precautionary measures were not as necessary and there was a certain freedom to talk at night, to stir in one's hammock; authorization was given to move into the villages of the Sierra and establish a closer relationship with the people. It was also affecting to see the reception given us by our old comrades.

At that time, the big names in the country were Felipe Pazos and Raúl Chibás. They were two totally different personalities. Raúl Chibás lived on his brother's name. His brother [Eddie Chibás], was a true symbol of an era in Cuba, but Raúl had none of his virtues; he was neither expressive, nor wise, nor intelligent. What allowed him to be a unique and symbolic figure in the Orthodox Party was precisely his absolute mediocrity. He spoke little and wanted to leave the Sierra as soon as possible.

Felipe Pazos had his own personality, and the reputation of being a good economist. Besides, he was known as an honest man, for, as President of the National Bank, he never dipped into the public treasury, in a country whose government (at the time, that of Prío Socarrás) was based on fraud and constant, systematic robbery.

133

How magnificent, one might think, to remain unpolluted during that period. A great merit perhaps in a mere functionary following his administrative career, insensible to the grave problems of the country. But how can we imagine a revolutionary who does not daily denounce the inconceivable outrages of that period? Felipe Pazos skillfully managed to avoid doing this and left the Presidency of the National Bank of Cuba after Batista's coup, adorned with the greatest prestige: his honor, his intelligence, and his great gifts as an economist. Arrogant, he wanted to come to the Sierra and take over; in his small Machiavellian mind he was the man clearly chosen to control the destiny of the country. Perhaps the idea of betraying the Movement had already taken root, or perhaps this happened later, but his attitude was never entirely frank.

Backed by the joint declaration which will be analyzed below, he named himself a delegate of the 26th of July Movement in Miami and was later slated for Provisional President of the Republic. Thus Prío would be assured of a right-hand man in the leadership of the provisional government.

We had little time to talk in those days, but Fidel told me of his efforts to make the document truly militant, to give it a basis as a declaration of principle. It was difficult to call for a popular uprising, however, in the face of those two troglodyte and insensitive mentalities.

Basically, the manifesto insisted upon "the creation of a broad civilian revolutionary front to include all political parties of the opposition, all civilian institutions, and all the revolutionary forces." A series of propositions was included: the "formation of a civilian revolutionary front for a common struggle"; the designation of "a figure to preside over the provisional government." The declaration expressed that the front would neither invoke nor accept the mediation of another nation in the internal affairs of Cuba; that "no type of military junta will be accepted as a provisional government of the Republic." It also announced the decision to totally separate the Army from politics and it guaranteed the armed forces their integrity. Furthermore, it declared that elections would be held after one year.

The program under which the provisional government was to rule provided freedom for all political prisoners, civilian and military; an absolute guarantee of freedom of information for the radio and the press, and all individual and political rights guaranteed by the Constitution; the appointment of provisional mayors in all the municipalities, after consultation with the civic institutions of the locality; the suppression of speculation in all forms and the adoption of measures which would tend to increase the efficiency of all state organisms; the establishment of administrative training; the democratization of trade union policy, promoting free elections in all unions and industrial federations; the immediate initiation of an intensive campaign against illiteracy and of civic education extolling the duties and rights of the citizen with regard to his society and his country; "the establishment of terms for an Agrarian Reform leading to the distribution of public lands, and the conversion of all sharecroppers, tenant farmers, and squatters possessing small parcels of land into proprietors, whether their land is state owned or privately owned, with prior indemnification to the previous owner"; the adoption of a healthy fiscal policy which would maintain the stability of our currency and lead to the utilization of the nation's credit for productive works; the acceleration of the process of industrialization and the creation of new jobs.

To this were added two especially important points: "First: the need to designate as of now the person called upon to preside over the provisional government of the Republic, in order to demonstrate before the world that the Cuban people are capable of uniting behind the call for liberty and of supporting this person, who will unite the qualities of impartiality, integrity, capacity, and decency, and who will embody that call. There are enough capable men in Cuba to lead the Republic." (Naturally, Felipe Pazos at least, as one of the signatories, knew in his heart of hearts that there were not enough men, that there was only one and that was he.)

"Second: that that person be designated by all civic, and thereby apolitical, institutions, whose support would free the provisional president from all party entanglements, allowing for absolutely clean and impartial elections."

Furthermore, it was declared: "It is not necessary to come to the Sierra to discuss this, we can be represented in Havana, in Mexico, or anywhere else."

Fidel had tried to influence them into making some of the declarations on the Agrarian Reform more explicit. However, it was difficult to break the monolithic front of the two troglodytes; the "establishment of terms for an agrarian reform which will lead to the distribution of public lands" was a policy which even the *Diario de la Marina* could support. The crowning touch was the "prior indemnification to the previous owner."

Some of the points here laid out were not carried out by the Revolution as planned originally. It must be emphasized that the enemy violated the tacit pact expressed in the manifesto by not recognizing the authority of the Sierra and by trying to bind the future Revolutionary government with *a priori* obligations.

We were not satisfied with the compromise but it was necessary; at that time, it was progressive. It could not last beyond the time when it became a brake on revolutionary development, but we were willing to go along with it. By their treachery the enemy helped us to break uncomfortable bonds and to show the people their true intentions.

We knew that it was a minimal program, a program which limited our efforts, but we also knew that it was not possible to assert our will from the Sierra Maestra and that we had, for a long time, to count on "friends" who tried to use our military force and the confidence which the people felt for Fidel for their own macabre devices. Above all they wanted to maintain the rule of imperialism in Cuba through its commercial bourgeoisie, which was tightly linked to the Northern masters.

The manifesto had some positive sides; it spoke of the Sierra Maestra and stated explicitly: "No one should be deceived by government propaganda with regard to the situation in the Sierra. The Sierra Maestra is already an indestructible bulwark of freedom which has captured the hearts of our compatriots and here we will know how to repay the faith and the confidence of our people." "Here we will know how" in reality meant that Fidel Castro knew how; the other two were incapable of following, even as spectators, the development of the struggle in the Sierra Maestra; they left the mountains almost immediately. One of them, Chibás, was surprised by the Batista police and somewhat mistreated; both of them later arrived in the United States.

It was a well-thought-out coup: a group of the most distinguished members of the Cuban oligarchy arrived in the Sierra Maestra "in defense of freedom," signed a joint declaration with the guerrilla chief, and went to Miami to play their trump card as they chose. What they did not realize was that political maneuvers have only the scope permitted by the strength of the adversary; in this case the adversary was the people armed. Quick action by our leader, who had the complete confidence of the Guerrilla Army, prevented the plot from developing, and Fidel's fiery answer, months later when the result of the pact in Miami was known, paralyzed the enemy. We were accused of being divisionists and of wishing to impose our will from the Sierra, but they had to vary their tactics and prepare a new trap, the Caracas Pact.

Our manifesto was dated July 12, 1957, and was published in the newspapers. For us this declaration was no more than a small halt along the way; we guerrillas would have to continue the fundamental task of defeating the oppressing army on the battlefield. In those days a new column was being formed which I was to lead. I was then a captain. There were also some other promotions:

Ramiro Valdés became captain, and with his platoon entered my column; Ciro Redondo was also made captain, leading another platoon. The column was composed of three platoons, the first led by Lalo Sardiñas, who led the vanguard and at the same time was Second Chief of the detachment. This column, which was known as "the dispossessed peasants," was made up of about seventy-five men, variously clothed and armed. Nevertheless, I was very proud of them. A few nights later I would feel much prouder, much closer to the Revolution, if that were possible, and more anxious to demonstrate that the promotions had been well-deserved.

We sent a letter of congratulations and gratitude to "Carlos" (Frank País' *nom de guerre*), who was living his last days. It was signed by all the officers of the Guerrilla Army who could write (the peasants of the Sierra were not very gifted in the art of writing and they were already an important part of the guerrilla troop). The letter was signed in two columns, the second being for rank. When my turn came, Fidel ordered simply: "Put down 'Major.'" In this informal and almost oblique manner I became major of the Second Column of the Guerrilla Army, which would later be called the Fourth Column.

It was in a peasant house, I do not remember which one, that this warm message was composed from the guerrilla fighters to their city brother who was fighting so heroically in Santiago itself to supply us and was relieving the pressures on us.

The vanity which we all have in us made me the proudest man in the world that day. The symbol of my rank, a small star, was given to me by Celia together with one of the wrist watches which they had ordered from Manzanillo. My first task as a major was to surround Sánchez Mosquera with my Column. But he, the most bestial of the thugs, had already left the region.

We had to do something to justify the semi-independent life which we were to lead in the new region toward which we were marching, the region of El Hombrito, and we began to hatch future actions.

We also were preparing to celebrate the glorious 26th of July which was approaching, and Fidel had given me a free hand in doing what I could, providing I was careful. At the last meeting we met the new troop doctor, Sergio del Valle, today Chief of the General Staff of our Revolutionary Army, who in those days practiced his profession as the conditions of the Sierra permitted.

It was essential to demonstrate that we were still alive, for our comrades in the plains had been seriously set back. The arms reserved for the opening of another front at the Miranda sugar mill fell into the hands of the police, who imprisoned many valiant leaders, among them Faustino Pérez. Fidel had opposed dividing our forces, but he gave in on the insistence of the city movement. The correctness of his position was clearly demonstrated by the capture of the arms, and we devoted ourselves to fortifying the Sierra Maestra as a first step in the expansion of the Guerrilla Army.

# The Attack on Bueycito

Our new independence brought with it new problems. Now we had to establish rigid discipline, to organize commands, and to establish some form of General Staff in order to assure success in any battle, a none too easy task given the men's lack of discipline.

No sooner had the detachment been formed than a beloved comrade left us. He was Lieutenant Maceo, who went to Santiago on a mission and whom we would never see again, for he died there in battle.

We also made a few promotions: Comrade William Rodríguez to lieutenant, also Raúl Castro Mercader. By this means we tried to give shape to our small guerrilla force. One morning we learned that a man had deserted with his rifle, a .22-caliber weapon which was precious in the deplorable conditions of that period. The deserter was known as "El Chino Wong," he was from the advance guard, and he had probably gone to his district in the foothills of the Sierra Maestra. Two men were sent after him; but we lost hope when Israel Pardo and Banderas returned after a fruitless search for other deserters. Israel, because of his familiarity with the terrain and his great physical resilience, was promoted to carry out special functions at my side.

We began to formulate a very ambitious plan, which consisted of first attacking Estrada Palma during the night and then going to the nearby villages of Yara and Veguitas to capture the small garrisons there, returning to the mountains by the same path. In this way we could take three barracks in one single assault, counting always on the element of surprise. We had some firing practice, using bullets sparingly, and we found that all our weapons were good, except for the Madzen automatic, which was very old and dirty. In a short note to Fidel we outlined our plan and asked for his approval or rejection. We did not receive an answer, but from a broadcast on July 27 we learned of the attack on Estrada Palma by two hundred men led by Raúl Castro, according to the official report.

The magazine *Bohemia,* in its only uncensored issue put out at that time, published a report on the damage inflicted by our troops at Estrada Palma, where the old barracks was burned down; it also mentioned Fidel Castro, Celia Sánchez, and an entire roster of revolutionaries who had come down from the mountains. Truth was mixed with myth, as happens in these cases, and the journalists were unable to disentangle them. In reality the attack was made not by two hundred men but by many fewer, and it was led by Major Guillermo García (captain in those days). In reality there was no real combat, for Barreras had retreated shortly before, fearing logically that there would be heavy attacks on July 26 and perhaps mistrusting his position. The Estrada Palma expedition was thus a wasted effort. The following day the Army troops chased our guerrillas and, since we did not yet have a top-flight organization, one of our men who had fallen asleep somewhere near San Lorenzo was captured. After hearing this news, we decided to move rapidly to an attack on some other barracks in the days immediately following July 26 and to continue maintaining an atmosphere appropriate to insurrection.

As we were walking toward the Maestra, one of the two men who had gone to look for the deserter caught up with us, near a place called La Jeringa; he told us that the other man had confided that he was an intimate friend of El Chino Wong and could not betray him; then the other invited him to desert and indicated that he himself was not returning to the guerrillas. The comrade ordered him to halt; but the new deserter continued walking and the comrade felt obliged to kill him.

I gathered the entire troop together on the hill facing the spot where this event had taken place. I explained to our men what they were going to see and what it meant; I explained once again why desertion was punishable by death and why anyone who betrayed the Revolution must be condemned. We passed silently, in single file, before the body of the man who had tried to abandon his post. Many of the men had never seen death before and were perhaps moved more by personal feelings for the dead man and by political weakness natural at that period than by disloyalty to the Revolution. These were difficult times and we used this man as an example. It is not important to give the men's names here; we will say only that the dead man was a young, poor peasant from the vicinity.

We now passed through some familiar territory. On July 30, Lalo Sardiñas made contact with an old friend, a merchant in the mining region named Armando Oliver. We made an appointment in a house near the California zone and there we met with him and Jorge Abich. We spoke of our intention to attack Minas and Bueycito. It was risky to put this secret in the hands of other people, but Lalo Sardiñas knew and trusted these comrades.

Armando informed us that Casillas came to the vicinity on Sundays, for, according to the inveterate habit of the soldiery, he had a sweetheart there. Naturally we were anxious to attack quickly before our presence was known, rather than trust to our luck, and capture Casillas. We agreed that on the following night, July 31, we would start the attack. Armando Oliver would take charge of getting us trucks, guides, and a miner who would blow up the bridges linking the Bueycito highway with that of Manzanillo-Bayamo. At two in the afternoon of the following day, we began our march. We spent a couple of hours getting to the crest of the Maestra, where we hid all our packs, continuing with only our field equipment. We had to march a long time and we passed a row of houses, in one of which a party was going on. We called all the people together and spoke to them, making clear that we would hold them responsible if our presence were discovered. We hurried on. Naturally, the danger of these encounters was not very great, for there was no telephone nor any means of communication in the Sierra Maestra in those days, and an informer would have had to run to arrive before us.

We reached the house of Comrade Santiestéban, who placed a light truck at our disposal; we also had two other trucks which Armando Oliver had sent us. Thus, with the entire troop in the trucks (Lalo Sardiñas in the first, Ramirito and I in the second, and Ciro with his platoon in the third), we reached the village of Minas in less than three hours. In Minas the Army had relaxed its vigilance, so the main task was to make sure no one moved toward Bueycito; here the rear-guard squad remained, under the command of Lieutenant Vilo Acuña, today a major in our Rebel Army, and we continued with the rest of the men to the outskirts of Bueycito.

At the entrance to the village, we stopped a coal truck and sent it on ahead with one of our men to see if there were army guards on watch, for sometimes at the entrance to Bueycito an army post inspected everything coming from the Sierra. But there was no one; all the guards were sleeping happily.

Our plan was simple, though a bit pretentious: Lalo Sardiñas would attack the west side of the barracks, Ramiro and his platoon would surround it, Ciro with the Staff's machine gun would be ready to attack from the front, and Armando Oliver would arrive casually in an automobile, flashing his headlights on the guards. At that moment, Ramiro's men would invade the barracks, taking everyone prisoner; at the same time precautions had to be taken to capture all the guards who were sleeping in their houses. Lieutenant Noda's squad (Noda died later in the attack on Pino del Agua) was charged with detaining all vehicles on the highway until firing began, and William was sent to blow up the bridge connecting Bueycito with the Central Highway, to detain the enemy forces.

The plan never materialized: it was too difficult for inexperienced men unfamiliar with the terrain. Ramiro lost part of his platoon during the night and came somewhat late; the car did not arrive; at one point some dogs barked loudly while we were putting our troops into position.

As I was walking along the main street of the village, a man came out of a house. I shouted: "Halt! Who goes there?" The man, thinking I was a soldier, identified himself: "The Guardia Rural!" When I aimed my gun at him he ran back into the house, slamming the door, and from within was heard the sound of falling tables and chairs and breaking glass as he ran through the house. There was, I suppose, a tacit agreement between the two of us: I could not shoot, since the important thing was to take the barracks, and he did not shout a warning to his companions.

We advanced carefully, and were putting the last men in position when the barracks sentinel moved forward, curious about the barking dogs and probably about the noise of my encounter with the Guardia Rural. We came face to face with each other, only a few meters apart; I had my Tommy gun cocked and he had his Garand. Israel Pardo was with me. I shouted: "Halt!" and the man made a movement. That was enough for me: I pulled the trigger with the intention of shooting him full on, but nothing happened and I was defenseless. Israel Pardo fired, but his defective .22 rifle did not discharge either. I don't really know how Israel came out of this alive. I only remember what I did under the shower of bullets from the soldier's Garand: I ran with a speed I have never again matched and turned the corner to reach the next street. There I put my Tommy gun back into firing order.

However, the soldier had unwittingly given the signal to attack, for his was the first shot our men heard. On hearing shots from all sides, the soldier, terrified, hid behind a column where we found him at the end of the short battle. While Israel went to make contact, the shooting stopped and we received the surrender. Ramirito's men, when they heard the first shots, had moved in and attacked the barracks from the rear, firing through a wooden door.

In the barracks there were twelve guards, of whom six were wounded. We had suffered one loss: Comrade Pedro Rivera, a recent recruit, was shot in the chest. Three of our men had slight wounds. We burned down the barracks, after removing everything that could be useful to us, and we left in the trucks, taking with us as prisoners the post sergeant and an informer named Orán.

The villagers along the way offered us cold beer and refreshments, for it was daylight now. The small wooden bridge near the central highway had been blown up. As we passed in the last truck, we blew up another small wooden bridge over a stream. The miner who did it was brought to us by Oliver as a new member of the troop and he was a valuable acquisition; his name was Cristino Naranjo. He later became a major and was murdered in the days following the triumph of the Revolution.

We continued on and reached Las Minas. We stopped there to hold a small meeting. In a rather theatrical scene, one of the Abich family, a shopkeeper in the area, begged us in the name of the people to free the sergeant and the informer. We explained that we held them prisoner only to guarantee that there would be no reprisals in the village. Abich was so insistent that we agreed to free them. So the two prisoners were released and the people's safety assured. As we headed for the Sierra we buried our dead comrade in the town cemetery. Only a few reconnaissance planes passed high over us. Just to make sure we were not spotted, we stopped in a small store, and there attended to the three wounded men: one had a surface wound in the shoulder but it had torn the flesh, so the treatment was somewhat difficult; the other had a small wound in the hand from a small-caliber weapon, and the third had a bump on his head. This he had gotten when the mules in the barracks, frightened by the shooting, had begun to kick wildly; at one point, according to the man, they had dislodged a piece of plaster which had fallen on his head.

In Alto de California, we left the trucks and distributed the new weapons. Although my participation in the battle had been minimal and not in the least heroic (since I had turned my back to the few shots I encountered), I took a Browning automatic, the jewel of the post, leaving the old Thompson, which never fired at the right moment. The distribution was made, the best arms being given to the best fighters, and we dismissed those men who had shown cowardice, including the *mojados* [the wet ones], a group of men who had fallen into the river while fleeing the first shots. Among those who had performed well we can name Captain Ramiro Valdés, who led the attack, and Lieutenant Raúl Castro Mercader who together with his men played a decisive role in the small battle.

When we reached the hills again, we learned that a state of siege had been declared and censorship established. We also heard that Frank País had been murdered in the streets of Santiago—a great loss to the Revolution. With his death one of the purest and most glorious lives of the Cuban Revolution ended; the people of Santiago, of Havana, and of all Cuba took to the streets in the spontaneous August strike. The semi-censorship of the government became total censorship, and we entered a new epoch characterized by the silence of the pseudo-opposition, who were no more than chattering magpies. The savage murders committed by Batista's thugs spread through the country, and the people of Cuba prepared for war.

In Frank País we lost one of our most valiant fighters; but the reaction to his murder demonstrated that new forces were joining the struggle and the fighting spirit of the people was growing.

# Lydia and Clodomira

I met Lydia only a few months after we had begun our revolutionary activities. I was new in the role of commander of the Fourth Column, and we went down to raid the hamlet of San Pablo de Yao, near Bayamo, in the foothills of the Sierra Maestra, in an effort to find provisions. One of the first houses we came to in the village belonged to a family of bakers. Lydia, one of the owners of the bakery, was a woman of forty-five, whose son had been a member of our column. From the first, she threw herself into revolutionary work with enthusiasm and exemplary devotion.

When I think of Lydia, I feel something more than just affectionate appreciation for this unblemished revolutionary, for she showed a special devotion to me and preferred working under my orders, regardless of the front to which I might be assigned. On countless occasions Lydia acted as special messenger for me and for the Movement. To Santiago and Havana she carried the most compromising documents, all of our column's communiqués, issues of our newspaper, *El Cubano Libre;* to us in the Sierra she brought paper, medicines, whatever we needed whenever we needed it.

Her infinite courage was such that male couriers avoided her. I remember very well the opinion—a mixture of admiration and resentment—of one of them, who told me: "That woman has more [balls] than Maceo* but she's going to get us all killed. The things she does are mad. This is no time for games." Lydia, however, went on crossing the enemy lines, again and again.

When I was transferred to the Mina del Frío zone, in Las Vegas de Jibacoa, she followed me. This meant leaving the auxiliary camp of which she had been the leader for a time and the men whom she had commanded with spirit and a touch of high-handedness, causing a certain resentment among them, since Cubans were not accustomed to taking orders from a woman. Her camp, at Cueva between Yao and Bayamo, was in the most exposed position of any of our bases; we wanted to remove her from that command because it was too dangerous a spot. After the enemy had located it, many was the time that our boys had to leave it under fire. I tried to have Lydia transferred from there once and for all; but I succeeded only when she followed me to the new fighting front.

Among the anecdotes that reveal Lydia's character, I remember this one: It was the day that Geilín, one of our best fighters—a mere boy—was killed. He was stationed at Lydia's advance post at that time. Returning to it from a mission, Lydia observed several men advancing stealthily toward the post, a result no doubt of some informer's tip. Lydia's reaction was unhesitating. She took out her little .32 revolver to give a couple of warning shots in the air; but friendly hands stopped her in time, for it would have cost the lives of all of them. Meanwhile, the men advanced and surprised Geilín, the camp sentry. Guillermo Geilín defended himself bravely until, twice wounded and knowing what would happen to him if he were to fall into the hands of these thugs, he committed suicide. The enemy soldiers advanced, burned everything that would burn, and left.

The following day I met Lydia. Her expression revealed the greatest despair over the death of the young fighter and resentment

---

* Antonio Maceo, a celebrated general from Oriente Province, who fought for Cuba's independence in the Ten Years' War (1868–1878) and in 1895.

against the person who prevented her from warning him. "Me, they would have killed," she said, "but the boy would have been saved. Me, I'm already old; he wasn't even twenty." She returned to this subject again and again. At times there seemed to be a kind of boasting in her constant expressions of contempt for death. However, the missions entrusted to her were carried out to perfection.

Lydia knew how fond I was of puppies and she was always promising to bring one from Havana, a promise not easy to keep. During the days of the great Army offensive, Lydia carried out her missions to the letter, she went up and down the Sierra, she carried the most important documents, she was our connection with the outside world. She was accompanied by another fighter of the same caliber, whose name is remembered by the entire Rebel Army, all of whom knew and revered her: Clodomira. Lydia and Clodomira had already become inseparable comrades-in-danger; they came and went constantly, always together.

I had asked Lydia to contact me as soon as I arrived from Las Villas, after the invasion, since she was to be our principal means of communication with Havana and with staff headquarters in the Sierra Maestra. I arrived and found her letter in which she announced that she had a puppy for me and that she would bring it on her next trip.

That was the trip that Lydia and Clodomira never took. Soon after, I learned that it was the weakness of a man—a hundred times their inferior as a fighter, as a revolutionary, as a human being—which had permitted the group to be spotted. In the group were Lydia and Clodomira. Our comrades defended themselves to the death; Lydia was wounded when she was captured. Lydia's and Clodomira's bodies have disappeared; they are sleeping their last sleep, side by side no doubt, as they were when they fought during the last days of their battle for freedom.

Someday, maybe, their remains will be found, perhaps in some lonely field in that enormous cemetery which the island became.

But, within the Rebel Army, among those who fought and sacrificed themselves in those anguished days, the memory will live forever of the women who, by the risks they took daily, made communications with the rest of the island possible. Among all of us —for us on the First Front, and for me personally—Lydia occupies a favored place. That is why I offer these reminiscences in homage to her today—a modest flower laid on the mass grave that this once happy island became.

# The Battle of El Hombrito

The Column was only a month old and we were already restless in our sedentary life in the Sierra Maestra. We were in the valley of El Hombrito, so named because from the plain one could see a pair of gigantic slabs of rock, one on top of the other, on the peak, resembling the figure of a small man.

The men were still very green and we had to prepare them before they faced really difficult situations. But the exigencies of our revolutionary war obliged us to be combat-ready at all times. We were obliged to attack any enemy columns which invaded that part of the Sierra Maestra which by then was looked upon as the Free Territory of Cuba.

During the night of August 29 a peasant informed us that there was a large troop preparing to ascend the Maestra, along the road to El Hombrito. We were wary of false information so I took the man hostage and ordered him to tell the truth, threatening him with dire punishment if he lied. He swore and re-swore that what he had said *was* true and that the soldiers were already at the farm of Julio Zapatero, a couple of kilometers from the Maestra.

That night we moved into position. Lalo Sardiñas' platoon was to occupy the eastern flank in a small grove of dry ferns, and open fire on the column when it stopped. Ramiro Valdés, leading those men with less firepower, was to be on the western flank in order to carry out an "acoustic skirmish," so as to spread alarm. Although lightly armed, their position was less dangerous because the guards would have had to cross a deep ravine to reach them.

The footpath on which the enemy would be coming bordered the hill on the side where Lalo was concealed. Ciro would attack them from the side; I, with a small column of the best-armed men, would open hostilities. The best squad was led by Lieutenant Raúl Mercader; it was to be used as a shock troop to gather the fruits of victory. The plan was very simple: when the enemy reached a small bend in the road, turning almost ninety degrees around a boulder, I was to let ten or twelve of the enemy pass and then shoot the last one, in order to separate those men from the rest. Then the others would be rapidly annihilated by my men, Raúl Mercader's squad would advance, the weapons of the dead would be taken, and we would retreat at once, protected by the fire of the rear guard led by Lieutenant Vilo Acuña.

At dawn I was in a coffee grove, the position assigned to Ramiro Valdés. We were facing Julio Zapatero's house, below us on the slope of the mountain. As the sun rose we saw men going in and out, in early morning rising routines. After a while some of them put on their army caps, which gave us tangible evidence of the truth of our hostage's information. All of our men were ready in their combat positions.

I went to my post and we watched the first men of the column climbing laboriously. The wait was interminable and my fingers played on the trigger of my new weapon, the Browning automatic, ready to fire it in combat for the first time. Finally word came that they were approaching, and we heard their unworried voices and their noisy shouts. The first one passed, then the second, then the third. I calculated that we wouldn't have enough time for the dozen to pass as planned. As I counted the sixth I heard a shout from up front, and one of the soldiers raised his head in a movement of surprise: I opened fire at once and the sixth man fell; then

# BATTLE OF EL HOMBRITO

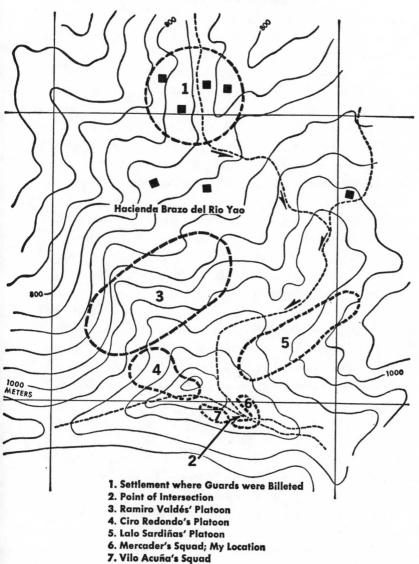

Hacienda Brazo del Rio Yao

1. Settlement where Guards were Billeted
2. Point of Intersection
3. Ramiro Valdés' Platoon
4. Ciro Redondo's Platoon
5. Lalo Sardiñas' Platoon
6. Mercader's Squad; My Location
7. Vilo Acuña's Squad

generalized firing began and, at the second burst from my automatic, the six men disappeared from the path.

I ordered Raúl Mercader's squad to attack, while some volunteers also moved in; the enemy was being fired on from both flanks. Lieutenant Orestes of the advance guard, Raúl Mercader himself, Alfonso Zayas, Alcibiades Bermúdez, and Rodolfo Vázquez, among others, advanced; from behind a large boulder they fired on the enemy column, which was of company strength and under the command of Major Merob Sosa. Rodolfo Vázquez took the weapon of the soldier I had wounded. To our regret he turned out to be a medic and carried only a .45 revolver with ten or twelve bullets. The other five men had escaped, scrambling off to the right of the path and retreating along a nearby river bed. After a while we began to hear the first bazooka shots, fired by the enemy troops, now recovered somewhat from their shock at our surprise attack.

The Maxim machine gun was the only weapon of any weight that we had, apart from my automatic rifle, but it had not yet been fired and Julio Pérez, who was using it, could not get it to work.

On Ramiro Valdés' flank, Israel Pardo and Joel Iglesias had advanced on the enemy with their almost primitive weapons; shotguns fired from both sides made an infernal racket and increased the enemy's confusion. I ordered the two lateral platoons to retreat, and when they began to move, we also began our retreat, leaving the rear guard in charge of maintaining fire until all of Lalo Sardiñas' platoon had passed, since we anticipated a second line of resistance.

As we withdrew, Vilo Acuña, having accomplished his mission, returned, announcing the death of Hermes Leyva, cousin of Joel Iglesias. In the course of our withdrawal we came upon a platoon sent by Fidel, whom I had notified of the imminence of a clash with superior enemy forces. Captain Ignacio Pérez led the group. We retreated about a thousand meters from the battlefield and planned a new ambush. The soldiers arrived at the small plateau where the battle had taken place and, before our very eyes, they burned Hermes Leyva's body, in that way taking their vengeance. In our impotent anger, we were limited to long-range firing, which they answered with bazookas.

It was then that I found out that the soldier who had provoked my hasty shot with his shout had yelled: "What a picnic!" He must have been referring to the fact that he was reaching the peak of the hill. This battle proved to us how poorly prepared our troop was, unable to fire accurately at a moving enemy line from close range. (There could not have been more than ten or twenty meters between the advance guard of the enemy's column and our positions.) However, it was a great triumph for us, for we had stopped Merob Sosa's column, which then retreated, and we had won a small victory over them. We had the minimal recompense of winning one small weapon, but we lost a valiant fighter. All this we had accomplished with a handful of weapons against an entire company, 140 men at least, all of them well armed for modern warfare, who had used bazookas and perhaps even mortars against our positions, although their shots had been as wild and haphazard as ours.

After this battle there were some promotions for bravery: Alfonso Zayas was named lieutenant, and there were some others whom I can't remember. That night, or the following day, after the soldiers had retreated, we had a conversation with Fidel in which he joyfully told us how they had attacked the Batista forces in the region of Las Cuevas, and I learned also of the deaths of some brave comrades in that fight: Juventino Alarcón, from Manzanillo, one of the first to join the guerrilla band; Pastor; Yayo; Castillo; and Oliva, son of a lieutenant in the government army, a brave fighter and a well-loved boy, as all of them were.

The battle won by Fidel was much more important than our own, since it involved not an ambush but an attack on a defended garrison. Although they did not destroy the enemy forces, they had caused many casualties, and the soldiers retreated from that position the next day. One of the heroes of the day was "El Negro Pilón." It is said that he arrived one day at a *bohío* where he saw "a pile of strange tubes with boxes next to them," which turned out to be bazookas abandoned by the enemy. However, none of us was familiar with this weapon except by name, and so Pilón, suffering from a leg wound, abandoned the *bohío*. Thus we lost the opportunity of acquiring these weapons which are so effective in attacks on small fortifications.

There were new repercussions of our battle; a day or two later we heard that an Army communiqué spoke of five or six dead; later we learned that, beside our comrade whose body they had abused, there were four or five murdered peasants for us to mourn. The sinister Merob Sosa had supposed them to be responsible for the ambush because they had not reported our troops' presence in the area to the Army. I remember their names: Abigaíl, Calixto, Pablito Lebón—of Haitian descent—and Gonzalo González, all of them completely or partially innocent of complicity with us. They knew of our presence and sympathized with our cause, as did all the peasantry, but they had been totally unaware of the maneuver we were preparing. Knowing the methods employed by the heads of Batista's army, we concealed our intentions from the peasants; if one of them happened to pass an area where an ambush was being prepared, we held him until it was over. The unfortunate peasants were murdered by Sosa's men in their *bohíos,* which were then set on fire.

This battle showed us how easy it was, under certain circumstances, to attack columns on the march. Furthermore, we again saw the tactical correctness of always aiming at the head of the marching troop, in an attempt to kill the first one or the first few, thus immobilizing the enemy force. Little by little this tactic crystallized and finally it became so systematic that the enemy stopped entering the Sierra Maestra, and the soldiers even refused to march in the advance guard. However, there had still not been enough battles for this tactic to be completely crystallized.

Reunited with Fidel, we were able to talk about our deeds, modest but nonetheless impressive because of the great disproportion of forces existing between our poorly armed soldiers and the very well-armed forces of repression.

This battle more or less marked the moment of the government troops' definitive withdrawal from the Sierra; thereafter it was penetrated, as a feat of daring, only by Sánchez Mosquera, the bravest, the most murderous, and one of the most thieving of all of Batista's military chieftains.

# The First Battle of Pino del Agua

After meeting up with Fidel on August 29 we marched for several days, sometimes together, sometimes separately, with the intention of arriving at the Pino del Agua sawmill together. We were informed that there were either no enemy forces there for the moment, or at the very most only a small garrison.

Fidel's plan was as follows: if there were a small garrison, to take it; if not, to show our faces there and then he would continue, with his troop, in the direction of the Chivirico sector, while we lay in wait for the Batista army. In such cases they always came on the double, so as to make a show of strength and thus dissipate, in the minds of the peasants, the revolutionary effects of our passage.

During those long days of marching before the battle of Pino del Agua, which led us from Dos Brazos del Guayabo to the battle site, various incidents occurred, the principal actors in which played a subsequent role in the history of the Revolution.

We suffered the blow of desertion by two local peasants, Manolo and Popo Beatón, who had joined the guerrilla ranks shortly before the battle of El Uvero. On that occasion they had been brothers in battle; today they abandoned our camp. Later these two returned to us. Fidel pardoned their treachery; but they never rose above their previous condition of semi-nomadic bandits. For some personal reason, Manolo killed Cristino Naranjo, after the Revolution was won. He succeeded in escaping from the Cabaña fortress where he had been confined and organized a small guerrilla force in the very place where he had fought alongside us in the Sierra Maestra. There he murdered Pancho Tamayo, a brave comrade who had joined us during the first days of the Revolution. Eventually a group of peasants captured Manolo and his brother Popo; both of them were shot at Santiago.

Another painful incident: A comrade named Roberto Rodríguez was disarmed for insubordination. He was very undisciplined and the lieutenant of his squad took his weapon, exercising a disciplinary right. Roberto got hold of a comrade's revolver and committed suicide. We had a small disagreement on the subject; in fact, I was opposed to rendering him military honors, whereas the men thought that he should be added to the list of their dead. I claimed that to commit suicide under such conditions was a criminal act, whatever good qualities the man might have possessed. Finally the men calmed down, and they were content to hold a wake, without rendering him honors.

One or two days earlier he had told me a part of his story. He was clearly a boy of excessive sensitivity, who made great efforts to adapt himself to guerrilla life and to discipline, to all that went counter to his physical weakness and his instinctive rebelliousness.

Two days later we sent a small detachment to Las Minas de Bueycito to make a show of force there, since it was September 4. The little group was commanded by Captain Ciro Redondo, who presented us with a prisoner, Leonardo Baró. Baró played an important role in the ranks of the counter-revolution. He remained our prisoner for a good while, and one day told me the sad story of his mother's illness. I took him at his word. I tried, however, to convince him to give political overtones to his liberation. I proposed that he take a bus, see his mother in Havana, and then demand asylum in an embassy, proclaiming his unwillingness to fight against us any more and denouncing the Batista regime. He didn't accept, alleging that he could not denounce the regime for which his brothers were fighting, and we agreed that he should limit himself, in demanding asylum, to declaring that he didn't want to fight any more.

We sent him off with four comrades. They had specific instructions not to allow him to see anyone on the way, since he was well acquainted with the names of a good many peasants who had visited us at our camp. Furthermore, the comrades were told to make the trip on foot, as far as the outskirts of Bayamo, where they were to leave him and return by another route.

These men did not obey their orders. They allowed themselves to be seen by many people; they even held a meeting at which Baró was present, as a liberated prisoner and an alleged sympathizer. Then they travelled to Bayamo by jeep. On the way they were intercepted by *batistiano* troops and the four comrades were murdered. We never knew for sure if Baró had dirtied his hands in this crime. It was he who installed himself forthwith at Las Minas de Bueycito, put himself under the orders of the assassin Sánchez Mosquera, and began to identify, among those who came to do their marketing, the peasants who had been in touch with our guerrilla group.

My error cost the people of Cuba countless victims.

Several days after the triumph of the Revolution, Baró was captured and executed.

Soon after the incident, we went down to San Pablo de Yao. The local people welcomed us with open arms. We occupied the hamlet without striking a blow for several hours (no enemy troops), and we made contacts, meeting many people from the area. We crammed the trucks provided for us by the merchants who sold us supplies (on credit; during that period we paid with bonds). It was on that occasion that I met Lydia Doce, whose memory I evoke in these pages.*

We had to arrange to transport the goods. This was not easy, since the road that ascends from San Pablo de Yao to Pico Verde,

---

* See the chapter entitled "Lydia and Clodomira."

The "Granma." (UPI)

Veterans of the "Granma" expedition—from left to right,
Raúl Castro, Juan Almeida, Fidel Castro, Ramiro Valdés. (UPI)

*Celia Sánchez counting money raised for the guerrillas.* (UPI)

*Members of the Rebel Army making Molotov cocktails.* (UPI)

Manzanillo: peasants assist Castro's surprise attack by widening a cow path into a passable road for vehicles. (UPI)

A wounded Cuban rebel is helped to the rear after the battle. (UPI)

Major Camilo Cienfuegos. *(UPI)*

CBS reporter Robert Taber interviewing three American youths in the Sierra Maestra. *(UPI)*

Two of the pictures, whose existence was denied by Batista government,
which Herbert Matthews took out of the Sierra after his interview with Fidel Castro.
(Courtesy of Herbert Matthews and The New York Times.)

Rebel soldiers wave "26th of July" banner over entrance of captured Army outpost in Fomento. (UPI)

Resting after the battle of Fomento. (UPI)

In Havana, January 3, 1959. (UPI)

past the Cristina mine, is very steep, and only trucks geared for the purpose, not too heavily loaded, can make the climb. Ours broke down en route, and the supplies had to be reloaded and brought up on mule back and man back.

Those days also witnessed a series of partings. A comrade, a good fighter, was expelled for drunkenness during the expedition to Yao, having thus endangered his comrades. Another, Jorge Sotús, left his post as squad chief and went to Miami with a letter of recommendation from Fidel. In reality, Sotús had never adapted himself to the Sierra, and his men disliked him because of his tyrannical nature. His career reached heights and depths. In Miami his attitude was a wavering one, to say the least. He rejoined the ranks of our army, was pardoned and his past errors forgiven. During Hubert Matos' time he betrayed us and was sentenced to twenty years' imprisonment. Aided by a jailer, he fled to Miami. He had made the final preparations for a pirate raid on Cuban territory when he died, apparently electrocuted in an accident.

Among the comrades who left us at that time was Marcelo Fernández, urban coordinator of the Movement, who returned to the Llano after a stay among us.

We reached Pino del Agua on September 10. Pino del Agua is a hamlet built around a sawmill in the middle of a forest in the Maestra. During that period it was managed by a Spaniard. There was a handful of workers, but not one soldier. We occupied the hamlet and Fidel disclosed his itinerary to the villagers, calculating that someone among them would pass the information on to the Army.

We engaged in a small diversionary maneuver, and while Fidel's column continued its march toward Santiago in full view of all, we made a detour during the night and laid an ambush for the enemy. We distributed the men in such a way that all the Army trucks would be under surveillance. We extended our surveillance to the road from Yao to Pico Verde, at some distance before Pino del Agua, but we did not neglect the more direct trail that went up to the Maestra, which could not be traversed by trucks. The Pico Verde group was very small, armed with hunting rifles, and charged with giving the alarm in case of need; since it was a good road for withdrawal, in fact, we counted on using it after the action. Efigenio Ameijeiras was in charge of keeping watch over one of the rear guard access roads, which also came from the Pico Verde sector. Lalo Sardiñas and his squad remained in the Zapato zone, guarding several lumber roads which end on the banks of the Peladero. But that was a superfluous precaution, since in order to reach these roads the enemy would have had to make a very long march up the mountain. Furthermore, it was not their custom to march through the forest in columns. Ciro Redondo and all his platoon were in charge of defending the access from Siberia.

We waited for the Army in a forest on the cliff, along the road that mounted from Guisa, so as to surprise the trucks and concentrate our fire power. The spot chosen permitted us to observe the arrival of the trucks from a great distance. The plan was simple: we would fire on them from both sides, immobilizing the first truck at a bend in the road, and firing on all the others in order to halt them. The platoon which was supposed to go into action had the best arms, and some of Captain Raúl Castro Mercader's men came to reinforce them.

We spent about seven days in ambush, waiting patiently, before anyone arrived. On the seventh day someone came to inform me that the enemy was approaching. Since the gradients are very steep, we heard the humming of the motors even before we saw them as the trucks attempted to clamber up the terrible slope. We prepared for battle. At the most important spot we placed those men who were under Captain Ignacio Pérez' command; they were to stop the first truck. Twenty minutes before the first confrontation, a torrential downpour fell, soaking us to the bone. Meanwhile, the enemy soldiers were advancing, more concerned with the rain than with the possibility of an attack. The comrade charged with opening hostilities fired his Tommy gun but hit no one. The fusillade became general and the soldiers in the first truck, more frightened and surprised than hurt by our attack, leaped to the road and disappeared behind the cliff, after killing José de la Cruz ("Crucito"), one of our great fighters and the poet of our column.

An enemy soldier took refuge under the truck at the bend in the road, and let no one raise his head. A minute or two passed before I arrived at the combat sites. I realized that many men were retreating, in obedience to a false order—a frequent accident in the midst of combat. Arquímedes Fonseca was wounded in the hand while retrieving a submachine gun abandoned by its gunner. We had to give orders for everyone to return to his combat post and to ask Lalo Sardiñas' and Efigenio Ameijeiras' forces to cooperate with us.

There was a fighter named Tatín on the road. As I walked down it he said to me, defiance in his voice: "He's there, under the truck! Let's go! Let's go!" I summoned up my courage, deeply disgusted by these cowardly cries. But when we tried to approach the enemy fighter who was firing on us from beneath the truck, we had to acknowledge that we were going to pay dearly for our display of courage.

The Army trucks numbered five and they transported one company. The squad led by Antonio López carried out precisely its orders not to allow anyone to pass after the opening of hostilities. Nevertheless, a group of soldiers, resisting energetically, impeded our advance. Lalo and Efigenio arrived to reinforce us; they charged the trucks and liquidated the seat of resistance. Some of the soldiers fled in dissarray, others in the two trucks they had salvaged, leaving behind them all the ammunition.

Thanks to Gilberto Caldero, we received some information concerning certain of their plans. This comrade had been taken prisoner during a reconnaissance mission in another sector. He had remained captive for a certain time and the enemy had brought him along to poison Fidel. All he had to do was empty the contents of a phial in Fidel's food. When he heard the shots, Caldero climbed down from the truck, like all the soldiers, but instead of fleeing the fusillade, he reported to us at once, and rejoined our ranks.

When we surrounded the first truck, we found two dead and one wounded soldier, who was still going through the motions of battle as he lay dying; the process was coldly terminated for him by one of our men. The combatant responsible for this act of barbarism had seen his family decimated by the Batista army. I reproached him violently, unaware that my remarks were overheard by another wounded soldier, concealed and motionless under some tarpaulins on the truck bed. Emboldened by my words and the way the comrade had asked to be excused, the enemy soldier made his presence known and begged us not to kill him. He had a fractured leg. Every time a fighter passed near him he would shout: "Don't kill me! Don't kill me! Che says not to kill prisoners!" When the battle was over, we transported him to the sawmill and gave him first aid.

As for the other trucks, we had inflicted only light losses, but a good number of weapons remained in our possession. The outcome of the battle: one automatic gun; five Garands; one tripod machine gun and its ammunition; and another Garand, which Efigenio Ameijeiras' troop, belonging to Fidel's column, made off with. Efigenio judged his platoon's participation in the battle to have been decisive; consequently, he felt they had a right to certain captured weapons. But Fidel had left this detachment under my orders, simply to lend us a helping hand. So that, regardless of all their protestations, I divided the trophies among the men of my column, except for the Garand which had already been appropriated.

The Browning went to Antonio López for his excellent performance. The Garands went to Lieutenant Joel Iglesias, Virelles (a member of the "Corintia" expedition, who had joined up with us), Oñate, and two others whose names I don't remember. We then set about burning the three captured trucks, since they were unsalvageable.

While we were assembling our troops, some planes passed over-head. But several bursts of gunfire from our direction sufficed to drive them away. Mingolo, one of the Pardo brothers, had been sent to warn Fidel of the approaching guards; but we decided to send another messenger (accompanied by Caldero, who would recount his adventure) to tell him the results of our battle. We sent word to Ciro to withdraw from his position; Mongo Martínez carried that message.

After a few minutes we heard gunfire. A group of our men, armed with hunting rifles, had discovered a soldier who was advancing surreptitiously. They shouted to him to halt; since he ignored the command, they fired at him. The man fled, abandoning his gun. They brought us a Springfield as evidence of their exploit. It seemed strange to us that there were still dispersed soldiers in the sector. Nevertheless, the gun was added to our tally. Two days later Mongo Martínez returned. He told us that some enemy soldiers had taken him by surprise, firing on him with hunting rifles, and that he had had to flee because he was wounded. His face was covered with powder marks. So he was the source of the Springfield which our comrades had seized from the enemy! The result had been that this wounded comrade, thinking the guards to be very near, had taken a cross road and got lost in the woods. He hadn't let Ciro Redondo know about our battle nor transmitted the withdrawal order to him. The next day Ciro sent a messenger to us and the order was conveyed to him.

While the B-26's were buzzing the sawmill in search of victims, we were calmly having our breakfast; installed in various parts of the building, we drank hot chocolate, brought to us by the mistress of the house—who was not exactly cheered by the sight of the B-26's passing and re-passing, almost grazing the roof. They finally flew off and we, utterly relaxed, were about to leave when we saw on the road from Siberia (the same one that Ciro had been watching a few hours earlier) four trucks, full of soldiers. But it was already too late; a good number of our men had fallen back

to safer positions. We fired in the air, twice—the retreat signal—
and we quietly left.

This battle, important for its repercussions (the news of it
spread throughout Cuba), took a toll among the enemy of three
dead and one wounded. In addition, we took a prisoner, captured
by Efigenio's platoon the next day, when we passed through the
riddled zone for the last time. It was Corporal Alejandro, who remained with us as our cook until the end of the war. Crucito was
buried at the site of our battle; our entire troop was grief-stricken,
having lost in him a noble comrade and its peasant bard.

Worthy of citation for this battle are: Efigenio Ameijeiras, Lalo
Sardiñas, Captain Victor Mora, Lieutenant Antonio López and
his squad, Dermidio Escalona, and Arquímedes Fonsecas. It is to
the latter that the tripod machine gun was entrusted. He would be
using it after his hand was healed. On our side we had one death,
one case of light wounds, some contusions, some scratches, not to
mention the bullets that poor Mongo stopped.

We left Pino del Agua by various routes, with plans to regroup
in the Pico Verde sector. There we would reorganize ourselves
while waiting for Comrade Fidel's arrival.

Analysis of the battle revealed that, although a political and military victory, it bore the traces nonetheless of our enormous shortcomings. The factor of surprise ought to have been exploited to the
hilt, so as to overwhelm the first three trucks; furthermore, after
hostilities had broken out, a false order to retreat had been circulated, leading the men to lose control and cooling their fighting
ardor. A lack of punch was evident in seizing trucks, which were
defended by a small number of soldiers. It must be added, too, that
by spending the night at the sawmill we were exposing ourselves
stupidly. And the final withdrawal was carried out in great dis-
order. All this proved the imperative necessity of improving battle
preparations and discipline among our troop, a task to which we
were to devote ourselves in the days to come.

# A Painful Episode

After the battle of Pino del Agua, we set about to improve the organization of our guerrilla force, strengthened at that point by several of Fidel's units. Our goal was to increase our usefulness and effectiveness in combat.

Lieutenant López, who had distinguished himself at Pino del Agua, was designated together with his squad (all of them very responsible boys) to be a member of the disciplinary commission. This commission would have the task of surveillance and would be charged with enforcement of respect for the rules of vigilance, general discipline, cleanliness, and revolutionary morality. But its life was ephemeral and it was dissolved a few days after its creation.

About this time, in the vicinity of the Botella, in a little camp that we ordinarily used as a way station, an earlier deserter named Cuervo, who had fled with his rifle two months before, was executed. What became of his gun we will never know; however, we were well-informed of his activities: under cover of fighting for the revolutionary cause and of executing spies, he simply victimized an entire section of the mountain population, perhaps in collusion with the Army.

The trial was speedy, in view of his desertion. We then had to proceed to his physical elimination. The execution of anti-social individuals who exploited their position of strength in the district in order to commit crimes was, unfortunately, not infrequent in the Sierra Maestra.

We learned that Fidel had completed his tour of the Sonador zone, after attacking Chivirico, and was once more in our sector. Consequently, we decided to march toward the Peladero in an attempt to join up with him as fast as we could. At that time there was a merchant in the coastal area, Juan Balansa, whose ties with the dictatorship and the *latifundistas* were known, but he had never shown any active hostility toward us. He had a mule, celebrated in the vicinity for its staying power; as a kind of war tax, we made off with it. With the mule, we arrived at Pinalito, near the Peladero.

On reaching its banks, we had to descend the steep cliffs. Should we sacrifice the beast, carve it up and carry the meat, should we simply abandon it in enemy territory, or should we have it go on as far as it was able? We opted for the last solution. Besides, carrying the meat would have caused problems.

The mule made his way downward, unhesitatingly, sure-footed, in places where we had to crawl along, to cling to lianas, or to hang on like grim death to rocky protuberances. He went on, even in places where our little mascot—a puppy—refused to walk, waiting to be picked up and carried. The mule gave an extraordinary display of acrobatic talent.

He continued his exploits by crossing the Peladero in a place full of boulders, by a series of incredible leaps from rock to rock. This is what won him his right to live. Later, he was mine to ride, my first regular mount, until the day he fell into the hands of Sánchez Mosquera, during one of our numerous clashes in the Sierra.

It was in the vicinity of the Peladero that the painful incident occurred that led to the abolition of the disciplinary commission. A group of comrades, hostile to the establishment of disciplinary standards, were constantly cutting the ground from under it and preventing it from functioning. Such a situation could not continue; we had to take Draconian measures. One of the rear guard squads played a tasteless practical joke on the members of the commission, which had dropped all other matters and was hastening to examine a very important problem. These jokers had stupidly deposited some ordure, in order to bait them. Following the incident, various members of the group were arrested, among them Humberto Rodríguez, of sad repute due to his penchant for playing the role of executioner whenever we found ourselves faced with the painful duty of executing a malefactor. After the Revolution triumphed, Rodríguez, with another rebel soldier as his accomplice, murdered a prisoner; they subsequently escaped from La Cabaña prison.

Two or three comrades were "imprisoned" along with Humberto. Under guerrilla conditions, prison didn't mean much. But when the crime was serious enough a prisoner guilty of a lack of discipline would be deprived of food for a day or two. This was indeed a punishment that struck home.

Two days after the incident, when the principal participants were still prisoners, it was announced that Fidel was in the vicinity, in the region known as "El Zapato." I went to welcome and talk with him. We hadn't been together for more than ten minutes when Ramiro Valdés came to us, bringing news: Lalo Sardiñas, in attempting with a slight excess of zeal to punish an undisciplined comrade, had held his pistol to the man's head as if he were going to shoot him. The gun went off unintentionally and the comrade was killed on the spot. I wasted no time in going back to the camp and putting Lalo under guard. Hostility against him was rife. The men demanded a summary trial and execution.

We began to take depositions and to look for evidence. Opinions were divided: some of the men expressed their explicit conviction that it was premeditated murder. Others favored the assumption that it was an accident. It must be emphasized, independently of these opinions, that it was expressly forbidden by guerrilla law to inflict corporal punishment on a comrade, and that this was not Lalo Sardiñas' first offense.

The situation was of the greatest delicacy. Comrade Lalo Sardiñas had always been a first-rate fighter, a strict supporter of discipline, a man highly endowed with a spirit of sacrifice. Those who were making fierce demands for the death penalty, on the other hand, were far from the best of the group.

The witnesses' declarations went on until nightfall. Fidel came to the trial. He was strongly opposed to the death penalty but he did not deem it wise to make a decision of this nature without consulting all the fighters. The next stage of the trial called for Fidel or me to defend the accused, who observed the deliberations impassively, without showing the slightest trace of fear. After a series of impassioned statements in which death was demanded, it was my turn to take the floor and beseech the comrades not to treat this problem lightly. I attempted to explain that our comrade's death had to be ascribed to our conditions of struggle, to the very fact that we were at war, and that it was after all the dictator Batista who was guilty. My words, alas, did not carry a convincing ring to this hostile audience.

It was already late; we had lit several pine torches and some candles so as to continue the discussion. Fidel then spoke, for a full hour. He presented all the reasons militating in favor of acquittal for Lalo Sardiñas. He enumerated our faults, our lack of discipline, the other errors we committed daily, the resultant weakness; and he explained that in the end this indefensible act had been committed in defense of the concept of discipline and that we should keep that fact in mind. As he spoke, illuminated by the light of the torches, standing tall against a background of shrubs, his voice took on emotional overtones, and many of our men were clearly convinced by our leader's opinion. His enormous power of persuasion was put to the test that night.

His eloquence, however, could not put an end to all opposition. We concluded that two possible punishments should be put to the vote: immediate death by shooting, or dismissal from the ranks. Inflamed spirits were influenced by a number of factors in the course of this vote, in which the life of a man was at stake. We had to suspend proceedings because some were voting twice and excited argumentation was fast distorting the terms of the solution. Once more the choices open to the voters were explained and everybody was asked to make his decision known at once. I was put in charge of tallying the votes cast, in a little notebook. Lalo was beloved by many among us; we recognized his transgression but we wanted his life to be spared, for he was a valuable cadre of the Revolution. I recall that Oniria, a young girl who had joined up with us, asked in an anguished voice if she too could vote in her capacity as a member of the column. She was permitted to do so and after all had cast their votes, we began to count the ballots. I recorded the results of this strange vote on little squares of paper, similar to those used in medical laboratories. It was extremely close. After the last hesitations, here is how opinion was divided among the 146 *guerrilleros* who voted: 70 declared themselves in favor of the death penalty; 76 for another type of punishment. Lalo was saved.

But that wasn't the end of it. The next day a group of men hostile to the majority vote announced their decision to leave the guerrilla movement. This group included many elements of questionable trustworthiness, but there were also some pretty good boys among them. Paradoxically, Antonio López, the chief lieutenant of the disciplinary commission, and various members of his squad were dissatisfied and left the Rebel Army. I remember several names: someone called Curro, a Pardo Jiménez (nephew of a Batista minister, which hadn't prevented him from taking part in the struggle). I don't know what happened to them. Leaving at the same time were the three Cañizares brothers. Their fate was less than glorious: one of them died at the Bay of Pigs, another was taken prisoner there, after the attempted invasion by the mercenaries. These men, who had not respected the majority and who dissociated themselves from the struggle, subsequently put themselves in the service of the enemy, and it was as traitors that they returned to fight on our soil.

Our leaders' and fighters' awareness was growing. The best among us felt deeply the need for an agrarian reform and an overturning of the social system, without which the country could never achieve health. But they always had to drag behind them the weight of those individuals who came to the struggle out of nothing but a hunger for adventure or in the hope of winning not only laurels but economic advantage.

A certain number of other malcontents withdrew. I don't remember their names any longer, except for Roberto, who subsequently spun out an interminable tale, chockful of lies; Conte Agüero lost face by publishing it in *Bohemia*. Lalo Sardiñas was dismissed and condemned to win his rehabilitation by fighting the enemy as a simple soldier. One of our lieutenants, Joaquín de la Rosa, Lalo's uncle, decided to accompany him. As a replacement for Captain Sardiñas, Fidel gave me one of his best fighters: Camilo Cienfuegos, who became a captain in our column's advance guard.

It was necessary to get moving without losing a moment, so as to neutralize a group of bandits who, using the name of our Revolution as a shield, committed their crimes in the region where we had begun our struggle; also in the Caracas sector and in Lomón. Camilo's first mission in our column was to advance by forced march so as to capture all those undesirables, who would subsequently be put on trial.

# The Morale and Discipline
## of Revolutionary Fighters

We all know what our Rebel Army was, and because we are
familiar with it we tend to undervalue the feat of our emancipation,
won with the blood of twenty thousand martyrs and the immense
surge of the people. There are, however, profound reasons that made
this triumph a reality. The dictatorship created the necessary fer-
ment, with its policy of oppression of the masses and maintenance
of a regime of privilege: privileges for the regime's lackeys, for para-
sitic *latifundistas* and businessmen, privileges for the foreign mo-
nopolies. Once the conflict broke out, the regime's repressive measures and its brutality, far from diminishing popular resistance, increased it. The demoralization and the shamelessness of the military
caste facilitated the task. The ruggedness of the mountains in Oriente, plus our enemy's tactical ineptitude, also did their share. But
this war was won by the people, through the action of its armed
fighting vanguard, the Rebel Army, whose basic weapons were
their *morale* and their *discipline.*

Discipline and morale are the foundations on which the strength
of an army rests, whatever its composition. Let us examine both
terms. The morale of an army has two aspects which complement
each other: there is morale in the ethical sense of the word, and

there is morale in its heroic sense. Any armed group, if it is to achieve excellence, must have both.

Ethical morale has changed with the passage of time, in accordance with the prevailing ideas of a given society. Pillaging homes and carrying off all objects of value was considered correct in feudal society, but carrying off women as a token of victory would have violated moral obligations; any army that behaved thus, as an established policy, would not be conducting itself according to the values of the epoch. However, prior to that period this was considered the correct thing to do, and the women of the conquered became part of the patrimony of the conquerors.

All armies must guard their ethical morale zealously, as a substantial element of their structure, as a factor of struggle, as a factor in toughening a soldier.

Morale in a heroic sense is that combative drive, that faith in the final victory and in the justice of their cause, which leads soldiers to carry out the most extraordinary deeds of valor.

The French *maquisards* who undertook their struggle—a seemingly hopeless one—under arduous conditions were faced by overwhelming adversity; yet the conviction with which they fought for a just cause, the indignation that the Nazi bestialities and crimes evoked in them, led them to carry on until victory. They had fighting morale.

The Yugoslav *guerrilleros,* their country occupied by a power fifty times their superior, threw themselves into the struggle and persisted, never wavering, until they conquered. They had fighting morale.

The defenders of Stalingrad, with forces many times inferior to those of the enemy, with the river at their backs, resisted the long and overwhelming offensive; they defended each hill and each ditch, each house and each room within, each street and each sidewalk of the city until the Soviet Army was able to mount an offensive and establish a huge blockade, destroying, overcoming, and making prisoners of their attackers. They had fighting morale.

If we want a more remote example, the defenders of Verdun repulsed one offensive after another and stopped an army many times their superior in number and in weaponry. They had fighting morale.

The Rebel Army on the battlefield of the *sierras* and the *llanos* had fighting morale. And that is just what the mercenary army lacked in its confrontation with the guerrilla deluge. We felt genuinely the forceful words of our national anthem: "To die for the fatherland is to live." They knew the words, but they did not feel them inside themselves. The sentiment of justice that prevailed in one cause, and the sentiment of not knowing why you were fighting in the other, created great differences between the soldiers of the two sides.

There is a nexus that transforms the two types of morale, the ethical and the fighting, into a harmonious unity: discipline. There are distinct forms of discipline but, fundamentally, there is an external discipline and an internal discipline. Militarist regimes are constantly working to procure the former. In this respect also, the difference between the two armies was observable: the dictatorship's army exercised its morale, its barracks-room discipline—external, mechanical, and cold. This produced a soldier of remarkable external discipline and an underdeveloped internal one. This automatically diminishes his fighting morale. Fighting for what and for whom? Fighting to preserve certain private sinecures for the soldier? Fighting for the right to plunder, to play the thief in uniform? For such rights people will fight only up to a certain point: until the sacrifice of their life is demanded of them.

On the other side: an army with an enormous ethical morale, a non-existent external discipline and an unbending internal discipline born of conviction. The rebel soldier did not drink, not be-

cause his superior officer would punish him but because he knew
he should not drink, because his morale imposed abstinence on him,
and his internal discipline strengthened that morale imposed by the
army. He had joined that army simply to fight, because he understood it to be his duty to give his life for a cause.

Morale was growing and discipline was becoming stronger; our
army was becoming invincible; but peace, the product of victory,
came and this led to the great clash between two concepts and two
organizations: the old form of organization, based on external,
mechanical discipline, forced into rigid patterns; and the new, based
on interior discipline, without pre-established patterns. From that
clash arose the difficulties familiar to all of us concerning the ulti-
mate structuring of our Army. Today the problem has been solved,
after we analyzed and understood it. We are trying to provide our
rebel armed forces with the minimum of necessary mechanical discipline required for the harmonious functioning of large units, with
the maximum of internal discipline growing out of the study and
understanding of our revolutionary duties. Today as yesterday, although an apparatus exists that is devoted specifically to punishing
offenses, discipline cannot derive totally from an external mechanism, but must be achieved through an internal eagerness to overcome all the errors committed. How to accomplish this? It is a task
requiring patience on the part of the revolutionary instructors who
are disseminating among the mass of our Army the great national
goals.

As with armies the world over, the members of our Army must
respect their superior officers, they must obey orders at once, they
must serve tirelessly wherever despatched. But they must also act
as both social researcher and judge. As social researchers, their contact with the people enables them to ascertain its prevailing sentiments which they can communicate to the upper echelons for constructive purposes; as judges, they have the duty to denounce any
kind of abuse committed within the army or outside it, in an effort

to eliminate it. This varied task of the Rebel Army proves the value of internal discipline, the goal of which is the perfecting of the individual. Just as it was in the Sierra, the Rebel soldier must not drink, not because of the punishment that may be inflicted by the disciplinary organism, but simply because the cause that we defend —the cause of the poor and of all the people—requires us not to drink, so that the mind of every soldier is alert, his body agile, and his morale high. He must remember that today, as yesterday, the Rebel is the cynosure of all eyes and constitutes an example for the people. There is and can be no great army if the bulk of the population is not convinced of the immense moral strength we possess today. Our armed strength is not limited to those who wear the uniform; the entire people is with us, and thus it must be. We must see to it that it shall be considered an honor by the people—workers, peasants, students, professionals—to carry the weapon which permits it to struggle in given cases alongside those who wear the uniform of the armed forces.

We must, then, serve as helmsman for the civilian population. Much more difficult than fighting, much more difficult than working at tasks of peaceful national construction, is the maintenance of the necessary direction, without deviating from it by an inch at any time. When sufficient cohesion is achieved in our armed forces, and our fighting morale is joined by a high ethical morale along with the indispensable complement of internal and external discipline, then we will have achieved the firm and lasting foundation for the great army of the future: the people of Cuba.

# The Struggle Against Banditry

Conditions in the Sierra permitted us to live freely in a quite vast territory. The army hardly ever occupied any of it; in many places, they had never set foot. But our system of government was not strongly organized nor rigorous enough to defeat the bands of marauders who, under the pretext of revolutionary activities, indulged in looting and banditry and a host of other offenses.

Besides, political conditions in the Sierra were still quite unsettled. The politicalization of the inhabitants was still superficial, and the presence in the vicinity of a threatening enemy army rendered useless all our efforts to correct this weakness.

Once again, the enemy tightened its vise. There were various signs indicating that they intended to march on the Sierra. That was sufficient to panic the people in the district. The least resolute among them did not rest until they had succeeded in finding a way to escape the dreaded invasion by the assassins of the dictatorship. Sánchez Mosquera had established his headquarters in the hamlet of Las Minas de Bueycito and it was becoming evident that a new invasion was in the making.

In spite of these threats we went about our business in the valley of El Hombrito, laying the groundwork for a free territory. We even initiated in this desolate Sierra the rudiments of industrial activity —a bakehouse. In this same sector of El Hombrito there was an encampment which served as a sort of gateway to the guerrilla forces. Young men wanting to join up with us arrived there in groups; they were placed under the authority of some peasants who were with us and in whom we had full confidence. Their leader, Aristidio, had been a member of our column as recently as a few days before the battle of El Uvero. But the battle took place without him, because he had fallen and fractured a rib. Besides, after this accident he had not expressed any desire to continue fighting.

Aristidio was a typical example of a peasant who joined the ranks of the revolution without having any clear understanding of its significance. His private estimate of this situation having convinced him that there were more advantages to waiting to see which way the wind would blow, he sold his revolver for a few pesos. Then he began to repeat to anyone who would listen that he was not off his rocker enough to allow himself to be quietly caught at home, after the guerrilla force left the sector, and that he was going to make contact with the Army. These declarations were brought to my attention from several sources. The revolution was undergoing difficult times; in virtue of the rights bestowed on me as chief of the sector, I called for an inquiry, very summary, and Aristidio was executed.

Today we may ask ourselves: was he really guilty enough to deserve death, or would it have been possible to save a life which could have been put to use by the revolution in its constructive phase? War is harsh, and at a time when the enemy's aggressiveness is on the rise, it is not possible to tolerate even the presumption of treason. He could perhaps have saved his skin, had this happened several months earlier, since the guerrilla movement was still insecure, or several months later, when we were much more firmly in control. But Aristidio had the bad luck to rat at the precise moment when we were sufficiently strong to punish pitilessly such an offense as his, but not strong enough to inflict any other kind of punishment, since we had no jail or facilities for any other kind of penalty.

Leaving the region for a time, the entire column set out toward Los Cocos on the Magdalena where we were to join up with Fidel and capture a gang which, led by "El Chino" Chang, was ravaging the Caracas region. Camilo, who had gone ahead with the advance guard, had already taken a certain number of prisoners before we arrived on the spot. The mopping-up operation lasted about ten days. It was there in a peasant hut that the notorious Chang, leader of the gang, was tried and condemned to death. By his order, peasants had been tortured, others murdered; he had sown terror in the district while usurping the name and stealing the possessions of the Revolution. At the same time, a peasant was condemned to death who, while boasting of his authority as a "messenger" for the Rebel Army, raped an adolescent. Subsequently we put on trial a good number of the members of the gang, consisting of boys from the cities and peasants seduced by the prospect of a carefree, prodigal life dangled before them by Chang.

Most of them were acquitted. However we decided, with regard to three of them, that we would stage a symbolic drama, which would surely make them think.

Chang and the peasant guilty of rape were tied to a tree in the forest and executed. They displayed a supreme calm. The first one, his large eyes wide open, faced the guns and shouted "¡Viva la revolución!" Chang faced death with absolute serenity but asked for the last rites to be administered by Father Sardiñas, who at that moment was nowhere near our encampment. We were unable to grant this request. Chang then asked us to be the eternal witnesses of his last prayer, as if public testimony would serve as an extenuating circumstance in the hereafter.

It was then that occurred the symbolic execution of three boys of the band. They had been deeply involved in Chang's shady dealings but Fidel felt they ought to be given a chance. We bandaged their eyes and subjected them to the anguish of a simulated execution. Three shots were fired in the air, and the boys realized that they were still very much alive. One of them threw himself on me and, in a spontaneous gesture of happiness and gratitude, gave me a big noisy kiss, as if I were his father.

These events had an eyewitness, Andrew St. George, agent of the CIA. His reportage, published in *Look* magazine and considered in the United States to be the most sensational of the year, won a prize for him.

In retrospect, this device as practiced in the Sierra might seem barbaric. The fact is that during that period no other form of punishment for these men was possible; true, they did not quite deserve death but they had on their record a series of serious offenses. All three of the "executed" men joined the Rebel Army. I later heard reports of the brilliant performance of two of them during the insurrectionary period; as for the third, he stayed in my column for a long time. Whenever the conversation touched on various episodes of the war in the course of talking with other soldiers, if he found a comrade who called into question any of his stories, he always said emphatically: "It's true I've never been afraid of death. Che's my witness."

Two or three days later, we captured another group. Their execution was especially painful. Among them was a *guajiro* named Dionisio and his brother-in-law Juan Lebrigio, two among the very earliest who aided our guerrilla troop. Dionisio, who had been instrumental in unmasking the traitor Eutimio Guerra, and who had aided us generously in one of the most difficult moments of our revolution, had later grossly abused our confidence, as had his brother-in-law. He had appropriated for his own purposes all the provisions that the urban organizations had sent us; he had set up several camps where he secretly slaughtered the cattle. Once on this slippery path, he had gone so far as to commit murder.

At that time in the Sierra, a man's wealth was measured essentially by the number of women he had. Dionisio, faithful to custom and taking himself for a pasha, had, by virtue of the powers conferred on him by the Revolution, taken over three houses, with a woman and a substantial food supply in each. In the course of his trial, faced with Fidel's indignant reproaches concerning his abuse of confidence, his treason, and his immoral conduct—was he not supporting three women with the people's money?—Dionisio maintained, with a good measure of peasant artlessness, that it was not three but two, since one of the three was his legitimate wife (which was true)!

At this trial we also executed two of Masferrer's spies, who had been caught red-handed, as well as a boy named Echeverría, who had been assigned to special missions in the Movement. The Echeverría family had furnished several fighters to the Rebel Army (one of the brothers had been in the "Granma" expedition), but this boy, after having formed a little troop while waiting for our arrival, succumbed to who knows what temptation, and began to organize armed attacks in guerrilla territory. His last moments were affecting. He recognized his errors, but he could not, however, accept the thought of death by execution. He begged us to let him die in the next battle; he swore that he would seek death there, that he wanted only to avoid dishonor to his family. Condemned to death by the tribunal, Echeverría (nicknamed "Squinty") wrote a long, moving letter to his mother, in which he explained the justice of his punishment and instructed her to remain loyal to the Revolution.

The last of the executed was a colorful character called "El Maestro," whom I had known well during some difficult hours when I had wandered aimlessly through these mountains, sick and alone except for him. He soon left us, using some illness as a pretext and coming to grief in a life of dissipation. One of his finest exploits was to pass himself off as me—"Dr. Guevara"—and to attempt the rape of a little peasant girl who had sought medical treatment. They all died proclaiming their commitment to the Revolution, except for Masferrer's two spies. I was not present at the scene, but witnesses have told me that when Father Sardiñas, who *was* present this time, approached one of the condemned in order to offer him the last rites, the man answered him: "Look, Father, see if anyone else needs you; frankly, I don't really go for that stuff."

With such men as these the revolution was being made. From the beginning, they had not taken to discipline; they were loners who ended by getting into the habit of busying themselves with their petty personal affairs, with no interest in overturning the social order. No matter how little or how briefly the revolution relaxed its control, they fell into errors that, with astonishing facility, led them into crime.

Dionisio and Juanito Lebrigio were no worse than other occasional delinquents whom the Revolution spared and who can be found today in the ranks of our army. But that moment called for an iron fist. We were obliged to inflict exemplary punishment in order to curb violations of discipline and to liquidate the nuclei of anarchy which sprang up in areas lacking a stable government.

Echeverría, then, could have become a hero of the Revolution, an activist and a leader like his two brothers, officers of the Rebel Army, but he had the bad luck to commit an offense in that particular epoch, and he had to pay with his life. I hesitated to name him in these pages, but his attitude in the face of death was so upright, so revolutionary, so firm—he recognized so clearly the justice of his punishment—that his end, it seemed to us, exalted him. It served as an example, tragic though it was, valuable in that it made clear to the eyes of others the need to make of our Revolution a healthy thing, free of all those acts of banditry which were the heritage of the Batista dictatorship.

During these trials a case was argued for the first time by a man who had taken refuge in the Sierra after various disputes with Llano leaders of the July 26th Movement. He became Minister of Agriculture after the Revolution, until the very moment when the Law of Agrarian Reform was signed (by others, since he did not wish to commit himself to it): Sorí Marín.

When we had performed the painful duty of establishing peace and moral order in all the territory over which the Rebel Army was moving to exercise administrative control, we headed back toward El Hombrito. Our column was divided into three platoons. The advance guard was led by Camilo Cienfuegos and four lieutenants: Orestes, Boldo, Leyva, and Noda. The second platoon was under the command of Captain Raúl Castro Mercader, whose lieutenants were: Alfonso Zayas, Orlando Pupo, and Pablo Cabrera. Ramiro

Valdés was in charge of our little staff headquarters, with Joel Iglesias as his lieutenant. Joel, not yet seventeen, was in command of men over thirty, whom he addressed respectfully as *usted* when giving them orders; they addressed him as *tú* but obeyed his orders with discipline. The rear guard platoon was led by Ciro Rodríguez, assisted by Vilo Acuña, Félix Reyes, William Rodríguez, and Carlos Mas.

It was toward the end of October 1957 that we re-established ourselves at El Hombrito. We had then to set up a defense groundwork for the territory under our control. With the aid of two students recently arrived from Havana—a future engineer and a future veterinarian—we began to lay plans for a miniature hydroelectric station, which we planned to construct at the little El Hombrito River. We also began production of our *mambi** newspaper, *El Cubano Libre.* An old but nonetheless precious mimeograph machine had been brought up from the *llano.* With its aid we printed the first issues of the paper, whose editors and printers were the students Leonel Rodríguez and Ricardito Medina.

Thus it was that we began to organize our life at this sedentary stage—which we were able to do thanks to the complicity and generous protection given us by the riverside residents, particularly by our gallant friend "Old Lady Chana" as we called her. We proceeded then to build a bakehouse in an old abandoned *bohío,* since we did not want to offer enemy aviation the target of a new building. We also had an immense July 26th flag made, bearing the inscription: "Happy 1958!" We planted it on the highest plateau of El Hombrito, in the hope that it would be seen from afar, as far as Las Minas de Bueycito. Meanwhile we travelled through the sector, reinforcing our authority and giving it concrete presence. At the same time we were preparing to face—any day—Sánchez Mosquera's invasion, by constructing fortifications around the access roads that he was likely to use.

---

* Name given to Cubans who fought against Spanish domination in the nineteenth century.

# Altos de Conrado

The days following the Mar Verde battle were days of intense activity. We knew very well that we didn't yet have sufficient fighting strength to maintain combat continuously, or to encircle the enemy effectively, or to resist frontal attacks. That is why we remained on the defensive while redoubling our precautions in the Hombrito Valley. This valley is a few kilometers from Mar Verde; to reach it you must take the road that goes up to Santa Ana and crosses the Guayabo, a little mountain stream. However, you can also reach it by going along the Guayabo to the south, past Botella Hill, then taking the road that comes from Mina del Frío.

We made sure that all these points of access were well defended. It was also necessary to establish a constant watch to avoid having the enemy swoop down and surprise us by moving their troops directly through the woods.

We had moved the bulkiest of our equipment to the La Mesa sector, to Polo Torres' house. We had also carried our wounded there, among them Joel Iglesias, the only one unable to walk, because he was wounded in the leg.

Sánchez Mosquera's troops were stationed at Santa Ana and there were other enemy troops who had taken the California road, headed for an unknown destination.

Four or five days after the Mar Verde confrontation, the combat alert sounded. Sánchez Mosquera's troops were advancing by the most usual route, the one that goes directly from Santa Ana to El

Hombrito. We immediately warned our men who had prepared an ambush, and they checked the mines. These first mines, made by us, had a rudimentary firing system: it consisted of a spring and a spike which, when released and thrust forward by the spring, struck the detonator. I must report here that they had not functioned during the Mar Verde battle and that this time they functioned no better.

A few moments later, the noise of firing reached our command post; someone came to advise us that since the mines weren't working and the enemy had arrived in force, our men had retreated, not without having first inflicted some damage on the enemy. Their first victim, according to the details they gave us, was a tall, fat sergeant armed with a .45 revolver, who led a mounted column. Lieutenant Enrique Noda and another fighter, "El Mexicano," fired at him from short range with their Garands, and their descriptions of the man coincided. Yet Sánchez Mosquera's troops had forced our retreat.

Two weeks later, a peasant by the name of Brito came to thank me for our generosity; he had been forced by the enemy to take a position at the head of the column, and he had clearly seen our boys pretend to take aim and shoot at him! I learned also, from him, that there had been no victim at that spot. However, there were some at Altos de Conrado.

The spot we occupied was so difficult to defend with our meager resources that we had not bothered to dig trenches worthy of the name; we had only the old defenses, put up to prevent access from Minas de Bueycito; furthermore, as it advanced along the road, the enemy endangered our ambushes so that we ordered them to withdraw. No one remained in the area but an occasional peasant, determined to resist extortion by the Guardia Rural or perhaps clandestinely in communication with the enemy.

Slowly we fell back to the road that leads to Altos de Conrado, [Conrad's Heights] which is nothing more than a small hill in the Sierra Maestra, on the heights of which lived a *guajiro* named

Conrado. This comrade was a member of the PSP,* who had been in contact with us from the beginning and had rendered us many noble services. He had evacuated his family, and his house was isolated: what a splendid spot for an ambush! There were only three narrow paths going in, which wound through the hilly forest perfectly protected by tropical foliage. All the rest was defended by sheer boulders and vertiginous cliffs, immensely dangerous to climb.

At one spot where there was a small area of felled trees, the road widened. This was the perfect place for preparing to resist Sánchez Mosquera's attacks. On the first day we had placed two bombs, with their fuses, in the oven of the little hut. It was the simplest possible trap: if we withdrew, the enemy would probably move into the house and use the oven. Covered completely by the ashes lay the two bombs; we assumed that the heat of a fire or a live coal would light the fuses, setting off an explosion which would surely have a number of victims. But of course, this would be useful only later; first, we would have to engage in battle on Conrad's Heights.

We stayed there, waiting patiently, for three days, with round-the-clock watches. At that altitude, and in that season of the year, nights were very cold and damp. And, it must be confessed, we were not yet toughened enough for the hardships of an entire night spent in the open in battle position.

We had mimeographed, on the machine on which we printed our newspaper, *El Cubano Libre* (the first issue of which had appeared a few days earlier), a leaflet for the Batista soldiers. Our intention was to post these on the trees along the road they would take.

On the morning of December 8, from the heights of our boulder, we heard the troop beginning its ascent; it wound along the road, arriving about two or three hundred meters below us. We sent someone to post the leaflets; it was comrade Luis Olazábal who

---

* Partido Socialista Popular, the name of the Communist Party at that time.

volunteered. We heard the shouts of a violent argument, in the midst of which I clearly heard (since I was on watch along the wall) the bellow of, apparently, an officer giving an order: "By my balls, move forward!" And the soldier, the other speaker (whoever he was), refused in a rage. The argument ceased and the troop began moving.

We could see the column advancing, in small groups, hidden among the trees. After observing them for a moment, I began to question the advisability of revealing our ambush to them by means of the leaflets. I called Luis again and asked him to remove them. He had only a few seconds in which to do it, for the first soldiers were arriving at a smart pace.

Battle arrangements were simple in the extreme: we assumed that when the enemy arrived in the open, a single man would come into view, quite cut off from his companions. That man, at least, had to fall. Camilo waited for him, hidden behind a large mastic tree; at the moment when the soldier passed him, looking attentively ahead, Camilo would fire his Tommy gun at him, at less than a meter's distance.

The sharpshooters whom we had concealed in the brush on both flanks would go into action. Lieutenant Ibrahim and someone else, at the edge of the road, some ten meters from Camilo, were to cover him by firing from in front, so that no one could approach him after he had felled the scout.

My post was some twenty meters distant, off to the side behind a tree trunk which protected half of me. My gun was pointed at the approach to the path along which the soldiers were coming. There were several of us who could not observe them at first, because we were in an exposed position where we risked being seen. We were supposed to wait for Camilo's shots. I sneaked a glance, violating the order that I myself had given. I could at that moment sense the tension prior to combat. I saw the first soldier appear. He looked around him suspiciously and advanced slowly. Actually, this place smelled of an ambush—with its untypical landscape, the little clearing and the spring in the midst of the forest's luxuriant vegetation. The trees, some cut down, others standing and charred by fire, gave an impression of desolation. I took cover, waiting for the fight to begin. There was the crack of gunfire and then shooting became generalized. I realized that it was not Camilo who had fired but Ibrahim, who had been unnerved by the waiting. He had fired ahead of time and this was instantly followed by general fire, although in reality we couldn't see a thing from any vantage point. Our isolated shots, all of which should have been lethal, and the firing by the soldiery, in wasteful bursts, joined but did not mingle. We could recognize from the noise which of the two facing armies was shooting. Several minutes later (five or six, not more), we heard overhead the first whistles of mortar shells or bazookas; their trajectory was too long and they burst well beyond us.

Suddenly I felt a disagreeable sensation, similar to a burn or the tingling of numbness. I had just been hit in the left foot, which had not been protected by the tree trunk. I fired my rifle at once (I had chosen one with a telescopic sight, to improve my aim); at the moment I was hit, I heard some men moving rapidly in my direction making a great noise as they pushed the tree branches aside. My rifle was of no further use to me, since I had just discharged it; and my pistol had fallen from my hand when I threw myself to the ground. It was underneath me, but I could not straighten up since I was directly exposed to enemy fire. In the quickness of despair, I rolled over and succeeded in grabbing the pistol; at that moment I saw one of our men, the one we called "Cantinflas," coming toward me. During those moments of distress and pain, poor Cantinflas came to tell me that he was withdrawing because his gun was screwed up. I snatched it from him and examined it, while he crouched near me. The gun had jammed simply because the trigger was out of line. I handed it over to him, in working order, along with a razor-sharp diagnosis: "The trouble with you is, you're a stupid ox!" Cantinflas, whose real name was Oñate, took the gun and threw himself into the fray. Leaving the protection of the

tree trunk, he hastened to empty his Garand; he wanted to give
proof of his courage. He could not follow through, however, because he was hit by a bullet, which penetrated his left arm and
came out through his shoulder-blade, following a path that was
bizarre, to say the least. Now we were both wounded, with no
chance to retreat under the rain of bullets. There was nothing for it
but to crawl toward the tree trunks near the felled trees, then
slip around them, all the while not knowing where the rest of our
group was. We made it, but Cantinflas fainted. In spite of the pain,
I was able to move more freely and I arrived where the others were,
to ask them for help.

We knew that there were deaths in the enemy ranks, but we
didn't know exactly how many. Our wounded (the two of us)
having been retrieved, we set off toward Polo Torres' house.
After the first moment of euphoria and the excitement of the
combat wore off, I began to feel the pain more sharply, and marching became unbearable. At last, halfway there, I mounted a horse
and thus arrived at our makeshift hospital. Cantinflas, meanwhile,
was carried on our field stretcher—a hammock.

The fusillade had ceased. It seemed likely to us that the enemy
had taken Conrad's Heights. We sent out sentries to check their advance, along a little stream in a place we had christened "Pata de la
Mesa," (Table Leg); at the same time we organized the withdrawal of the peasants and their families. I sent a long letter to
Fidel explaining the situation.

I sent the column commanded by Ramiro Valdés to join up with
Fidel. In effect, defeat and fear were blowing in the wind among
our troop, and I wanted to stay there with a minimum of men so as
to preserve a maximum of mobility for our defense. Camilo remained at the head of a small defense group.

Such an apparent calm reigned in the vicinity on the morning
after the battle that we sent Lien, one of our best scouts, to find out
what the enemy was cooking up. That is how we learned that they
had withdrawn from the sector, lock, stock, and barrel. Lien went

as far as Conrado's house but saw no trace of the soldiers. He even brought us, as proof of his search, one of the bombs we had hidden in the *bohío*.

When the time came for troop inspection, we noticed that comrade Guile Pardo's gun was missing. He had swapped his gun for another, and in retreating he had taken only the second, leaving the first on the battle premises. That was one of the gravest crimes he could have committed. The rule was explicit: he had to go out equipped only with small arms to retrieve the gun from the hands of the enemy, or else bring in another. Crestfallen, Guile went out to fulfil his obligation, but he returned several hours later, a smile on his lips and his own gun in his hands! The mystery was eventually cleared up: the Army had never moved from the place where it had dug itself in to resist our attack. Each had retreated to its own side, so that not a living person had reached our comrade's post. The gun had been caught in a downpour, nothing more.

This was, for a good while, the furthest point of penetration by the Army in the Sierra. In any case, in this particular zone, it never went beyond this point. A trail of burned-down huts— typical of Sánchez Mosquera's passing—that was all that remained of El Hombrito, among other villages. Our bakehouse had been conscientiously destroyed; in the midst of the smoking ruins we found nothing but some cats and a pig; they had escaped the destructive fury of the invaders only to fall into our gullets. A day or two after the battle Machadito, the present Minister of Public Health, operated on me with a razor and extracted an M-1 rifle bullet. From that time on, my recovery was rapid.

Sánchez Mosquera had carried off everything he could, from sacks of coffee to furniture, which his soldiers had to carry. We had the impression that it would be a long time before he would poke his nose into the Sierra again.

It then became necessary to tackle the political preparation of the sector and to begin once more to organize our basic industrial center, which would no longer be at El Hombrito but in a more remote place, in the same zone as the Mesa.

# War and the Peasant Population

To live in a continual state of war and to adapt to this new phenomenon creates an attitude of mind in the popular consciousness. The individual must undergo an adaptation to enable him to resist the bitter experience that threatens his tranquility. The Sierra Maestra and other newly liberated zones had to undergo this bitter experience.

The situation in the rugged mountain zones was nothing less than frightful. The peasant, migrated from afar, eager for freedom, working to root out his sustenance from the newly dug land, had by dint of his labors coaxed the coffee plants to grow on the craggy slopes where creating anything new entails sacrifice—all this by his own sweat, in response to the age-old longing of man to possess his own plot of land, working with infinite love this hostile crag, an extension of the man himself.

Soon after, when the coffee plants began to blossom with the fruit that represented his hope, the lands were claimed by a new owner. It might be a foreign company, a local land-grabber, or some other speculator taking advantage of peasant indebtedness. The political *caciques,* the local army chieftains, worked for the company or the land-grabber, jailing or murdering any peasant who was unduly rebellious against these arbitrary acts. Such was the scene of defeat and desolation that we found, paralleling our own defeat at

Alegría de Pío, the product of our inexperience (our only misadventure in this long campaign, our bloody baptism of fire).

The peasantry recognized those lean men whose beards, now legendary, were beginning to flourish, as companions in misfortune, fresh victims of the repressive forces, and gave us their spontaneous and disinterested aid, without expecting anything of the defeated ones.

Days passed and our small troop of now seasoned soldiers sustained the victories of La Plata and Palma Mocha. The regime responded with all its brutality, and there were mass assassinations of peasants. Terror was unleashed in the rustic valleys of the Sierra Maestra and the peasants withdrew their aid; a barrier of mutual mistrust loomed up between them and the *guerrilleros,* the former out of fear of reprisals, the latter out of fear of betrayal by the fearful. Our policy, nevertheless, was a just and understanding one, and the *guajiro* population began to return to their earlier relationship with our cause.

The dictatorship, in its desperation and criminality, ordered the resettlement of thousands of *guajiro* families from the Sierra Maestra in the cities.

The strongest and most resolute men, including almost all the youth, preferred liberty and war to slavery and the city. Long caravans of women, children, and old people took to the roads, leaving their birthplaces, going down to the *llano,* where they huddled on the outskirts of the cities. Cuba experienced the most criminal page of its history for the second time: the Resettlement. The first time it was decreed by Weyler, the bloody general of colonial Spain, this time by Fulgencio Batista, the worst traitor and assassin known to America.

Hunger, misery, illness, epidemics, and death decimated the peasants resettled by the tyranny. Children died for lack of medical attention and food, when a few steps away there were the resources that could have saved their lives. The indignant protest of the

Cuban people, international scandal, and the inability of the dictatorship to defeat the rebels obliged the tyrant to suspend the resettlement of peasant families from the Sierra Maestra. And once again they returned to the land of their birth, miserable, sick, decimated. Earlier they had experienced bombardments by the dictatorship, the burning of their *bohíos,* mass murders; now they had experienced the inhumanity and barbarism of a regime that treated them worse than colonial Spain treated the Cubans in the war of Independence. Batista had surpassed Weyler. The peasants returned with an unbreakable will to struggle until death or victory, rebels until death or freedom.

Our little guerrilla band, of city extraction, began to don palm leaf hats, the people lost their fear, decided to join the struggle and proceed resolutely along the road to their redemption. In this change, our policy toward the peasantry and our military victories coincided, and this already revealed us to be an unbeatable force in the Sierra Maestra.

Faced by the choice, all the peasants chose the path of revolution. The change of mental attitude, of which we have already spoken, now showed itself fully. The war was a fact—painful, yes, but transitory, a definitive state within which the individual was obliged to adapt himself in order to exist, When the peasants understood this, they made the adjustments necessary for the confrontation with the adverse circumstances that would come.

The peasants returned to their abandoned plots of land; they stopped the slaughter of their animals, saving them for worse days; they became used to the savage machine gunning, and each family built its own shelter. They also accustomed themselves to periodic flights from the battle zones, with family, cattle, and household goods, leaving only their *bohíos* for the enemy, which displayed its wrath by burning them to the ground. They accustomed themselves to rebuilding on the smoking ruins of their old dwellings, uncomplaining but with concentrated hatred and the will to conquer.

When the distribution of cattle began in the struggle agair
dictatorship's food blockade, they cared for their animals witⁱⁱ loving solicitude and they worked in groups, establishing what were
in effect cooperatives in their efforts to move the cattle to a safe
place, giving over all their pasture land and their mules to the
common effort.

It is a new miracle of the Revolution that the staunchest indi-
vidualist, who zealously protected the boundaries of his property,
joined—because of the war—the great common effort of the struggle. But there is an even greater miracle: the rediscovery by the
Cuban peasant of his own happiness, within the liberated zones.
Whoever has witnessed the timorous murmurs with which our
forces were received in each peasant household, notes with pride
the carefree clamor, the happy, hearty laughter of the new Sierra
inhabitant. That is the reflection of his self-assurance which the
awareness of his own strength gave to the inhabitant of our liberated
area. That is our future task: that the concept of their own strength
should return to the Cuban people, and that they achieve absolute
assurance that their individual rights, guaranteed by the Constitution, are their dearest treasure. More than the pealing of the bells,
it will be the return of the old, happy laughter, of carefree security,
lost by the Cuban people, which will signify liberation.

# One Year of Armed Struggle

By the beginning of 1958 we had been fighting for more than a year. A brief recapitulation is necessary—of our military, organizational, and political situation, and our progress.

Concerning the military aspect, let us recall that our troops had disembarked on December 2, 1956 at Las Coloradas Beach. Three days later we were taken by surprise and routed at Alegría de Pío. We regrouped ourselves at the end of the month and began small-scale actions, appropriate to our current strength, at La Plata, a small barracks on the banks of the La Plata river, on the southern coast of Oriente.

During this period between the disembarkation and prompt defeat at Alegría de Pío and the battle of El Uvero, our troop was composed primarily of a single guerrilla group, led by Fidel Castro, and it was characterized by constant mobility. (We could call this the nomadic phase.)

Between December 2 and May 28, the date of the battle of El Uvero, we slowly established links with the city. These relations, during this period, were characterized by lack of understanding on the part of the urban movement's leadership of our importance as the vanguard of the Revolution and of Fidel's stature as its leader.

Then, two distinct opinions began to crystallize regarding the

196

tactics to be followed. They corresponded to two distinct concepts of strategy, which were thereafter known as the *Sierra* and the *Llano*. Our discussions and our internal conflicts were quite sharp. Nevertheless, the fundamental concerns of this phase were survival and the establishment of a guerrilla base.

The peasantry's reactions have already been analyzed many times. Immediately after the Alegría de Pío disaster there was a warm sentiment of comradeship and spontaneous support for our defeated troop. After our regrouping and the first clashes, simultaneously with repressive actions by the Batista army, there was terror among the peasants and coldness toward our forces. The fundamental problem was: if they saw us they had to denounce us. If the Army learned of our presence through other sources, they were lost. Denouncing us did violence to their own conscience and, in any case, put them in danger, since revolutionary justice was speedy.

In spite of a terrorized or at least a neutralized and insecure peasantry which chose to avoid this serious dilemma by leaving the Sierra, our army was entrenching itself more and more, taking control of the terrain and achieving absolute control of a zone of the Maestra extending beyond Mount Turquino in the east and toward the Caracas Peak in the west. Little by little, as the peasants came to recognize the invincibility of the guerrillas and the long duration of the struggle, they began responding more logically, joining our army as fighters. From that moment on, not only did they join our ranks but they provided supportive action. After that the guerrilla army was strongly entrenched in the countryside, especially since it is usual for peasants to have relatives throughout the zone. This is what we call "dressing the guerrillas in palm leaves."

The column was strengthened not only through aid given by peasants and by individual volunteers but also by the forces sent from the National Committee and by the Oriente Provincial Committee, which had considerable autonomy. In the period between the disembarkation and El Uvero, a column arrived consisting of some fifty men divided into five fighting squads, each with a weapon, although the weapons were not uniform and only thirty were of good quality. The battle of La Plata and El Arroyo del Infierno took place before this group joined us. We had been taken by surprise in the Altos de Espinosa, losing one of our men there; the same thing almost happened in the Gaviro region, after a spy, whose mission it was to kill Fidel, led the Army to us three times.

The bitter experiences of these surprises and our arduous life in the mountains were tempering us as veterans. The new troop received its baptism of fire at the battle of El Uvero. This action was of great importance because it marked the moment in which we carried out a frontal attack in broad daylight against a well-defended post. It was one of the bloodiest episodes of the war, in terms of the duration of the battle and the number of participants. As a consequence of this clash the enemy was dislodged from the coastal zones of the Sierra Maestra.

After El Uvero I was named Chief of Column Two, later called Column Four, which was to operate east of Turquino. It is worth noting that the column led by Fidel personally was to operate primarily to the west of Mount Turquino, and ours on the other side, as far as we could extend ourselves. There was a certain tactical independence of command, but we were under Fidel's orders and kept in touch with him every week or two by messenger.

This division of forces coincided with the July 26th anniversary, and while the troops of Column One, the José Martí Column, attacked Estrada Palma, we marched rapidly toward Bueycito, a settlement which we attacked and took in our column's first battle. Between that time and January 1958, the consolidation of rebel territory was achieved. The Army, in order to penetrate this territory, had to concentrate forces and advance in strong columns; preparations were extensive and results limited, since they lacked mobility. Various enemy columns were encircled and others decimated, or at least stopped. Our knowledge of the zone and our maneuverability increased, and we entered the sedentary, fixed-encampment period. In the first attack on Pino del Agua we used subtler methods, hoodwinking the enemy completely, since we were by then familiar with their habits. It was as Fidel had anticipated: a few days after he let himself be seen in the area, the punitive expedition would arrive, my men would ambush it; meanwhile Fidel would pop up elsewhere.

At the end of the year the enemy troops retreated from the Sierra again, and we remained in control of the territory between Caracas Peak and Pino del Agua, on the west and east; on the south was the sea, and the Army occupied the small villages on the slopes of the Maestra to the north.

Our zone of operations was to be broadly extended when Pino del Agua was attacked for the second time by our entire troop under the personal command of Fidel. Two new columns were formed, the "Frank País," commanded by Raúl, and Almeida's column. Both had come out of Column One, commanded by Fidel, which was a steady supplier of these offshoots, created for the purpose of establishing our forces in distant territories.

This was a period of consolidation for our army, lasting until the second battle of Pino del Agua on February 16, 1958. It was characterized by deadlock: we were unable to attack the enemy's fortified and relatively easily defended positions, while they did not advance on us.

We had suffered the deaths of the "Granma" martyrs; we mourned the loss of all of them but especially of Ñico Márquez. Other fighters who, because of their intrepidity and their moral qualities, had acquired great prestige among the troops had also lost their lives during this first year. Among them we can mention Nano and Julio Díaz, not brothers, both of whom died in the battle of El Uvero; Ciro Redondo, who fell at Mar Verde; Captain Soto, who met his death in the battle of San Lorenzo. In the cities, among the many martyrs of our struggle, the greatest loss to the Revolution until that time was Frank País, who died in Santiago de Cuba.

To the list of military feats in the Sierra Maestra must be added the work carried out by the Llano forces in the cities. There were groups fighting against the Batista regime in the principal towns of the nation, but the two focal points of the struggle were Havana and Santiago.

Full liaison between the Llano and the Sierra was always lacking, due to two fundamental factors: the geographical isolation of the Sierra, and tactical and strategic divergencies between the two groups. This latter situation arose from differing social and political conceptions. The Sierra was isolated because of natural conditions and also because the Army's cordon was sometimes extremely difficult to pass.

In this brief sketch of the country's struggle during the course of a year we must mention the activities, generally fruitless and culminating in unfortunate results, of other groups of fighters.

March 13, 1957, the Student Directorate attacked the [Presidential] Palace in an attempt to bring Batista to justice. In that action a choice handful of fighters fell, headed by the president of the FEU [Federación Estudiantil Universitaria]—a great fighter, a real symbol of our young people, "Manzanita" Echeverría.

A few months later, in May, a landing was attempted. It had probably already been betrayed before setting out from Miami, since it was financed by the traitor Prío. It resulted in a virtual massacre of all its participants. This was the "El Corintia" expedition, led by Calixto Sánchez, who was killed together with his comrades by Cowley, the assassin from northern Oriente, who was later brought to justice by members of our Movement.

Fighting groups were established in El Escambray, some of them led by the 26th of July Movement and others by the Student Directorate. The latter groups were originally led by a member of the Directorate who betrayed first them and then the Revolution itself—Gutiérrez Menoyo, today in exile. The fighters loyal to the Directorate formed a separate column that was later commanded by Major Chomón; those who remained set up the Second National Front of Escambray.

Small nuclei were formed in the Cristal and Baracoa mountains which were sometimes half guerrilla, half belly-soldiers; Raúl cleaned them up when he invaded with Column Six. Another incident in the armed struggle of that period was the uprising at the Cienfuegos Naval Base on September 5, 1957, led by Lieutenant San Román, who was assassinated when the coup failed. The Base was not supposed to rise alone, nor was this a spontaneous action. It was part of a large underground movement among the armed forces, led by a group of so-called pure military men, untainted by the crimes of the dictatorship, which was penetrated by—today it is obvious—*yanqui* imperialism. For some obscure reason the rising was postponed to a later date but the Cienfuegos Naval Base did not receive the order in time and, unable to stop the rising, decided to go through with it. At first they were in control but they committed the tragic mistake of not heading for the Escambray mountains, only a few minutes distant from Cienfuegos, at a time when they controlled the entire city and had the means to form a solid front in the mountains.

National and local leaders of the 26th of July Movement participated. So did the people; at least they shared in the enthusiasm that led to the revolt, and some of them took up arms. This may have created moral obligations on the part of the uprising's leaders, tying them even closer to the conquered city; but the course of events followed a line characteristic of this type of coup, which history has seen and will see again.

Obviously an important role was played by the underestimation of the guerrilla struggle by Academy-oriented military men, by their lack of confidence in the guerrilla movement as an expression of the people's struggle. Thus it was that the conspirators, probably assuming that without the aid of their comrades-in-arms they were lost, decided to carry on a fight to the death within the narrow boundaries of a city, their backs to the sea, until they were virtually annihilated by the superior forces of the enemy, which had mobilized its troops at its convenience and converged on Cienfuegos. The 26th of July Movement, participating as an unarmed ally, could not have changed the picture, even if its leaders had seen the outcome clearly, which they did not. The lesson for the future is: he who has the strength dictates the strategy.

Large-scale killing of civilians, repeated failures, murders committed by the dictatorship in various aspects of the struggle we have analyzed, point to guerrilla action on favorable terrain as the best expression of the technique of popular struggle against a despotic and still strong government, the least grievous for the sons of the people. After the guerrilla force was set up, we could count our losses on our fingers—comrades of outstanding courage and tenacity in battle, to be sure. But in the cities it was not only the resolute ones who died, but many among their followers who were not total revolutionaries, many who were innocent of any involvement at all. This was due to greater vulnerability in the face of repressive action.

By the end of this first year of struggle, a generalized uprising throughout the country was looming on the horizon. There were acts of sabotage, ranging from those which were well-planned and carried out on a high technical level to trivial terrorist acts arising from individual initiative, leaving a tragic toll of innocent deaths and sacrifices among the best fighters, without their signifying any real advantage to the people's cause.

Our military situation was being consolidated and the territory we occupied was extensive. We were in a state of armed truce with Batista; his men did not go up into the Sierra and ours hardly ever went down. Their encirclement was as effective as they could make it but our troops still managed to evade them.

Organizationally, our guerrilla army had developed sufficiently to have, by the year's end, elementary organization of provisions, certain minimal industrial services, hospitals, and communications services.

The *guerrillero's* problems were very simple: to subsist as an individual he needed small amounts of food, certain indispensable items of clothing and medicaments; to subsist as a guerrilla force, that is, as an armed force in struggle, he needed arms and ammunition; for his political development he needed channels of propaganda. In order to assure these minimal necessities, a communications and information apparatus was required.

In the beginning the small guerrilla units, some twenty men, would eat a meager ration of Sierra vegetables, chicken soup on holidays; sometimes the peasants provided a pig, for which they were scrupulously paid. As the guerrilla force grew and groups of *pre-guerrilleros* were trained, more provisions were needed. The Sierra peasants did not have cattle and generally theirs was a subsistence diet. They depended on the sale of their coffee to buy indispensable processed items, such as salt. As an initial step we arranged with certain peasants that they should plant specified crops —beans, corn, rice, etc.—which we guaranteed to purchase. At the same time we came to terms with certain merchants in nearby towns for the supplying of foodstuffs and equipment. Mule teams were organized, belonging to the guerrilla forces.

As for medicines, we obtained them in the cities, not always in the quantity or quality we needed; but at least we were able to maintain some kind of functioning apparatus for their acquisition.

The problem of supplying ourselves with arms was another story. It was difficult to bring arms from the *llano;* to the natural dif-

ficulties of geographical isolation were added the arms requirements
of the city forces themselves, and their reluctance to deliver them
to the guerrillas. Fidel was constantly involved in sharp discussions
in an effort to get equipment to us. The only substantial shipment
made to us during that first year of struggle, except for what the
combatants brought with them, was the remainder of the arms used
in the attack on the Palace. These were transported with the co-
operation of a large landowner and timber merchant of the zone,
Babún, whom I have already mentioned.

Our ammunition was limited in quantity and lacking in the
necessary variety, but it was impossible for us to manufacture it or
even to recharge cartridges in this first period, except for bullets for
the .38 revolver, which our gunsmith would recharge with a little
gunpowder, and some of the .30–06's which were used in the single-
shot guns, since they caused the semi-automatics to jam and inter-
fered with their proper functioning.

Certain sanitary regulations were established at this time, and the
first hospitals were organized, one of them set up in the zone under
my command, in a remote, inaccessible place, offering relative
security to the wounded, since it was invisible from the air. But,
since it was in the heart of a dense forest, its dampness made it
unhealthy for the wounded and the sick. This hospital was organized by Comrade Sergio del Valle. Drs. Martínez Páez, Vallejo,
and Piti Fajardo organized similar hospitals for Fidel's column,
which were improved during the second year of the struggle.

The troop's equipment needs, such as cartridge boxes and belts,
knapsacks, and shoes were met by a small leather-goods workshop
set up in our zone. When we turned out the first army cap I took it
to Fidel, bursting with pride. It caused quite an uproar; everyone
claimed that it was a *guagüero's** cap, a word unknown to me until
then. The only one who showed me any mercy was a municipal

---

* Cuban (and Caribbean) slang for "bus driver."

councillor from Manzanillo, who was visiting the camp in order to make arrangements for joining us and who took it with him as a souvenir.

Our most important industrial installation was a forge and armory, where defective arms were repaired and bombs, mines, and the famous M-26 [Molotov cocktail] were made. At first the mines were made of tin cans and we filled them with material from bombs frequently dropped by enemy planes which had not exploded. These mines were very faulty. Furthermore they had a firing pin, which struck the detonator, that frequently missed. Later a comrade had the idea of using the whole bomb for major attacks, removing the detonator and replacing it with a loaded shotgun; we would pull the trigger from a distance by means of a cord, and this would cause an explosion. Afterward, we perfected the system, making special fuses of metal alloy and electric detonators. These gave better results. Even though we were the first to develop this, it was given real impetus by Fidel; later, Raúl in his new operations center created stronger industries than those we had during the first year of war.

To please the smokers among us we set up a cigar factory; the cigars we made were terrible but, lacking better, we found them heavenly.

Our army's butcher shop was supplied with cattle which we confiscated from informers and *latifundistas*. We shared equitably, one part for the peasant population and one part for our troop.

As for the dissemination of our ideas, first we started a small newspaper, *El Cubano Libre,* in memory of those heroes of the jungle.* Three or four issues came out under our supervision; it was later edited by Luis Orlando Rodríguez. After him, Carlos Franqui gave it new impetus. We had a mimeograph machine brought up to us from the *llano,* on which the paper was printed.

---

* A newspaper by this name was published by the *Mambis,* independence fighters against Spain in 1868–1878, and 1895.

By the end of the first year and the beginning of the second, we had a small radio transmitter. The first regular broadcasts were made in February 1958; our only listeners were Palencho, a peasant who lived on the hill facing the station, and Fidel, who was visiting our camp in preparation for the attack on Pino del Agua. He listened to it on our own receiver. Little by little the technical quality of the broadcasts improved. It was then taken over by Column One and by December 1958 had become one of the Cuban stations with the highest "rating" [in English in the original].

All these small advances, including our equipment—such as a winch and some generators, which we laboriously carried up to the Sierra so as to have electric light—were due to our own connections. To cope with our difficulties we had to begin creating a network of communications and information. In this respect Lydia Doce played an important part in my column, Clodomira in Fidel's.

Help came in those days not only from the people in the neighboring villages; even the city bourgeoisie contributed equipment. Our lines of communication reached as far as the towns of Contramaestre, Palma, Bueycito, Las Minas de Bueycito, Estrada Palma, Yara, Bayamo, Manzanillo, Guisa. These places served as relay stations. Goods were then carried on muleback along hidden trails in the Sierra up to our positions. At times, those among our men who were in training but were not yet armed went down to the nearest towns, such as Yao or Las Minas, with some of our armed men, or they would go to well-stocked stores in the district. They carried supplies up to our retreat on their backs. The only item we never—or almost never—lacked in the Sierra Maestra was coffee. At times we lacked salt, one of the most important foods for survival, whose virtues we became aware of only when it was scarce.

When we began to broadcast from our own transmitter, the existence of our troops and their fighting determination became known throughout the Republic; our links began to become more extensive and complicated, even reaching Havana and Camagüey in the west, where we had important supply centers, and Santiago in the east.

Our information service developed in such a way that the peasants in the zone immediately notified us of the presence, not only of the Army, but of any stranger; we were easily able to detain any such person while investigating his activities. Thus were eliminated many Army agents and spies who infiltrated the zone for the purpose of prying into our lives and actions.

We began structuring a legal service, but no law of the Sierra was yet promulgated. Such was our organizational situation at the beginning of the last year of the war.

As for the political struggle, it was very complicated and contradictory. The Batista dictatorship was supported by a Congress elected by so many frauds that it could count on a comfortable majority to do its bidding.

Certain dissident opinions were allowed expression—when there was no censorship—but official spokesmen for and officials of the regime, calling for national unity, spoke with powerful voices and the networks transmitted their messages throughout the island. The hysterical voice of Otto Meruelo alternated with the pompous buffooneries of Pardo Llada and Conte Agüero. The latter, repeating in writing what he had broadcast, called on "brother Fidel" to accept coexistence with the Batista regime.

The opposition groups were varied and dissimilar, even though most had as a common denominator the wish to take power (read: public funds) for themselves. This brought in its wake a sordid internal struggle to win that victory. The groups were all infiltrated by Batista agents who, at key moments, reported their main activities. Although these groups were often characterized by gangsterism and opportunism, they also had their martyrs.

In effect, Cuban society was in such total disarray that brave and honest men were sacrificing their lives to maintain the comfortable existence of such personages as Prío Socarrás.

The Student Directorate took the path of insurrectional struggle, but their movement was independent of ours and they had their own line. The PSP [Partido Socialista Popular] joined with us in certain concrete activities, but mutual distrust hampered joint action and, fundamentally, the party of the workers did not understand with sufficient clarity the role of the guerrilla force, nor Fidel's personal role in our revolutionary struggle.

In fraternal discussion I once made an observation to a PSP leader which he later repeated to others as a true characterization of that period: "You are capable of creating cadres who can silently endure the most terrible tortures in jail, but you cannot create cadres who can take a machine gun nest." As I saw it from my vantage point as a *guerrillero,* this was the consequence of a strategic concept: the decision to struggle against imperialism and the excesses of the exploiting classes, together with an inability to envision the possibility of taking power. Later, some of their men, of guerrilla spirit, were to join us, but by then the end of the armed struggle was near; therefore its influence on them was slight.

Within our own movement there were two quite clear-cut tendencies, which we have already referred to as the Sierra and the Llano. Differences over strategic concepts separated us. The Sierra was already confident of being able to carry out the guerrilla struggle, to spread it to other places and thus, from the countryside, to encircle the cities held by the dictatorship; by strangulation and attrition to provoke the breakup of the regime. The Llano took an ostensibly more revolutionary position, that of armed struggle in all the towns, culminating in a general strike which would topple Batista and allow the prompt taking of power.

This position was only apparently more revolutionary, because in that period the political development of the Llano comrades was incomplete and their conception of a general strike was too narrow. A general strike was called on April 9 of the following year, secretly, without warning, without prior political preparation or mass action. It ended in defeat.

These two tendencies were represented in the National Committee of the Movement, which changed as the struggle developed. In the preparatory stage, until Fidel left for Mexico, the National Committee was constituted by: Fidel, Raúl, Faustino Pérez, Pedro Miret, Ñico López, Armando Hart, Pepe Suárez, Pedro Aguilera, Luis Bonito, Jesús Montané, Melba Hernández, and Haydée Santamaría—if my information is exact. My personal participation at that time was very limited and documentation is scarce. Later, for reasons of incompatibility, Pepe Suárez, Pedro Aguilera, and Luis Bonito withdrew; while we were in Mexico the following people joined the committee: Mario Hidalgo, Aldo Santamaría, Carlos Franqui, Gustavo Arcos, and Frank País.

Of all these comrades the only ones to go to the Sierra during the first year and remain there were Fidel and Raúl. Faustino Pérez, member of the "Granma" expedition, was put in charge of work in the city, Pedro Miret was jailed a few hours before we were to leave Mexico. He remained there until the following year, when he arrived in Cuba with an arms shipment. Ñico López died only a few days after the landing; Armando Hart was jailed at the end of that year (or early in the next); Jesús Montané was jailed after the landing; so was Mario Hidalgo; Melba Hernández and Haydée Santamaría worked in the cities; Aldo Santamaría and Carlos Franqui joined the struggle in the Sierra the following year; Gustavo Arcos remained in Mexico, in charge of political liaison and supplies; and Frank País, assigned to political work in Santiago, died in July 1957.

Later, the following were to join us in the Sierra: Celia Sánchez, who was with us during all of 1958; Vilma Espín, who had first worked in Santiago and afterward, until the end of the war, with Raúl Castro's column; Marcelo Fernández, coordinator of the Movement, who replaced Faustino after the April 9 strike, stayed with us only a few weeks, since his work was in the towns; René Ramos Latour, assigned to the organizing of the militia in the Llano came up to the Sierra after the April 9 fiasco and died heroically as a major, during the second year of the struggle; David Salvador, in charge of the labor movement, on which he left the imprint of his opportunist and divisive actions. He was later to betray the Revolution and is now in prison. Some of the Sierra fighters, such as Almeida, were to join some time later.

As can be seen, during this stage the Llano comrades constituted the majority, and their political background, which had not been very much influenced by the process of revolutionary maturation, led them to favor a certain type of "civil" action, and to a kind of resistance to the *caudillo* they saw in Fidel and to the "militarist" faction represented by us in the Sierra. The divergencies were already apparent, but they were not yet strong enough to provoke the violent discussion which characterized the second year of the war.

It is important to point out that the fighters against the dictatorship in both the Sierra and the Llano were able to sustain opinions on tactics that were at times diametrically opposed without allowing this to lead to an abandonment of the insurrectional struggle. Their revolutionary spirit continued to increase until the moment in which, victory having been won and followed by the first experiences in the struggle against imperialism, we all united closely in one organism, led indisputably by Fidel. This group then joined together with the Directorate and the PSP to form the PURSC [Partido Unido de la Revolución Socialista Cubana, which in October 1965 became the Communist Party of Cuba]. When we encountered pressures from outside our movement, attempts to divide or infiltrate it, we always presented a common front; even

those comrades who at that moment saw the Cuban Revolution
with imperfect perspective were wary of opportunists.

When Felipe Pazos, availing himself of the name of the 26th of
July Movement, took over for himself and for the most corrupt
oligarchical interests of Cuba the positions offered by the Miami
Pact, including the post of Provisional President, the entire Movement turned out to be solidly united against such an attitude and
supported the letter that Fidel sent to the organizations involved in
the struggle against Batista. We reproduce this document here in
its entirety. It is a historic document. It is dated December 14, 1957
and was copied out by Celia Sánchez, since during that period it
was impossible to print it.

CUBA
December 14, 1957

To the leaders of:
The Revolutionary Party
The Party of the Cuban People
The Organization of *Auténticos*
The Federation of University Students
The Revolutionary Directorate
The Revolutionary Workers Directorate

It is my moral, patriotic, and even historic duty to address this
letter to you; the events and the circumstances which have profoundly troubled us during this time, which have been, furthermore,
the most disturbing and the most difficult since our arrival in Cuba,
have made the drafting of this statement indispensable. Wednesday, November 20th, a day when our forces sustained three battles
during six consecutive hours, a day which suggests the sacrifices and
the efforts which, without the slightest aid from other organizations, our men have made, was the very day when we received in
our area of operations the surprising news and the document con-

taining the public and the secret terms of a so-called Unity Pact which, it appears, has been signed in Miami by the July 26th Movement and the organizations to whom I am addressing myself. The arrival of these papers—one has to see in this the irony of fate, since what we needed was arms—coincides with the strongest offensive the dictatorship has launched against us.

In conditions of struggles such as ours, communications are difficult. In spite of everything, it was necessary to convene, right out in the field, the leaders of our organization to discuss this matter, in which not only the prestige but the historic justification of the July 26th Movement is at stake.

For those who struggle against an enemy incomparably superior in number and in weapons, and who for a whole year have not been supported by anything other than the dignity with which one must fight for a truly cherished cause and the conviction that it is a cause worth dying for; for these men bitterly isolated by the neglect of their comrades who, even when they had the means, have systematically, not to say criminally, refused all aid; for these comrades who have witnessed at close range daily sacrifice in its purest and most disinterested form, and have so frequently suffered the pain of seeing the best among them fall, at a moment when one asks with anguish who will be the next victim in the next and inevitable holocaust; in this dark hour, when one cannot even see the day of triumph for which we struggle with such steadfastness, with no other hope or solace than that of not sacrificing ourselves in vain— how can one not understand that the news of a pact, deliberately broadcast, which commits the Movement to a future course without that consultation by the signatories with the leaders and fighters which propriety, not to say simple courtesy, demands . . . well, this news can only wound us to the quick and provoke our indignation. To act in an improper fashion always brings with it the worst consequences. And those who consider themselves capable of overthrowing a tyranny and of the even harder enterprise of achieving

the reorganization of a country after the revolutionary overturn—
they would do well not to forget it.

The July 26th Movement has never appointed a delegation nor
granted authority to anyone to participate in the negotiations in
question. The Movement, however, would not have been opposed
to such a step if it had been consulted on this, and it would have
been concerned to give concrete instructions to its representatives
on a matter so important to the present and future activities of our
organization. Instead, our information concerning relations with
these various groups was limited to a report by Sr. Lester Rodríguez
—whom we had commissioned exclusively to settle with them certain problems of a military nature—who told us the following: "I
can report to you on the subject of Prío and of the Directorate
that I have had a series of conferences with them exclusively for
the purpose of coordinating military plans right up to the formation
of a provisional government guaranteed and respected by the three
groups. Of course, I pointed out that it was necessary first of all to
accept the principles of the Sierra Letter, which specifies that this
government should be formed in accord with the will of the political forces of the country. First hitch.

"During the general strike, we had an emergency meeting. I
then proposed that considering the circumstances we utilize all the
forces at hand in an effort to resolve Cuba's problem once and for
all. Prío answered that he did not have enough forces to go into
the enterprise with assurance of victory, and that it would be mad-
ness to go along with my proposal. To which I retorted that he
should please let me know when everything was in readiness to
weigh anchor; then we would be able to speak of the possibility of
pacts. That he should be so kind, in the meanwhile, to let me work
—me and consequently those whom I represent as part of the 26th
of July Movement—with complete independence. My firm opinion
is that there is no way to come to an understanding with these gen-
tlemen and that it is better even to refrain from trying to do so in

the future because, at the moment when Cuba most needed it, they denied having the material which they had never stopped accumulating and with which they are glutted."

This report needs no commentary, and confirms our suspicion; we could not expect any outside aid.

We recognize that the organizations that you represent have considered it advisable to discuss the terms of unity with certain members of our Movement: it was inconceivable that you should publicize these as settled agreements without having advised the national leaders of the Movement and without their consent, all the less so since these agreements changed the very institutional foundations to which we had subscribed in the Sierra Manifesto. To behave so is to make a pact for publicity purposes, and to usurp the name of our organization.

The situation is paradoxical to say the least: at the very moment when the national leadership, with its underground headquarters somewhere on the island, is preparing to oppose, from the outset, the terms which are publicly and privately proposed as the basis for an agreement, this leadership learns through underground circulars and through the foreign press that it had been shouted from the rooftops that these very terms constituted the basis for agreement. It thus found itself presented with a public *fait accompli,* and compelled either to deny it, with all the confusion and injury to morale which that would involve, or to accept it without even having expressed its opinions. And, as might be expected, a copy of the document only reached us in the Sierra several days after it had been published.

Faced with this dilemma, the national leadership, before making a public denial concerning the agreements in question, asserted to you the need to return to the principles of the Sierra Manifesto; meanwhile holding a meeting in rebel territory where the views of each member of the leadership were expressed and analyzed, and where as a result a unanimous resolution was adopted which forms the basis for this letter.

It goes without saying that any unity agreement must be well received by national and international public opinion. Because, among other reasons, the real situation of the political and revolutionary anti-Batista forces is not known; because in Cuba itself the word unity possessed great prestige in the days when the relationship of forces was really very different from what it is today; and finally because it is always best to unite all efforts, from the most enthusiastic to the most lukewarm.

However, what is important for the Revolution is not unity in itself, but the groundwork of this unity, the form it assumes, and the patriotic intentions which animate it.

To decide in favor of this unity on terms that we have not even discussed, to have them ratified by people who are not qualified to do so, and to proclaim unity without further ado, from the comfortable refuge of a foreign city, and thus to put the Movement under the necessity of confronting a public opinion which has been deluded by a fraudulent pact, that is a dirty trick of the worst sort —one which, however, will not destroy a truly revolutionary organization; it is a fraud against the country, a fraud against the world.

And here is what made the operation possible: while the leaders of the various organizations which subscribed to this pact met abroad and made an imaginary revolution, the leaders of the 26th of July Movement were in Cuba, leading a very real revolution.

These lines are superfluous? So be it. I would not have written them were it not for this bitterness and this mortification that we feel because of the way you tried to associate the Movement with this pact, even given the fact that differences over procedure should never prevail over the essential. We would have accepted it in spite of everything, for the positive value that unity always offers, for the value of certain projects of the Liberation Junta, for the aid offered us which we really need, if we did not find ourselves in pure and simple disagreement with some of its essential principles.

Even if our situation were to become desperate, if the dictatorship were to mobilize as many thousands of soldiers as they wanted in an effort to annihilate us, we would never accept the sacrifice of certain fundamental principles and of our conception of the Cuban Revolution.

And these principles are clearly stated in the Sierra Manifesto.

To suppress, in a unity declaration, the principle of hostility toward foreign intervention in the internal affairs of Cuba is an act of the most lukewarm patriotism and of manifest cowardice.

To declare that we are opposed to such intervention, is not only to oppose it on behalf of the Revolution—for it would be an offense against our sovereignty and, let it be said, against a principle dear to all the peoples of Latin America—it is equally to oppose intervention in support of the dictatorship, in the form of shipments of planes, bombs, modern tanks and weapons, thanks to which it maintains itself in power and by reason of which no one, with the exception of the peasant population of the Sierra, has suffered more than we. Finally, to enforce respect for the principle of non-intervention would in itself overturn the dictatorship. Are we going to be so cowardly concerning this point as not to dare demand the withdrawal of pro-Batista foreign intervention? Or so insincere as to make a behind-the-scenes request for our chestnuts to be pulled out of the fire? Or so feeble as not to risk pronouncing a single word on the question? How, under these conditions, can we have the temerity to declare ourselves revolutionaries and endorse the claim to historic significance of this unity declaration?

The unity declaration has likewise eliminated the formal commitment to reject any form of military junta as the provisional government of the Republic.

The worst thing that could befall the nation at this moment, however much it may let itself be deluded by the false illusion that Cuba's problem will be resolved by the elimination of the dictator, would be the replacement of Batista by a military junta. And certain civilians of the worst sort, who were actually accomplices on March 10th* and who subsequently broke away, perhaps because of their consuming ambition and their immoderate fondness for the blackjack, envisage a solution of this nature, which only the enemies of our country's progress could view with favor.

American experience has proved that all military juntas slip toward autocracy; the worst of the evils which have martyrized this continent is the entrenchment of military castes in countries which have fewer wars than Switzerland and more generals than Prussia; one of the most legitimate aspirations of our people at this crucial hour when its democratic and republican destiny is being either salvaged or destroyed for many years to come is to preserve, as the most precious legacy of its liberators, the civilian tradition which was born in the struggles for emancipation and which would be trampled underfoot at the very instant when a uniformed junta put itself at the head of the Republic (something that none of our generals in the independence struggle, not even the most vainglorious among them, was tempted to do, neither in wartime nor peacetime). If all this is so, then just how far shall we have gone along the road of renunciation if, out of a fear of wounding sensibilities (more imaginary than real among the honest military men who may support us), we devote ourselves to suppressing the statement of so important a principle? Or is it, then, that one does not understand that a timely statement would avert the danger of a military junta which would certainly prolong the civil war? Well: we have no hesitation in stating that if a military junta replaces Batista, the July 26th Movement will resolutely continue its liberation cam-

---

* March 10, 1952, date on which Batista carried out a coup d'état.

Ve prefer to struggle harder today rather than fall into omless abysses tomorrow. No plaything for the military: neither a military junta nor a puppet government!

Are we perhaps waiting for the generals of March 10, before whom Batista would gladly give way once he felt himself strongly menaced, seeing in this step the most viable means of effecting the necessary transfer of powers with a minimum of damage to his own interests and those of his coterie? To what delusions this lack of foresight, lack of an ideal, lack of will to fight, lead the Cuban politicians!

If you do not have faith in the people, if you do not count on their great reserves of energy and combativeness, you do not have the right to lay hands upon their destiny in order to block and frustrate it at the most heroic and hopeful moment for its Republican existence. Let the politicos, with their deals, their puerile ambitions, their desperate greed, their advance division of the spoils, not meddle with the revolutionary process, because in Cuba men are dying for something more than that. Let the hack politicians become revolutionaries, if they wish! But let them not transform the Revolution into degenerate politics, because too much of our people's blood is being spilled today and too many enormous sacrifices have been made to deserve such a worthless deception tomorrow.

Aside from these two fundamental principles which were omitted from the unity document, we are likewise in disagreement on other points:

If we are to accept sub-section B of secret clause II, relating to the powers of the Liberation Junta, which provides for naming "the President of the Republic who will fill that office in the Provisional Government," then we cannot accept sub-section C of the same clause, which includes among those powers: "To approve or disapprove, in its totality, the Cabinet to be named by the President of the Republic, as well as the changes that may arise in the case of a total or partial crisis."

How can it be imagined that the President's right to appoint and remove his collaborators should remain subject to the approval of a body not connected with the state power? Is it not clear that inasmuch as the Junta is composed of representatives of different parties and sectors and, consequently, of different interests, the appointment of Cabinet members would be nothing more than the search for the least common denominator, as the only means of reaching agreement on diverse questions? Is it possible to accept a clause which implies the establishment of two executives within the state? The only guarantee that all the sectors of the country must demand of the Provisional Government is that it base its mission on a minimum fixed program and that it play its role of moderator with absolute impartiality during the transitional stage leading to complete constitutional normality.

To attempt to interfere in the appointment of each minister is tantamount to wanting to control the public administration so as to subjugate it to political interests. This procedure has meaning only for the parties and organizations which, lacking mass support, can expect to survive only within the canons of traditional politics, but it is incompatible with the exalted political and revolutionary goals pursued by the 26th of July Movement for the Republic.

The mere existence of secret agreements referring not to organizational questions of the resistance nor to plans for action, but to problems concerning which the nation should have its say—such as the structure of the future government—and which for this reason should be publicly proclaimed, is in itself unacceptable. Martí said: "In the Revolution, methods are secret but the ends must always be public."

Another point which is equally inadmissible for the July 26th Movement is secret clause VIII, which says: "The revolutionary forces, with their weapons, will become part of the regular armed institutions of the Republic."

First of all, what is meant by revolutionary forces? Does this mean that one accepts into the police force, or as a sailor or soldier, those whose arms are today carefully hidden, but who will not hesitate to brandish them on the day of victory, and who fold their arms while a handful of compatriots fight against the organized forces of the tyranny? Are we thus going to shield, in a revolutionary document, the very virus of gangsterism and anarchy which was the scourge of the Republic in a still-recent past?

Experience in the territory which we occupy has taught us that the maintenance of public order is an important problem for the country. Facts have proved to us that from the time the existing order is suppressed, a number of bonds are dissolved and delinquency, if it is not stopped in time, flourishes everywhere. It is by the timely application of stringent measures, with the full and total approval of the population, that we have put an end to the first manifestations of banditry. The peasants, formerly accustomed to consider an agent of authority as an enemy of the people, used to offer protection from prosecution to a fugitive who had problems with the authorities. Today, they see our soldiers as the defenders of their interests and order reigns solidly, its best guardians being the citizenry itself.

Anarchy is the worst enemy of the revolutionary process. To combat it henceforth is a fundamental necessity. He who does not understand this should not concern himself with the fate of the Revolution; it is natural that those who have not sacrificed themselves for it should not care about its survival.

The nation must know that justice will be done and that crime will be punished, wherever it appears.

The July 26th Movement claims for itself the duty of maintaining public order and reorganizing the armed institutions of the Republic.

1) Because it is the only organization possessing disciplined militia throughout the country and an army in the field which has won more than twenty victories over the enemy.

2) Because our fighters have given proof a thousand times of their generosity and the absence of hate toward the soldiers by always sparing their lives, by caring for those wounded in battle, by never torturing an opponent even if it were known that he had important information. And they have maintained this wartime conduct with a magnanimity which commands admiration.

3) Because it is necessary to infuse the armed institutions with that spirit of justice and nobility which the July 26th Movement has spread among its own soldiers.

4) Because the equanimity which we have displayed in this war is the best guarantee that honorable military men have nothing to fear from the Revolution, and they will not have to pay for the misdeeds of those who, by their crimes and their shame have brought disgrace to the military uniform.

Certain other aspects of the unity declaration remain difficult to grasp. How is it possible to achieve agreement without having defined a strategy of struggle? Were the *auténticos* still thinking of a *putsch* in the capital? Were they going to continue accumulating arms and more arms which would surely sooner or later fall into the hands of the police, rather than pass them on to the fighters? Lastly, have they accepted the proposition of the general strike as advocated by the July 26th Movement?

In addition, we have the impression that the military importance of the Oriente struggle has been woefully underestimated. Today in the Sierra Maestra, we are no longer making guerrilla war but a war of confrontation. Our forces, inferior in number and armament, take as much advantage as possible of the terrain, of constant surveillance of the enemy, and greater rapidity of movement. It is superfluous to stress the unique importance of the moral factor in this struggle. The results have been astonishing and some day they will be known in detail.

The entire population is in revolt. If it were armed, our detachments would not have to worry about the smallest corner of the country; the peasants would not allow a single enemy to pass. The

defeats of the dictatorship, which persists in sending large-scale reinforcements, could be turned into disasters. Anything I might say to
you concerning the way in which the courage of the people has
been aroused would fall short of the reality. The dictatorship is engaging in barbarous reprisals. The mass murder of peasants rivals
the butchery perpetrated by the Nazis in Europe. They make the
defenseless population pay for each of their defeats. The communiqués of the General Staff announcing rebel losses are always
preceded by a massacre. Such practices have awakened a spirit of
fierce revolt among the people. And the heart bleeds, the spirit is
afflicted at the thought that no one has sent this people a single
gun; at the thought that while here the peasants wait, powerless,
for their homes to be burned down and their families to be murdered, and call for guns with all the strength of despair, arms caches
exist in Cuba which are not being used to destroy even one miserable lackey, and which await seizure by the police or the collapse
of tyranny or the extermination of the rebels.

The conduct of many of our fellow citizens could not have been
more ignoble. There is still time to change and to aid those who
are struggling. From our personal point of view, this has no importance. You should not think that it is self-interest or pride that
dictates these words: our fate is sealed and we are not afflicted with
doubts. Either we will die here, to the last rebel, and in the cities
an entire young generation will perish, or else we shall triumph
over the most incredible obstacles. For us, defeat is not possible.
The year of sacrifices and of heroic deeds which our men have
experienced will not be obliterated by anyone or anything. Our
victories are also real, and cannot easily be erased. Our men, more
resolute than ever, will fight to the last drop of their blood.

It is those who have refused to help us who will suffer defeat;
those who were with us at the beginning and have abandoned us;
those who, having lacked faith in dignity and ideals, squandered
their time and their prestige in shameful deals with the Trujillo
despotism; those who, possessing arms, were led by their own

cowardice to hide them at the moment of combat. They are the ones who blundered, not we.

There is one thing that we can say, loudly and clearly: if we had seen other Cubans fighting for freedom, pursued and on the point of being exterminated, if we had seen them resisting day after day without surrendering or weakening in their resolve, we would not have hesitated for a moment to fly to their assistance and to die with them if necessary. Because we are Cubans and Cubans cannot remain unmoved by the struggle for liberty, even in any other country of Latin America. The Dominicans were mustering their island forces to liberate their people? For each Dominican there were ten Cubans. Somoza's followers invaded Costa Rica? The Cubans hastened there to join the battle. To think that today, when their own country is undergoing an arduous battle for liberty, there are some Cubans in exile, expelled from their fatherland by the dictatorship, who deny their aid to their brothers who fight!

Or, if they are to aid us, will they set unfair conditions? Perhaps, in order to repay their aid, we should offer them a plateau of the Republic as booty? Or else, should we renounce our ideals and make of this war a new art of killing one's fellow men, plunging the country into a useless blood bath which does not redeem the promise with the reward which the country expects from such a sacrifice?

The leadership of the struggle against tyranny is, and will continue to be, in Cuba itself and in the hands of revolutionary fighters. Those who, now or later, wish to be considered leaders of the revolution must be inside the country and must accept directly the responsibilities, risks, and sacrifices required by the situation in Cuba today.

The exiles have a role to play in this struggle, but it is absurd that they should attempt to tell us from abroad which peak we should storm, which sugar plantation we are permitted to burn, which acts of sabotage we can carry off successfully and at which moment, under which circumstances, and in what form we can call a general strike. This is more than absurd, it is ridiculous. Help us abroad by collecting funds among Cuban exiles and émigrés, by leading a publicity campaign for the Cuban cause, denounce from there the crimes of which we here are victims; but do not try to lead from Miami a revolution that is taking shape in all the cities and the fields of the island, amid struggle, tumult, sabotage, strikes, and a thousand other forms of revolutionary activity which the fighting strategy of the July 26th Movement has set into motion.

The national leadership is ready, as it has repeatedly made known, to enter into talks in Cuba with the leaders of any opposition organization whatsoever, for the purpose of coordinating specific plans and carrying out concrete activities deemed to be useful in the overturning of the dictatorship.

The general strike will take place with effective coordination of efforts among the Movimiento de Resistencia Cívica [Movement for Civic Resistance], the Frente Nacional Obrero [National Workers' Front] and any other group which has rejected the spirit of sectarianism and entered into contact with the July 26th Movement, which today finds itself to be the only opposition organization fighting within the country.

The Workers' Section of the July 26th Movement is now organizing strike committees in every labor and industrial center, together with those opposition elements who show support for a work stoppage and who do not seem likely to disappear at the crucial moment. These strike committees will constitute the Frente Nacional Obrero, which will be the only representative of the proletariat which the July 26th Movement will recognize as legitimate.

The overturn of the dictator necessarily implies the removal of an inglorious Congress, of the leadership of the Confederación de Trabajadores Cubanos [Confederation of Cuban Workers], and of all the mayors, governors and other functionaries who, directly or otherwise, relied on the "elections" of November 1, 1954 or on the military *coup d'état* of March 10, 1952 to win their posts. It likewise implies the immediate freeing of political prisoners, whether civil or military, as well as bringing to trial all the accomplices of the crimes, of the dictatorship's despotism.

The new government shall rest on the Constitution of 1940 and will guarantee all the rights recognized by it and will hold itself aloof from all political sectarianism.

The Executive shall assume the legislative functions that the Constitution assigns to the Congress of the Republic and shall have for its principal task the holding of general elections in accordance with the Electoral Code of 1943 and the Constitution of 1940, and putting into effect the ten-point minimum program of the Sierra Manifesto.

The present Supreme Court shall be declared dissolved on account of its inability to resolve the illegal situation created by the *coup d'état;* this does not preclude the subsequent re-appointment of some of its present members who have always defended constitutional principles or have maintained a firm attitude toward the crimes, the absolutism, and the abuses of these years of tyranny.

The President of the Republic shall determine the manner of constituting the new Supreme Court and it shall, in its turn, be charged with reorganizing all the courts and autonomous institutions, dismissing all those who are convicted of involvement in the shady dealings of the dictatorship. The appointment of new functionaries shall be done according to the law. The political parties, under the provisional government, shall enjoy this sole right: namely, the freedom to defend their program before the people, to mobilize and organize the citizens within the framework of our Constitution, and to participate in the general elections.

The necessity of appointing the person called on to occupy the presidency of the Republic has already been elucidated in the Sierra Maestra Manifesto, and our Movement has declared that in its opinion said person should be chosen by all civic institutions. Be that as it may, although five months have passed this question has not yet been resolved and it is becoming increasingly urgent to give the nation the answer to the question: Who shall succeed the dictator? And it is not possible to wait one more day in the face of this large question mark. The July 26th Movement is answering the question. It presents its proposal to the people, as the only possible formula for guaranteeing legality and the development of the preconditions for unity and provisional government. This man must be that upright magistrate of the Oriente Court of Justice, Dr. Manuel Urrutia Lleo. It is not we, but his own conduct, that singles him out, and we expect that he will not refuse this service to the Republic.

The grounds for appointing him are:

1) He has been the member of the judiciary who has most respected the Constitution by declaring, in court chambers after the trial of the "Granma" expeditionaries, that to organize an armed force against the regime does not constitute a crime and was perfectly licit, in accordance with the spirit and the letter of the Constitution and the law—a declaration unprecedented for a magistrate in the history of our struggles for freedom.

2) His life, dedicated to the true administration of justice, assures us that he is professionally and personally sufficiently equipped to maintain the balance among all legitimate interests at the moment when the tyranny is overturned by the people.

3) No one is as free of party spirit as Dr. Manuel Urrutia. In fact, by virtue of his role of judge, he does not belong to any political group. And there exists no other citizen of equal prestige who, without active involvement, is so much identified with the revolutionary cause.

If our conditions—the disinterested conditions of an organization that has assented to the greatest sacrifices, which has not even been consulted before its name was used in a unity manifesto it has not ratified—are rejected, we shall continue the struggle alone, as we have always done, with no other arms than those we take from the enemy in each battle, with no other aid than that of the sorely tried people, with no support other than our ideal.

For, after all, it is the July 26th Movement and it alone th
struggled actively throughout the country and continues to
It is the militants of the Movement and nobody else who have
brought the revolt from the rugged mountains of Oriente all the
way to the western provinces; it is they alone who have carried
out sabotage, burned sugar cane fields, executed the political thugs;
it is the July 26th Movement alone which has been able to organize
the workers of the nation in a revolutionary way; it alone has cooperated in the organization of the movement for civil resistance
in which all civic groups from virtually every region of Cuba are
united.

We would have you know that we have withdrawn from bureau-
cratic entanglements and from participation in the government;
but you must understand once and for all that the July 26th militants have not given up and will never give up guiding and leading
the people—from underground, from the Sierra Maestra or from the
graves where the enemy may fling our dead. We will not give it
up because it is not we but an entire generation which has promised
the people of Cuba to give concrete solutions to their momentous
problems.

We shall conquer or die, alone. The struggle will never be harder
than it was when we were only twelve men, when we did not
have the support of a people inured to war and organized in all
the Sierra, when we did not have as we have today a powerful and
disciplined nationwide organization, when we could not count
on tremendous support from the masses, such as that which was
displayed on the day our unforgettable Frank País died.

In order to die with dignity, company is not necessary.

FIDEL CASTRO RUZ
Sierra Maestra
December 14, 1957

# The Second Battle of Pino del Agua

Fidel felt it was important to strike a resounding blow to take advantage of the fact that censorship had now been lifted, and we prepared ourselves for this.

Once again, Pino del Agua was chosen as the spot where we would execute our plan. We had once attacked Pino del Agua successfully; from then on it had been occupied by the enemy. Even when the troops did not move about very much, their position on the crest of the Sierra Maestra made wide detours necessary, and passing near the area was always dangerous. The elimination of Pino del Agua as an advance position of the Army could be of great strategic importance and, given the new press conditions in the country, could have national repercussions.

From the first days in February, feverish preparations and reconnoitering began, chiefly by Roberto Ruiz and Félix Tamayo (both officers in our present army) for they were from the region. Furthermore, we speeded up preparations on our latest weapon, the M-26, also called "sputnik," to which we attributed an exceptional importance. It was a small bomb made of tinplate, which we first launched by means of a complicated apparatus, a kind of catapult made with the lines from an underwater spear gun. Later we perfected it so that we could launch it by means of a rifle and cartridge, which made the device go much further.

These little bombs made a great deal of noise and were really frightening, but since they had only a tinplate casing, their lethal power was small and they inflicted only minor wounds when they exploded close to some enemy soldier; in addition, it was very difficult to time the moment in which the fuse was lit so that the end of the trajectory and explosion would coincide perfectly. Because of the launching shock, the fuse was apt to go out and the little bomb would not explode, falling intact into enemy hands. When the enemy learned how it worked, they no longer feared it; in this first battle, though, it had its psychological effect.

We made our preparations with great care and on February 16 the attack took place.

The strategic plan was very simple: Fidel, knowing that there was an entire company in the lumber camp, doubted that our troops could take the camp; our goal was to attack it, destroy their posts, surround it, and watch for their reinforcements, for we knew very well that troops on the march are much more alert than quartered troops. We established various ambushes, expecting great results from them. At each one we stationed the number of men necessary to deal with the expected enemy strength.

The attack was directed personally by Fidel, whose Staff was on a hill to the north, commanding a clear view of the lumber camp. The battle plan: Camilo was to advance along the road which comes from Uvero, passing through the Bayamesa; his troops, the advance guard platoon of the Fourth Column, were to take the posts, advance as far as the terrain would permit, and hold on. The retreat of the guards was to be harassed by Captain Raúl Castro Mercader's platoon, situated on the edge of the road to Bayamo; in case the enemy tried to reach the Río Peladero, Captain Guillermo García with some 25 men were waiting for them.

When firing started, our mortar, which had exactly six shells and was manned by Quiala, would come into action; then the siege would begin. An ambush led by Lieutenant Vilo Acuña on the

Loma de la Virgen would aim at intercepting the troops coming from Uvero; and farther away, to the north, waiting for the troops who would come from Yao by way of Vega de los Jobos, was Lalo Sardiñas with some men.

In this ambush we first tested a special type of mine, with results which were far from encouraging. Comrade Antonio Estévez (later killed during an attack on Bayamo) had contrived a system for exploding undetonated airplane bombs, using a gunshot as a detonator. We installed the device, foreseeing that the Army would advance through the area where we had so little strength. There was a lamentable mistake: the comrade in charge of announcing the arrival of the enemy, very inexperienced and nervous, gave the signal at the moment a civilian truck was approaching; the mine worked, and the driver became the innocent victim of this new weapon which, after it was developed, was to be so effective.

At dawn on the 16th Camilo moved to take the posts; but our guides had not foreseen that the guards would pull back during the night until they were very close to the camp, so there was quite a delay before the attack began. The men thought they had come to the wrong place and they moved forward very cautiously without realizing what the enemy had done. It took Camilo and his twenty men in Indian file no less than an hour to cover the five hundred meters between the two positions.

Finally they reached the settlement; the guards had installed a simple alarm system consisting of some string with tin cans tied to it, around ground level. The cans would rattle when stepped on or when the string was touched. But they had also left some horses grazing, so that when the column's advance guard bumped into the string, this was confused with the noise of the horses. Thus, Camilo was able to get close to the soldiers.

On the other side, our vigil was made anxious by the hours that passed before the long-awaited attack began; finally we heard the first shot that marked the beginning of the battle, and we opened with a bombardment—the six mortar shells—which ended very soon, without sorrow and without glory.

The guards had seen or heard the first attackers, and with the burst of gunfire which initiated the battle they wounded Comrade Guevara, who later died in our hospital. In a few minutes Camilo's forces had wiped out the resistance, taking eleven weapons (among them two automatic rifles) and three prisoners, and killing seven or eight; but resistance in the barracks was immediately organized and our attacks were held off.

Lieutenants Noda and Capote and the fighter Raimundo Lien died one after the other while attempting to advance; Camilo was wounded in the thigh, and Virelles had to retreat, abandoning the machine gun he had been manning. Despite his wound, Camilo returned at dawn to try and rescue the weapon. In the dawn's first light, caught in a hail of fire, he was wounded again, but luckily the bullet which penetrated his abdomen left his body through his side without touching any vital organs. Camilo was rescued, the machine gun was lost, and in all this another wounded comrade named Luis Macías dragged himself through the bushes in the opposite direction from his comrades' line of retreat, and there found his death. Some isolated fighters, from positions close to the barracks, were bombarding it with the "sputniks" or M-26's, sowing confusion among the soldiers. Guillermo García could not participate at all in this battle, since the soldiers made no attempt to leave their refuge; as we had foreseen, they immediately radioed for help.

At mid-morning the situation was calm throughout the region, but from our command post we heard some shouts which filled us with anguish: "There goes Camilo's machine gun," followed by a volley. Along with the abandoned tripod machine gun Camilo had left his cap which had his name on the back, and the guards were making fun of us. We had a hunch that something had happened, but we could not make contact with the troops on the other side; Camilo, attended by Sergio del Valle, refused to retreat and they remained there awaiting further developments.

Fidel's predictions were coming true: the company led by Captain Sierra sent units of its advance guard from Oro de Guisa to investigate what was happening at Pino del Agua; Paco Cabrera's entire platoon was waiting for them, with about thirty to thirty-five men stationed by the roadside on the hill called El Cable because of the cable to help vehicles make the difficult climb.

Our squads were posted under the command of Lieutenants Suñol, Alamo, Reyes, and William Rodríguez; Paco Cabrera was also there as leader of the platoon, but the people in charge of holding off the forward units of the advance guard were Paz and Duque, who faced the road. The small enemy force advanced and was completely destroyed: eleven dead, five wounded prisoners who were treated in a house and left there; Second Lieutenant Laferté, who today is one of us, was also taken prisoner; twelve rifles were captured, among them two M-1's and an automatic rifle as well as a Johnson.

One or two soldiers who were able to flee reached Oro de Guisa with the news. On receiving word, people in Oro de Guisa must have asked for help, but between Guisa and Oro de Guisa was precisely where Raúl Castro was posted with all his forces, for that was where we had assumed the guards would arrive to relieve the besieged men at Pino del Agua.

Raúl organized his men so that Félix Pena and the advance guard would close the road to enemy reinforcements, and then his squad with Ciro Frías' and the one commanded by Raúl would immediately attack the enemy, while Efigenio would close the encirclement in the rear.

One detail went unnoticed at that moment: two inoffensive and bewildered peasants, who passed all our positions with roosters under their arms, turned out to be Army soldiers from Oro de

Guisa who had been sent to explore the road. They were able to observe our troop's positions, and they reported to their comrades in Guisa. As a result, Raúl had to bear the brunt of the Army's offensive, since they knew his position. They attacked him from a height they had taken, and Raúl had to make a long retreat, during which one man was wounded and one man, Florencio Quesada, was killed.

The road from Bayamo, passing through Oro de Guisa, was the only route taken by the Army in its attempt to advance. Although Raúl was obliged, given his disadvantaged position, to retreat, the enemy troops advanced very slowly along the road and did not appear during the whole day.

That day we underwent constant attack by the Army's B-26's which machine gunned the hills with no greater result than that of inconveniencing us and obliging us to take certain precautions.

Fidel was euphoric over the battle; at the same time, he was worried about the fate of our comrades and at various times he took greater risks than he should have. Because of this, days later a group of officers and I sent him a letter asking him in the name of the Revolution not to risk his life needlessly. This rather infantile letter, which was inspired by the most altruistic motives, did not, I believe, warrant even a reading on his part, and needless to say, he did not pay the least attention to it.

That night I insisted that an attack of the type Camilo had carried out was possible, and we could overcome the guards who were posted in Pino del Agua. Fidel was not in favor of the idea, but he finally agreed to try it, sending a force under the command of Escalona, composed of Ignacio Pérez' and Raúl Castro Mercader's platoons. The comrades approached and did everything possible to reach the barracks, but they were repelled by heavy fire and they retreated without trying to attack again. I asked that I be given the command of the force, and Fidel granted this, not without grumbling.

My idea was to get as close as possible and, with Molotov cocktails made with gasoline from the lumber camp itself, set fire to the wooden houses and oblige the men to surrender or at least to come pouring out to face our fire. As we approached the battle site and prepared to take positions, I received this short note from Fidel: "February 16, 1958. CHE: If everything depends on the attack from this side, without support from Camilo and Guillermo, I do not think that anything suicidal should be done, because there is a risk of too many casualties and of failing to achieve the objective. I seriously urge you to be careful. You yourself must not take part in the fighting: this is a strict order. The crucial need of the moment is that you lead the men well. FIDEL."

Furthermore, Almeida, who had brought the message, told me that I could attack on my own responsibility, according to the terms of the note, but that he, Fidel, was not in agreement. The strict order not to enter into combat weighed on me; the likelihood if not the certainty that several men would be killed; the slim chance of taking the barracks; our lack of information concerning the placement of Guillermo's and Camilo's isolated forces; all this and also taking all the responsibility on my shoulders was too much for me, and, crestfallen, I took the same path as my predecessor Escalona.

The following morning, amidst continual aerial attack, the order for a general retreat was given. After a few shots aimed by telescopic sight at the soldiers who were beginning to leave their shelters, we began to retreat along the Maestra road.

As can be noted in the official dispatch which we issued at the time, the enemy suffered from eighteen to twenty-five deaths and we captured thirty-three rifles, five machine guns, and abundant ammunition. To the list of casualties must be added the name of Luis Macías, whose fate was not known at the time, and other comrades such as Luis Olazábal and Quiroga, wounded in different actions of the prolonged battle. In the newspaper *El Mundo* of February 19 appeared the following dispatch:

"EL MUNDO, WEDNESDAY FEBRUARY 19, 1958.—Loss of 16 Insurgents and 5 Soldiers is Reported.—Not Known if Guevara Was Wounded. —The Army's General Staff issued a communiqué at five o'clock yesterday afternoon denying that an important battle with the rebels had taken place at Pino del Agua, south of Bayamo. It was further admitted in the official report that 'there have been a few skirmishes between Army reconnaissance patrols and groups of rebels,' and also that at the time of the report, 'the rebels' casualties rose to sixteen, while the Army as a result of those skirmishes had five casualties.' As for whether the well-known Argentine communist Che Guevara was wounded, adds the communiqué, this has not yet been confirmed. Concerning the presence of the insurrectional leader at those encounters, nothing has been confirmed, but it *is* known that he remains hidden in the cave maze of the Sierra Maestra."

A little later, or perhaps even at that moment, came the massacre of Oro de Guisa carried out by Sosa Blanco, the assassin who in the first days of January 1959 was to die before a firing squad. While the dictatorship could only confirm that Fidel "remains hidden in the cave maze of the Sierra Maestra," the troops under his personal command begged him not to risk his life needlessly, and the enemy army avoided our strong points. Some time later Pino del Agua was cleared and thus we completed the liberation of the western part of the Maestra.

A few days after that battle occurred one of the most important actions of the struggle: the Third Column, under the command of Major Almeida, moved toward the region of Santiago, and the Sixth "Frank País" Column, under the command of Major Raúl Castro Ruz, crossed the eastern plains, penetrated the Mangos de Baraguá, west on to Pinares de Mayarí, and then formed the Second (Eastern) Front, called "Frank País."

# Camilo

Memory is a way of reviving the past, the dead. To remember Camilo is to remember things which are past or dead, and yet Camilo is a living part of the Cuban Revolution, immortal by his very nature. I would like simply to give our comrades of the Rebel Army an idea of who this invincible guerrilla fighter was. I am able to do so, since, from the sad hours of the first setback at Alegría de Pío on, we were always together, and it is my duty to do so, because, far more than a comrade in arms, in joys and victories, Camilo was a real brother. I never got to know him in Mexico, as he joined us at the last minute. He had come from the United States without any previous recommendation, and we didn't have any confidence in him—or in anyone else, in fact—in those risky days. He came on the "Granma," just one among the eighty-two who crossed the sea at the mercy of the elements to carry out a feat that was to shake the entire continent. I realized what he was like before I actually got to know him through hearing a representative exclamation of his during the disastrous battle of Alegría de Pío. I was wounded, stretched out in a clearing, next to a comrade covered with blood who was firing his last rounds, ready to die fighting. I heard someone cry weakly: "We're lost. Let's surrender." And a clear voice from somewhere among the men shouted in reply: "Nobody surrenders here!" followed by a four-letter word.

The battle ended, we survived, and I went on breathing, thanks to the help of Comrade Almeida. Five of us wandered around the steep cliffs near Cabo Cruz. One clear, moonlit night we came upon three other comrades sleeping peacefully, without any fear of the soldiers. We jumped them, believing them to be enemies. Nothing happened, but the incident served later as the material for a joke between us: the fact that I was among those who had caught them by surprise, and the fact that it was I who had to raise the white flag so that they would not shoot us, mistaking us for Batista soldiers.

And so then there were eight of us. Camilo was hungry and wanted to eat; he didn't care what or where, he simply wanted to eat. This led to some serious disagreements with him, because he continually wanted to approach *bohíos* to ask for food. Twice, for having followed the advice of "the hungry ones," we nearly fell into the hands of enemy soldiers who had killed dozens of our comrades. On the ninth day "the hungry ones" won out, and we approached a *bohío,* ate, and all got sick. And among the sickest was, naturally, Camilo, who, like a hungry lion, had gulped down an entire kid.

During that period I was more a medic than a soldier. I put Camilo on a special diet and ordered him to stay behind in the *bohío,* where he would receive proper attention. That trouble passed, and we were together again, and the days lengthened into weeks and months during which many comrades were killed. Camilo showed his mettle, earning the rank of lieutenant of the vanguard of our one and only beloved Column, which would later be called the José Martí First Column, under Fidel's personal command. Almeida and Raúl were captains; Camilo, lieutenant of the vanguard; Efigenio Ameijeiras, leader of the rear guard; Ramiro Valdés, lieutenant in one of Raúl's platoons; and Calixto, soldier in another platoon. In other words, all our forces were born there, where I was the group's lieutenant medic. Later, following the battle of Uvero, I was given the rank of captain, and, a few days later, the rank of major and the command of a column. One day Camilo was made captain of the column which I commanded, the Fourth Column. We bore that number to deceive the enemy, as actually there were only two. And it was there that Camilo began his career of exploits, and it was with untiring effort and extraordinary zeal that, time and again, he hunted down enemy soldiers. Once he shot a soldier of the enemy's scout at such close range that he caught the man's rifle before it even hit the ground. Another time he planned to let the first of the enemy soldiers go by until he was abreast of our troop, and then open flank fire. The ambush never materialized, because someone in our group got nervous and opened fire before the enemy got close enough. By then Camilo was "Camilo, Lord of the Vanguard," a real guerrilla fighter who was able to assert himself through his own colorful way of fighting.

I recall my anxiety during the second attack on Pino del Agua, when Fidel ordered me to stay with him and gave Camilo the responsibility of attacking one of the enemy's flanks. The idea was simple. Camilo was to attack and take one end of the enemy camp and then surround it. The firing started, and he and his men took the sentry post and continued advancing, entering the settlement, killing or taking prisoner every soldier in their path. The town was taken house by house until finally the enemy organized its resistance and the barrage of bullets began to take its toll among our ranks. Valuable comrades, among them Noda and Capote, lost their lives in this battle.

An enemy machine gunner advanced, surrounded by his men, but at a given moment he found himself amidst a veritable storm of gunfire. The machine gunner's assistants were killed, and the soldier manning the gun dropped it and fled. It was dawn. The attack had begun at night. Camilo hurled himself across the machine gun to seize and defend it, and was shot twice. A bullet pierced his left thigh, and another hit him in the abdomen. He got away, and his comrades carried him. We were two kilometers away, with the enemy between us. We could hear machine gun bursts and shouting: "There goes Camilo's gun!" "That's Camilo firing!" and vivas for Batista. We all thought that Camilo had been killed. Later we praised his luck that the bullet had entered and left his abdomen without hitting his intestines or any vital organ. Then came the tragic day of April 9,* and Camilo, the trailblazer, went to the Oriente plains and became a legend, striking terror into the heart of the enemy forces mobilized in the Bayamo area. Once he was surrounded by 600 men, and there were only 20 in the rebel force. They resisted an entire day against an enemy advance that included two tanks, and at night they made a spectacular escape.

Later came the offensive, and in the face of imminent danger and the concentration of forces Camilo was called, as he was the man Fidel trusted to leave in his place when he went to a specific front. Then came the marvelous story of the invasion and his chain of victories on the plains of Las Villas—a difficult feat, as the terrain afforded little natural protection. These actions were magnificent for their audacity, and at the same time one could already see Camilo's political attitude, his decision regarding political problems, his strength and his faith in the people. Camilo was happy, down-to-earth, and a joker. I remember that in the Sierra a peasant, one of our great, magnificent, anonymous heroes, had been nicknamed by Camilo, who accompanied this with an ugly gesture. One day the peasant came to see me as head of the column, complaining that he shouldn't be insulted and that he was no ventriloquist. As I didn't understand, I went to speak with Camilo so that he could explain the man's strange attitude. What happened was that Camilo had looked at the man with an air of disrespect and called him a ventriloquist, and, as the peasant didn't know what a ventriloquist was, he was terribly offended.

---

* Date of the unsuccessful general strike.

Camilo had a little alcohol burner, and he used to cook cats and offer them as a delicacy to new recruits who joined us. It was one of the many tests of the Sierra, and more than one failed this preliminary "examination" when he refused to eat the cat proffered. Camilo was a man of anecdotes, a million anecdotes. They were a part of his nature. His appreciation of people and his ability to get along with them were a part of his personality. These qualities, which today we sometimes forget or overlook, were present in all his actions, something precious that few men can attain. It is true, as Fidel has said, that he had no great amount of "book learning," but he had the natural intelligence of the people who had chosen him from among thousands to place him in that privileged place earned by his audacity, his tenacity, his intelligence and devotion. Camilo was uncompromisingly loyal to two things, and with the same results: he had unlimited loyalty and devotion to Fidel and the people. Fidel and the people march together, and Camilo's devotion was projected toward them both.

Who killed Camilo? Who killed the man who, in the lives of others like him, lives on in the people? Such men do not die so long as the people do not authorize it. The enemy killed him, killed him because they wanted him to die, because there are no completely safe airplanes, because pilots are not able to acquire all the necessary experience, because he was overloaded with work and had to be in Havana as quickly as possible. He was killed by his drive. Camilo did not measure danger. He utilized it as a game, he played with it, he courted it, he attracted and handled it and, with his guerrilla's mentality; a mere cloud could not detain or deviate him from the line he was following. It happened at a time everyone knew him, admired and loved him; it could have happened before, and then his story would have been known only as that of a mere guerrilla captain. There will be many Camilos, as Fidel has said; and there have been Camilos, I can add—Camilos who died before completing the magnificent work he had managed to complete so as to enter the pages of history. Camilo and the other Camilos—the ones who fell early and those still to come—are the index of the people's strength; they are the most complete expression of the heights that can be reached by a nation fighting to defend its purest ideals and with complete faith in the fulfillment of its noblest goals. There is too much to be said to allow me to put his essence into a lifeless mold, which would be equivalent to killing him. It is better to leave it like this, in general descriptive terms, without spelling out in black and white his socio-economic ideology, which was not precisely defined. But we must always bear in mind that there was never a man—not even before the Revolution—comparable to Camilo: a complete revolutionary, a man of the people, an artist of the Revolution, sprung from the heart of the Cuban nation. His mind was incapable of the slightest slackening or disappointment. He is an object of daily remembrance; he is the one who did this or that, something by Camilo; he who left his exact and indelible imprint on the Cuban Revolution, who is present among those who fell early in their revolutionary careers and those heroes who are yet to come. In his constant and eternal rebirth, Camilo is the image of the people.

# The General Strike,
# the Final Offensive,
# and the Battle of Santa Clara

The entire *llano* Movement was feverishly preparing a revolutionary general strike. An organization was formed, the Frente Nacional Obrero [National Workers Front], led by remote control by the 26th of July Movement. From its inception it was a victim of the malady of sectarianism. The workers displayed a certain indifference toward this budding organization, obviously sired by the July 26th Movement, whose objectives were too radical for prevailing conditions. Several days before the strike date of April 9th, 1958, Fidel Castro issued a manifesto in which he had harsh words for those who had not taken the path of revolution. He was soon to issue another manifesto to the workers, calling for unity, either within the Frente Nacional or outside it, because he clearly understood that the Frente alone would be powerless to call a strike.

Our troops flung themselves into the fray; and Camilo Cienfuegos, captain of the Fourth Column at that time, went down to the low country in Oriente, near Bayamo, where he sowed confusion and death in the enemy's ranks. However, April 9th arrived and our efforts came to naught: the National Committee of the Movement, having blundered utterly concerning the rudiments of mass struggle, had attempted to start the strike by surprise, with no advance notice—with shooting. As could be expected, the workers refused to participate, and a certain number of exemplary comrades all over the country died in vain. April 9th was a painful failure which did not for a moment succeed in threatening the regime's stability. Far from it: after this tragic date the government was able to withdraw its forces and send them little by little to Oriente, to sow destruction as far as the Sierra. We had to reinforce our defenses constantly and to move deeper into the forests. The government, for its part, increased the number of regiments sent to confront us, until finally they had ten thousand men in the field. It was then that the May 25th offensive began, in the village of Las Mercedes, which was our outpost.

The poverty of our resources was flagrant: two hundred guns in good condition against ten thousand weapons of all types—what an enormous handicap! But there was another side to the picture: the half-heartedness which the Batista army had shown in combat. Our boys fought like lions, one of us against ten or fifteen of them. The enemy had to throw in everything it had—tanks, mortars, aviation—to force them to abandon the village. Our little group was led by Captain Angel Verdecia, who was to die a month later in combat.

By this time Fidel had received a letter from the traitor Eulogio Cantillo* who, maneuvering like a typical maggotty politician, wrote to the rebel leader as chief of enemy operations, announcing that the offensive would be pursued without quarter, except that "The Man's" (Fidel's) life would be spared while waiting for the final outcome. In fact, the offensive took its course. After two and a half months of steady skirmishing, the enemy had a thousand casualties—dead, wounded, captured, and deserters. They had abandoned to us six hundred weapons, including one tank, twelve mortars, twelve tripod machine guns, and an impressive quantity of automatic arms, not counting an incredible amount of equipment

---

* General of the Batista forces who in the final days of the regime tried to play both sides.

and ammunition of all sorts, plus four hundred and fifty prisoners, whom we turned over to the Red Cross at the end of the campaign.

This famous final offensive in the Sierra Maestra broke the back of the Batista army, but it had not yet said its last word. The struggle resumed. We planned our final strategy, deciding that we would attack at three points: Santiago de Cuba, under loose encirclement; Las Villas, where I was to go; and Pinar del Río, at the other end of the island, which Camilo Cienfuegos and his Second Column, known as the "Antonio Maceo," were to take. Camilo was unable to carry out the latter part of the program because imperatives of the war obliged him to remain at Las Villas.

When we had smashed the regiments that had stormed the Sierra Maestra and had re-established the front along its normal lines, we decided to begin the march on Las Villas, the central province. From the point of view of strategy, my principal task was to cut systematically all the roads between the two ends of the island. I had received the order, furthermore, to establish contacts with all the existing political groups we could find in the mountain districts. And, finally, I had broad powers to set up a military government over the sector for which I was responsible. Thinking to make the trip in four days, we planned to set off by truck on August 30, 1958, but our plans were unexpectedly upset. On that night a courier arrived, bringing uniforms and the gasoline we needed for the trucks, which were all set to move. But at the same time a plane carrying a shipment of weapons landed at an airfield near the road. The plane had been spotted just as it landed, in spite of the blackness of the night, and the airfield underwent an intense bombardment, beginning at ten in the evening and going on until five in the morning; at that time we set the plane afire to avoid its falling into enemy hands and to stop them from continuing to bomb in daylight, which would have had even worse consequences for us. Enemy troops advanced on the airfield, and intercepted the courier and his cargo of gasoline. We found ourselves on foot once more.

Then the march began, on August 31st, sans trucks, sans horses. We expected to meet up with them again after crossing the Manzanillo-Bayamo road, and so we did; but on September 1st a terrible cyclone struck the area, making all roads impassable except for the Carretera Central, the only tar-surfaced road in this part of Cuba. Well, we had to give up the idea of truck transport. From that moment on, we had to travel on horseback or on foot. We were heavily loaded with ammunition, with a forty-rocket bazooka, and everything necessary for a long march and a quick setting up of camp.

Came difficult days, in the still-friendly territory of Oriente Province. We had to cross rivers in flood, creeks and brooks converted into rivers; we had to struggle unendingly to keep ammunition, guns, and rockets dry; we had to find fresh horses to replace the tired ones; we had increasingly to avoid populated areas as we moved beyond Oriente Province. We marched toilsomely through flooded terrain, attacked by hordes of mosquitoes which made rest stops unbearable. We ate little and badly, we drank water from streams that wound through the marshes, or even swamp water itself. We dragged ourselves along, in a pitiable state, during appalling days. A week after we had set out, we crossed the Jobabo, which divides Camagüey from Oriente. We were quite enfeebled and furthermore lacked footwear: many comrades walked barefoot through the mud of southern Camagüey.

During the night of September 9th, on entering La Federal, our advance guard fell into an enemy ambush. Two courageous comrades met their death there. But the worst was that we were spotted by enemy forces who, from that moment on, harassed us without letup. After a small clash, we reduced their little garrison, at the cost of four of our men taken prisoner. We had to redouble our caution, all the more so now that the enemy's aviation knew our general course.

One or two days later we arrived at Laguna Grande; at the same time Camilo and his column reached there, too. They were in better shape than we were. I remember the place well: it was absolutely infested by mosquitoes, to the point that without mosquito nets—and not all of us had them—it was impossible to get a moment's rest.

Came days of grueling trudging across desolate stretches where we came upon nothing but water and mud. We suffered from thirst and hunger and we were scarcely able to move ahead. Our legs were like lead and our weapons weighed us down oppressively. We continued the march with some better horses, which Camilo left us when he went to fetch the trucks, but we had to abandon them in the vicinity of the Macareño sugar mill. Since the guides who were to meet us had not appeared we simply plunged ahead, feeling our way blindly.

Our advance guard came upon an enemy post at Cuatro Compañeros and this was the beginning of a grueling battle. Dawn came. We succeeded—not without difficulties—in mustering the majority of the troop in a densely wooded grove, but the enemy flanked us and we had to carry on a long battle in order to permit those who had fallen behind to cross over a railroad track in the direction of the woods. It was then that their planes spotted us. B-26's, C-47's, large reconnaissance C-3's, small planes, all spitting fire within a perimeter of two hundred meters or less. After this saturation, they withdrew. We had lost one man to the bombs and we had several wounded, among them Major Silva, who made the rest of the expedition with a fractured shoulder.

By the next day things were not quite so bad, since some of our stragglers appeared and we were able to muster the whole troop, except for ten men who joined Camilo's column and went with him to Yaguajay, in northern Las Villas.

In the midst of our troubles we never lacked for support from the peasants. There was always one to serve us as guide or keep us from starving. To be sure, we did not find unanimous support such as that given us by the population of Oriente, but nonetheless there were always people to help us. Sometimes we were betrayed, while passing through an estate. This by no means signified a concerted peasant action against us. It must be understood that their conditions of existence turned these men into slaves. Terrified at the thought of losing their daily crust, they would inform the proprietor that we were passing through the estate property, and he had nothing better to do than warn the military authorities.

One afternoon we heard, on our little field radio, a report made by General Francisco Tabernilla Dolz. With his customary fire-eating bombast, he announced the annihilation of the hordes led by Che Guevara and presented a list divided into dead, wounded, and unscathed. All of this came from papers taken from our haversacks after our disastrous encounter with the enemy some days earlier. He had interlarded what he found there with false information that had been collected by the Army's General Staff.

The news of our demise provoked delight among our little troop. However, little by little they began to be attacked by pessimism: thirst, hunger, fatigue, a feeling of impotence in the face of the encircling enemy forces, and especially a terrible foot ailment which made each step a torment, had transformed our group into an army of shadows. Day after day our physical condition deteriorated and our meals—one day yes, another day no, the third day perhaps—were not such as to improve our condition. Our hardest days were those we spent under siege, near the Baraguá sugar mill, in pestilential swamps, without a drop of potable water, harassed by planes, without a single horse to aid the feebler among us to cross that unfriendly slough, our shoes completely rotted by this brackish, muddy water full of vegetation that lacerated our bare feet. When we broke through the encirclement of Baraguá in order to reach the famous road from Júcaro to Morón—a historic spot, the scene of bloody battles between patriots and Spaniards in the War of Independence—we were truly in a disastrous situation. We had no time to recover, because torrential downpours and the general inclemency of the weather, together with enemy attacks, obliged us to resume our march. The troop became more and more exhausted and disheartened. However, at the most critical moment, when insults, entreaties, and tongue lashings were the only way to get the weary men to advance, a distant vision sufficed to restore their courage and give new spirit to the group: a blue spot on the horizon toward the west, the blue of the Las Villas cordillera, glimpsed for the first time by our men. From that moment on, privations were more bearable, everything seemed easier. We escaped the second ring of encirclement by swimming the Júcaro, which separates the provinces of Camagüey and Las Villas. We felt as if we had emerged from darkness.

Two days later we were safe in the heart of the Trinidad-Sancti Spíritus mountain range, ready to enter the new stage of the war. Two days later we were able to rest; we had had to keep going without delays, because we proposed to prevent the elections scheduled for November 3rd. We had reached the mountains of Las Villas on October 16th; we had very little time for an enormous task.

From the time we arrived in the Sierra Escambray, we were supposed to harry the military apparatus of the dictatorship, especially its communications network. Our immediate objective was to impede the elections. A tough job, considering that we had so little time and that there were internal dissensions in the revolutionary movement for which we were to pay a high price, including that in human lives.

We were supposed to attack the neighboring hamlets so that election meetings could not be held. We planned a simultaneous attack on Cabaiguán, Fomento, and Sancti Spíritus, on the rich central plains. Meanwhile the little mountain garrison of Güinía de Miranda surrendered, and we then attacked the Banao garrison, without substantial result. During the days before November 3rd we engaged in a torrent of activity: our columns were everywhere, reducing attendance at the polls to almost nothing. Camilo Cienfuegos's troops, in the northern part of the province, paralyzed the electoral farce. Nothing could move: neither *batistiano* troop transports nor commercial traffic.

In Oriente there was no voting to speak of; in Camagüey the percentage was slightly higher; in the western zone, in spite of everything, there were mass abstentions. Abstention in Las Villas was spontaneous, since we hadn't had time to organize both passive resistance and guerrilla activity.

The increasing number of attacks on communications made the situation of Las Villas a very critical one. On arrival, we instituted a complete new system of urban struggle: on each march we took with us some of the best among the city *milicianos* to a training camp where they were taught sabotage tactics. This bore fruit in the suburban areas.

During November and December 1958 we gradually closed down all the roads. Captain Silva blocked the road from Trinidad to Sancti Spíritus completely, and the central highway was seriously damaged when we cut the bridge over the Tuinicú, without however succeeding in destroying it completely. The central railroad line was cut at several points; service on the southern division was interrupted by the Second Front, and the northern division was closed down by Camilo Cienfuegos's troops. Thus the island found itself split in two. Only Oriente, the most disturbed region, received governmental aid, by air and by sea; and this aid became increasingly uncertain. Symptoms of enemy disintegration were multiplying everywhere.

After December 16, the systematic closing of the roads and blocking of the bridges put the enemy in a tight spot. How, under these conditions, could they defend their advance positions, or even those on the central highway? At dawn on the 16th we blew up the bridge over the Falcón, and communications between Havana and the cities to the east of Santa Clara were virtually cut off. Likewise, a series of hamlets—among them Fomento, the southernmost of them—was besieged and attacked by our forces. The commander of the fortress defended it fairly effectively; but in spite of the pounding given our Rebel Army by enemy aviation the demoralized troops of the dictatorship did little to bring relief to their comrades. Realizing the futility of resistance, they surrendered—and more than a hundred guns passed over to the side of freedom.

Not allowing the enemy troops to catch their breath, we decided to knock out the central highway at once. On December 21st we attacked Cabaiguán and Guayos simultaneously. After several hours Guayos surrendered; two days later Cabaiguán and its ninety soldiers followed suit. At Cabaiguán the dictatorship's inefficiency was clear to see; it never sent infantry reinforcements to the aid of the beleaguered men.

Camilo Cienfuegos attacked a series of villages north of Las Villas while organizing the encirclement of Yaguajay, the last bastion of the dictator's troops. Its commanding officer was a captain of Chinese descent [Abón Lee] who resisted for eleven days, immobilizing the revolutionary troops in the sector. Meanwhile, our group made for the central highway, going in the direction of Santa Clara, capital of the province.

After the fall of Cabaiguán we set about attacking Placetas, which surrendered at the end of one day. The Revolutionary Directorate gave us valuable assistance. After Placetas was taken we soon liberated Remedios and Caibarién (an important port) on the northern coast. The situation was a gloomy one for the dictatorship: we continued to win victories in Oriente, the column on the Escambray front routed all the small garrisons in their area, and Camilo Cienfuegos controlled the North.

When the enemy retreated from Camajuaní, having offered no resistance whatsoever, we were ready for the final assault on the capital of Las Villas. (Santa Clara is the hub of the central plain of

Cuba. A city of 150,000 inhabitants, it is a railroad center and possesses an important communications network. It is surrounded by low, bare hills, which the enemy troops had already occupied.)

By the time of the attack we had increased our stock of guns considerably; we had even regained some heavy weapons—but without ammunition. We had a bazooka but no rockets, and we were fighting against ten or more tanks. We realized that the best way of combatting them was to go deep into the densely populated neighborhoods, where tank effectiveness is considerably diminished.

While the Directorate's troops undertook to capture Barracks No. 31 of the Guardia Rural, we were busy laying siege to virtually all the strongholds of Santa Clara. We turned our attention to the defenders of the armored train, which stood on the track at the Camajuaní junction, a position solidly defended by the Army.

On December 29th the battle began. At the beginning, the university had served as our base of operations. Later, we set up our GHQ nearer the center of the city. Our men were battling against troops supported by tank units, which they drove out, though many paid for their gallant acts with their lives. The dead and wounded began to fill our improvised cemeteries and hospitals.

I recall an episode highly characteristic of the spirit of our troops during this last assault. I had reprimanded one of our soldiers whom I found asleep at the height of a battle. He told me that he had been disarmed because he had accidentally let his gun go off. I answered, with my customary dryness: "Go to the front lines barehanded, and come back with another gun . . . if you're man enough." Later, I went to visit our wounded in a military hospital; a dying man touched my hand and said: "Remember, major? You sent me to find a gun at Remedios. . . . I brought it here." It was the soldier who had fired in the air, who was to die a few minutes later. It seemed to me that he was pleased to have proved his courage. Such was our Rebel Army.

The hills of Cápiro were still resisting and the battle lasted all day on the 30th. Meanwhile, we took several other parts of the city. Communications were already cut between the center of Santa Clara and the armored train. Its occupants, finding themselves encircled in the hills of Cápiro, tried to flee by rail, and they arrived, along with their magnificent cargo, at the junction, which we had taken the precaution to blow up. The locomotive and several carriages were derailed. A very interesting battle ensued: the men in the armored train had been dislodged by our Molotov cocktails; in spite of their excellent protection they were prepared to fight only at long range, from comfortable positions, and against a virtually disarmed enemy—in the true style of colonizers versus the Indians of the North American West. Harassed by our men who, from nearby train carriages and other close-range positions, were hurling bottles of flaming gasoline, the train—thanks to its armor-plate—became a veritable oven for its soldiers. After several hours, the entire crew surrendered, with their twenty-two armored cars, their anti-aircraft guns, their DCA machine guns, their fabulous quantities of ammunition (fabulous, that is, to us).

We had succeeded in taking the electric-power station and the entire northwestern section of the city. We went on the air to announce that virtually all Santa Clara was in the hands of the Revolution. During the broadcast, which I made as commander-in-chief of the armed forces of Las Villas, I had the sad duty of informing the Cuban people of the death of Captain Roberto Rodríguez, "El Vaquerito," small in height and years, the leader of the Suicide Squad who had risked his life a thousand times in the struggle for freedom. The Suicide Squad, composed strictly of proven volunteers, was a model of revolutionary vigor. Every time one of its men died—and this happened during every combat —and a new candidate was accepted, those who were not chosen could not hide their disappointment nor hold back their tears. How strange it was to see these noble, battle-hardened warriors reveal their youthfulness by shedding tears of despair on not having the honor of being chosen for a position in the front ranks of combat and death.

The police station fell next, along with the tanks that had defended it. There was quick capitulation by Barracks No. 31 to Major Cubela; the prison, the courthouse, and the provincial government headquarters fell to us, as well as the Grand Hotel where the besieged men continued their fire from the tenth floor almost until the cessation of hostilities.

At this point only the Leoncio Vidal Barracks, the largest fortress of Central Cuba, remained in the hands of the dictatorship. But by January 1st, 1959, the signs of collapse were evident among its defenders. During the morning of January 1st we sent Captain Núñez Jiménez and Rodríguez de la Vega to negotiate the surrender of the barracks. The news was astonishing and contradictory: Batista had just fled, causing the collapse of the Armed Forces Command. Our two delegates contacted Cantillo by radio and informed him of the surrender offer, but he refused to go along, since it constituted an ultimatum and since he had taken over command of the army in strict accordance with Fidel Castro's instructions. We immediately contacted Fidel, told him what was happening and gave him our opinion of Cantillo's questionable attitude. Fidel's mind was already made up: he was also sure that Cantillo was a traitor. (Cantillo, in those decisive hours, allowed all the top officials of the Batista government to flee. His attitude was all the more lamentable if we take into account the fact that he had made contact with us as an *officer*; we had trusted him, thinking naively that a military man's word is as good as his bond.)

The rest is well known: Fidel Castro's refusal to take Cantillo's advice; Fidel's order to march on Havana; the taking over of the army command by General Barquín upon his release from jail on the Isle of Pines; the taking of Camp Columbia by Camilo Cienfuegos, and of the Cabaña fortress by our Eighth Column; and, several days later, the installation of Fidel Castro as Prime Minister of the Provisional Government. All that is part of the contemporary political history of the nation.

We are now in a situation in which we are much more than simple instruments of one nation; we constitute at this moment the hope of unredeemed America. Today all eyes—those of the powerful oppressors and those of the hopeful—are fixed on us. On our future attitude, our capacity to resolve manifold problems, depends to a large extent the growth of people's movements in America. And each step that we take is observed by the ever-watchful eyes of the powerful oppressor and by the optimistic eyes of our American brothers.

We all know that it will not be easy, and we all recognize the enormous historic responsibility of the 26th of July Movement, of the Cuban Revolution, of the nation at large, to be an example for all the peoples of America, for those we must not disappoint.

Our friends of the indomitable continent may be sure that, if necessary, we shall struggle to the last economic consequence of our acts. And if the fight goes even further, we shall fight to the very last drop of our rebel blood, to make this land a sovereign republic, with the real attributes of a nation that is happy, democratic, and a true brother to the other peoples of America.

# letters by
# che guevara

FIDEL,

At this moment I remember many things—when I met you in Maria Antonia's house, when you suggested my coming, all the tensions involved in the preparations.

One day they asked who should be notified in case of death, and the real possibility of that fact affected us all. Later we knew that it was true, that in revolution one wins or dies (if it is a real one). Many comrades fell along the way to victory.

Today everything is less dramatic because we are more mature. But the fact is repeated. I feel that I have fulfilled the part of my duty that tied me to the Cuban revolution in its territory, and I say good-by to you, the comrades, your people, who are already mine.

I formally renounce my positions in the national leadership of the party, my post as minister, my rank of major, and my Cuban citizenship. Nothing legal binds me to Cuba. The only ties are of another nature; those which cannot be broken as appointments can.

Recalling my past life, I believe I have worked with sufficient honor and dedication to consolidate the revolutionary triumph. My only serious failing was not having trusted more in you from the first moments in the Sierra Maestra, and not having understood quickly enough your qualities as a leader and a revolutionary.

I have lived magnificent days and I felt at your side the pride of belonging to our people in the brilliant yet sad days of the Caribbean crisis.

Rarely has a statesman been more brilliant than you in those days. I am also proud of having followed you without hesitation, identified with your way of thinking and of seeing and of appraising dangers and principles.

Other nations of the world call for my modest efforts. I can do

---

This letter was sent in April, 1965.

that which is denied you because of your responsibility as the head of Cuba and the time has come for us to part.

I want it known that I do it with mixed feelings of joy and sorrow: I leave here the purest of my hopes as a builder, and the dearest of those I love. And I leave a people that received me as a son. That wounds me deeply. I carry to new battlefronts the faith that you taught me, the revolutionary spirit of my people, the feeling of fulfilling the most sacred of duties: to fight against imperialism wherever it may be. This comforts and heals the deepest wounds.

I state once more that I free Cuba from any responsibility, except that which stems from its example. If my final hour finds me under other skies, my last thought will be of this people and especially of you. I am thankful for your teaching, your example, and I will try to be faithful to the final consequences of my acts.

I have always been identified with the foreign policy of our revolution and I will continue to be. Wherever I am, I will feel the responsibility of being a Cuban revolutionary, and as such I shall behave. I am not sorry that I leave my children and my wife nothing material. I am happy it is that way. I ask nothing for them, as I know the state will provide enough for their expenses and education.

I would like to say much to you and to our people, but I feel it is not necessary. Words cannot express what I would want them to, and I don't think it's worth while to banter phrases.

Ever onward to victory! *Patria o muerte!*

I embrace you with all my revolutionary fervor.

CHE

DEAR FOLKS—

Once again I feel between my heels the ribs of Rosinante; once more I hit the road with my shield upon my arm.

Almost ten years ago today, I wrote you another letter of farewell. As I remember, I lamented at not being a better soldier and a better doctor. The latter no longer interests me; I'm not such a bad soldier.

Nothing has changed in essence, except that I am much more aware, my Marxism has taken root and become purified. I believe in the armed struggle as the only solution for those peoples who fight to free themselves, and I am consistent with my beliefs. Many will call me an adventurer—and that I am, only, one of a different sort—one of those who risks his skin to prove his platitudes.

It is possible that this may be the finish. I don't seek it, but it's within the logical realm of probabilities. If it should be so, I send you a last embrace.

I have loved you very much, only I haven't known how to express my fondness. I am extremely rigid in my actions, and I think that sometimes you didn't understand me. It hasn't been easy to understand me. Nevertheless, please just take me at my word today.

Now, a wil which I have polished with delight is going to sustain some shaky legs and some weary lungs. I will do it.

Give a thought once in a while to this little soldier-of-fortune of the twentieth century. A kiss to Celia, to Roberto, Juan Martín and Pototín, to Beatriz, to everybody.

An *abrazo* for you from your obstinate and prodigal son.

ERNESTO

---

This letter was written in mid-1965, to his parents. (*Translation by Lee Lockwood*.)

# Index*

*Note: where first names are unknown, members of the Rebel Army, the Reunified Revolutionary Army, or the guerrilla Army are described in parentheses as "guerrilla fighter"; members of Batista's military are noted either as "officer" or by rank.